READING THE GRAPHIC SURFACE

This book critically engages with the visual appearance of prose fiction where it is manipulated by authors with devices that range from alterations in typography to the deconstruction of the physical form of the book. It reappraises the range of effects it is possible to create through the use of graphic devices and explores why literary criticism has dismissed such features as either unreadable experimental gimmicks or, more recently, as examples of the worst kind of postmodern decadence. Through the examination of problematical novels which utilise their graphic surface in innovative and unusual ways this book demonstrates that an awareness of the graphic surface can make significant contributions to interpretation.

The introductory chapters show how and why the graphic surface has been neglected, examine critical assumptions about the transformation of manuscript to novel, tackle theoretical obstacles to the perception of the graphic surface and investigate critical 'blindness' to its mimetic usage. The later chapters offer substantial, extended readings of key works by four significant authors including Samuel Beckett's *Murphy and Watt*, B. S. Johnson's *Albert Angelo*, Christine Brooke-Rose's *Thru* and Alasdair Gray's *Lanark: A Life in Four Books*. Each of these chapters identifies and analyses the weaknesses of previous criticism and attempts to fully account for the use of the graphic surface in new interpretations of the novels in question.

This book will be of interest to anyone intrigued by novels which test the possibilities of the book as a medium for prose fiction from students of literature to adventurous readers.

Glyn White is a Lecturer in the Department of Humanities at the University of Central Lancashire

For Gilbert and Muriel

READING THE GRAPHIC SURFACE

THE PRESENCE OF THE BOOK IN PROSE FICTION

Glyn White

Manchester University Press

Manchester and New York

distributed exclusively in the USA by Palgrave

Published by Manchester University Press
Oxford Road, Manchester M13 9NR, UK
and Room 400, 175 Fifth Avenue, New York, NY 10010, USA
www.manchesteruniversitypress.co.uk

Distributed in the United States exclusively by
Palgrave Macmillan, 175 Fifth Avenue,
New York, NY 10010, USA

Distributed in Canada exclusively by
UBC Press, University of British Columbia, 2029 West Mall,
Vancouver, BC, Canada V6T 1Z2

British Library Cataloguing-in-Publication Data is available

Library of Congress Cataloging-in-Publication Data is available

ISBN 978 0 7190 6969 7 paperback

First published by Manchester University Press in hardback 2005

This paperback edition first published 2014

The publisher has no responsibility for the persistence or accuracy of URLs for any external or
third-party internet websites referred to in this book, and does not guarantee that any content on
such websites is, or will remain, accurate or appropriate.

Printed by Lightning Source

CONTENTS

Contents

LIST OF FIGURES

ACKNOWLEDGEMENTS

Reading the graphic surface is the product of research over a long period and I have accumulated a lot of debts along the way. I take this opportunity to acknowledge the following with thanks:

Professor Victor Sage, without whom this project would not have happened. His help has been vital, painstaking and inspirational at every stage. He is in no way, however, responsible for the recklessness of the undertaking or any weaknesses which may remain.

The late Professor Lorna Sage for bracing encouragement and support at key moments.

Authors Christine Brooke-Rose and Alasdair Gray for replying to my communications generously and helpfully and granting permissions.

At the University of East Anglia: The English and American Studies postgrad research group (1995–2000), for providing a friendly testing ground for the beginnings of each chapter. Aileen Davies, for making sure I jumped through the right hoops at the right time. EAS Graduate Studies, the UEA Graduate Students Association and The Dean of Students Office for timely and much-needed financial help.

The Organisers of the Ma(r)king the Text Conference (Cambridge 1998), Joe Bray, Miriam Fraser and Anne C. Henry, who created an event which made me realise that scholars of all periods in literature and related disciplines were also confronting issues discussed here.

Those who have actively gathered or otherwise provided resources for me at various points over the years; Evin Aslan, Richard Beard, Dr Stephen Carver, Dr Ivy Dennett-Thorpe, Judith Eberstein, Dr Andrew Folkard, Dr Ilham Ibnouzahir, Dr Helen Jones, Kenneth and Julia Monkman, Dr Petra Rau, Dr Philip Tew, Dr Aliki Varvogli, Dr Kate Webb and Dr Chiharu Yoshioka.

Those who have read and commented on sections at various stages: Ian W. White, Micaela Schoop, James Russell, Mick Gornall, Phil Tew and everyone else who has contributed suggestions or asked questions while I have been pursuing this.

Dr Sarah Cardwell whose interdisciplinary enthusiasm prompted an early viable proposal.

My Uncle Woodruff for gasping the advice 'keep working' from his deathbed (aged 94), and my family for not doubting the eventual completion of this long and (to them) mysterious project.

Matthew Frost and all at Manchester University Press who have helped bring about the presence of *this* book.

INTRODUCTION

Aside from the fact that they are all novels of the twentieth century there may seem to be little to link Samuel Beckett's *Watt*, B. S. Johnson's *Albert Angelo*, Christine Brooke-Rose's *Thru* and Alasdair Gray's *Lanark: A Life in Four Books*, and the other novels discussed in this book, but a fundamental similarity will present itself to the reader of all these texts: they do not wholly follow the graphic conventions that arrange words on a page, and pages in a book, in the usual neutral way. These novels foreground the process by which they are presented to the reader and make emphatic use of the visual possibilities of the page through typographic and other means. Connecting such texts on these grounds alone may still seem perverse, in that each is idiosyncratic in other ways too; each has its own contexts, intertexts and specific problems to offer the reader. The reason these novels are linked here is because a critical awareness of the graphic surface, as I call it, allows us to recognise useful and vital contributions to the experience of reading of such complex and difficult texts.

The immediate purpose of this book is to construct a vocabulary for the literary study of graphic textual phenomena. I am not, however, proposing to offer a history of typographic devices, noting development and lineages of influence (a difficult but worthy task for a bibliographer). My intention is to examine such devices within a very particular context: that of the interpretation of prose fiction. This should not be read as an attempt to establish these phenomena as governors of a text's meanings, or of its message, but as a potentially significant contributing factor in both. Nor am I simply intent on producing an awareness of the book as object; that would be too obvious and too easy. Ultimately the materiality of the text is only one contributory factor in the complexity of what a book actually is. As Jerome McGann states: 'Literary production is not an autonomous and self-reflexive activity; it is a social and institutional event' (1983: 100). Just as the text is embedded in a physical book, so the book, and its reader, are embedded in a complex environment in which the text is received, read and reacted to. Such concerns cannot be divorced from the interpretation of texts and the need for them to be addressed is readily justified if, instead of explaining why we should want to refer to the typographical design of any particular text, we turn the question around and ask how is it possible for the reader, interpreter or critic to neglect or marginalise the very form and substance of the book he or she reads?

Bray, Handley and Henry (2000) is a significant collection of work which reveals the range of approaches already adopted and the breadth of historical material that is beginning to be addressed. Cairns Craig devotes a chapter (1999: 167–99) to the role of 'the typographic muse' in contemporary Scottish writing. Nevertheless, there is still a lack of sustained critical work on the use of the graphic surface in British twentieth-century fiction, and, indeed, little recognition that there is anything about variations in the printed presentation of text that might need critical work, despite a large body of texts which may be grouped with those which are studied in detail in this book. However, because the *proportion* of texts that alter or reject the graphic conventions of the novel is still small, there has been a strong tendency within criticism to regard such texts as difficult, unreadable and gimmicky, and thus deserving only to be forgotten, ignored or, at best, treated in a way which denies that what happens on the graphic surface might play any role in their literary/textual interpretation. This has certainly been the attitude in Britain, particularly in the three decades after the Second World War, where a traditional criticism, with a strong conservatism in favour of realism and against any writing that might diverge from those conventions, has been dominant. More recent 'postmodern' criticism seems much more willing to acknowledge graphic devices, and often cites graphic disruption as a postmodern aesthetic strategy, but it too sells the graphic surface short. Caught up in debates over what constitutes postmodern literature and whether it is of value, graphic devices are often dismissed as symptoms of the most decadent kind of postmodernity. Neither the traditionalist nor the postmodern critical approach is anything other than reductive with regard to our subject, and in developing an awareness of the graphic surface we shall necessarily expose flaws in critical approaches that wilfully neglect it.

The structure of this book is straightforward: there are eight chapters each divided into sections. The first four chapters set out to demonstrate both how and why the graphic surface has been neglected. In the first we will look at perception of the graphic surface during reading and how it may be obscured by other concerns or automatised until unnoticed. The second chapter examines some critical assumptions about the transformation of manuscript to novel and what our familiarity with the printed form of the book leads us to take for granted. The third chapter looks at theoretical approaches to the graphic surface, particularly those which see printed text as either an idealised sign-system or a representation of spoken language. The fourth chapter moves on to look at how 'blindness' to the graphic surface, and particularly to its mimetic usage, is reflected and perpetuated in literary criticism. Chapters 5 to 8 deal with the work of specific authors, their texts and the relevant critical background, before a concluding summary which touches on some of the implications of these analyses.

In keeping with the subject of this book the graphic surface of each chapter is varied by the use of different typefaces. These are listed, as is customary, near the foot of the title verso or biblio page. Apart from reinforcing points made about the effect of typographic choices in Chapter 1 the variations in the appearance between chapters will also assist navigation within the book.

References for each chapter appear in a consistent form at the end of each chapter, as below, while the Further Reading at the end of the book includes other examples of literary fiction which make special use of the graphic surface.

References

Bray, Joe, Handley, Miriam and Henry, Anne C. (eds) (2000) Ma(r)king the Text: The Presentation of Meaning on the Literary Page, Aldershot: Ashgate

Craig, Cairns (1999) The Modern Scottish Novel: Narrative and the National Imagination, Edinburgh: Edinburgh University Press

McGann, Jerome (1983) A Critique of Modern Textual Criticism, Chicago: University of Chicago Press

CHAPTER 1

Reading the graphic surface

The term 'graphic surface' relates to the face of any page of printed text. We are all familiar with a page of text, and we know how to use it, yet it is just this familiarity that makes the graphic surface a little too close for analytical comfort. It will be helpful, therefore, to step back momentarily in order to remind ourselves what sort of a medium we, as readers and critics, are dealing with.

Imagine an archetypal page of printed text, before reading begins. The words on this model page are irrelevant; we do not need to differentiate letters, read words or lines; they only form the apparent *texture* of the surface, going back to the Latin origin of the word in *to weave*.[1] Text is nothing but marks on paper here, and thus the graphic surface is essentially abstract, like a page of Arabic or oriental script to the average occidental reader, meaningless lines subject to a play of pattern and coincidence. Nevertheless our attitude to this printed page will be completely different to that with which we might approach a wholly blank page: our model page of text offers itself to be read rather than to be written upon.

Once we have conceived our archetypal page of text, we can begin to focus on the specific details of actual pages which such a model obscures. Conventionally, perception of the graphic surface is effaced during reading by our interest in the words that compose it, but this does not mean it does not have an influence on us. As Gérard Genette notes: 'The typesetting – the choice of typeface and its arrangement on the page – is obviously the act that shapes a text into a book ... typographical choices may provide an indirect commentary on the texts they affect ... no reader should be indifferent to the appropriateness of particular typographical choices' (1997: 34). If we think about our experiences as readers it should be possible to remember examples of perception of the graphic surface of texts, even if it was simply bad typography. An example in prose would be the 'rivers' of white space we have

---

1 Structuralists and post-structuralists have been quick to spot the origin of the word 'text' but use it with regard to meaning. See, for example, Barthes (1986: 59–60): 'the Text depends ... on the stereographic plurality of the signifiers which weave it (etymologically the text is a fabric)'. I shall contest this appropriation of text into an ideal non-specific form in Chapter 3.

all observed involuntarily, usually in older printed material, where our eye links the gaps between words vertically and/or diagonally.

The general appearance of any specific page will be largely dependent on the design and technology of the day in which it is printed (or re-printed). The terms that would be used by a designer or a typographer to describe the appearance of a specific page (or indeed to design one) include page format, text area, type size, line length, line spacing, indents, titles, running heads, etc. (see Figure 1.1 for clarification of these terms). All these considerations are generally governed by the conventions of publishing and printing, which vary from language to language, nation to nation and genre to genre, throughout the history of the book. It is not, however, my intention to study the implications and effects of these general typographic and publishing conventions (Genette 1997 does so), only to note them as the influences on the appearance of our model page. I will refer to these conventions only when they form specific departure points for our chosen texts.

The interest in the graphic surface lies at a greater level of specificity still: the appearance of specific pages of specific prose texts.[2] As a rule, in any particular text (and some different editions of the same text) each page will be different. The groupings of letters and paragraph breaks that compose the text determine the individual graphic surface of each page of text. Thus all authors determine the graphic surface of their texts to some degree by choosing the words which form it, but authors conscious of the visual aspect of their texts and who fully exploit their input are able to disrupt the conventional layout and create what I shall call 'graphic devices'.

This term is somewhat broader than *typo*graphic device because it is not limited to the alphabet and the related marks available in a typical western font (or collection of fonts). What I mean by a graphic device is simply an intentional alteration or disruption of the conventional layout of the page of a text which adds another layer of meaning. Some devices may be comparable to the paralinguistic features of speech: pauses, volume, hesitation, etc. Others may be visually iconic, forming images which directly illustrate or conceptually support the prose. Some devices offer facsimiles of embedded texts, while some are mimetic in less direct ways. Others may reorganise the page simply to convey information in more concise forms. In all cases where graphic devices appear they are noticeable because they alter the conventional form of the text which usually is perceived as neutral.

By defining a model page of text at first vaguely and then adding detail I have been trying to show what is usually elided in the process of reading. The elision of the conventional graphic surface by readers happens because the

---

2 Prose, not poetry, because there is a critical blindspot over the layout of prose in comparison. See below.

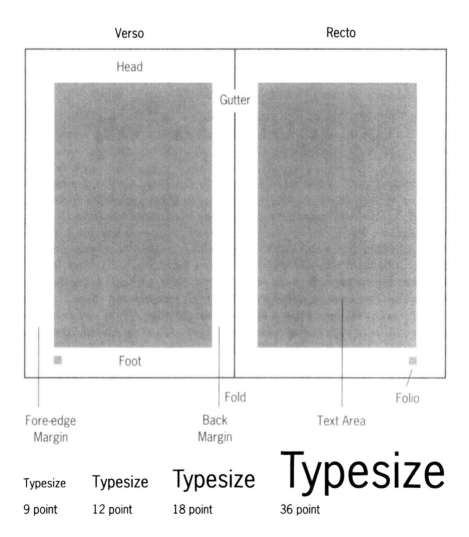

Verso · Recto

Head

Gutter

Foot

Fold · Folio

Fore-edge Margin · Back Margin · Text Area

Typesize
9 point

Typesize
12 point

Typesize
18 point

Typesize
36 point

Indent
→ The graphic surface of the page is free two-dimensional space on which text appears either mechanically (as a result of the translation of the manuscript into print) or consciously (when the author wishes to use it for specific purposes).

←Line-
←spacing

Line length

Serif: Roman *Italic* **Bold**   Sans-serif: Roman *Italic* **Bold**

Figure 1.1: The anatomy of a page

process of reading is automatised. Once we have gained a reasonable competency in reading we do not read words letter by letter but by their shape and length. This is easily demonstrated, using a graphic device as an example:

demonstration

If we obscure half of this word horizontally (looking at either the tops or bottoms of each letter) it does not seriously inhibit our ability to read it (though it is noticeable that the top half of the word with its ascenders is most recognisable). But if half of the word was obscured vertically, leaving only either the beginning or end visible, the remainder would probably not provide us with enough information to identify the word authoritatively. Here, by de-automatising the perception of a single printed word, we begin to see the way that the eye reads words; not letter by letter but by horizontal shape.

This is not to suggest that reading is a simple matter of the eye travelling left to right over each line of text. In *A History of Reading* Alberto Manguel describes the complexity of the visual perception of text:

> It is usually assumed that, when we are reading, our eyes travel smoothly, without interruptions, along the lines of a page, and that, when we are reading Western writing, for instance, our eyes go from left to right. This isn't so. A century ago, the French ophthalmologist Émile Javal discovered that our eyes actually jump about the page; these jumps or saccades take place three or four times per second, at a speed of about 200 degrees per second. The speed of the eye's motion across the page – but not the motion itself – interferes with perception, and it is only during the brief pause between movements that we actually 'read'. Why our sense of reading is related to the continuity of the text on the page ..., assimilating entire sentences or thoughts, and not to the actual saccadic movement of the eyes, is a question which scientists have not yet been able to answer. (1997: 37)

Without claiming to have a scientific answer I do think it is possible to construct a viable theory of how reading operates by reference to the graphic surface, or, as Roy Harris calls it, graphic space: 'writing begins with graphic space. In that space written forms have to be arranged in such a way that they can be read' (1995: 129). On the page, written marks are not seen in isolation: 'Writing does *not* typically depend on establishing a fixed value for any absolute position in graphic space. Instead, what is sought is the establishment of the *relative* position of any scriptorial form to other forms sharing the graphic space in question' (124, Harris's italics). This would seem to me to explain why the eye ranges so widely while reading a line of text. However, the process of moving our eyes is so automatised (our eyes are not static while we look at another person's face, for example) that such movement does not impinge upon our reading.

Thus, when reading, we are perceiving the whole page, as well as the linear, left to right, continuation of the text. Nevertheless, although we might sometimes accumulate enough awareness of the individual features of a text which we have read to help us navigate our way when flipping through the book which contains it, ordinarily the specific differences between one page of prose and the next go unnoticed.

There is, however, a form of literature in which the graphic surface of the page does not go unnoticed: poetry. This is because, as Viktor Shklovsky states in his essay 'Art as Technique', 'the rhythm of prose is an important automatizing element; the rhythm of poetry is not' (1988: 29). Conventional prose is undifferentiated by comparison with poetry, or, as Steve McCaffery puts it, 'Prose as print encourages an inattention to the right hand margin as terminal point ... In poetry, by contrast, the end of each line is integral to the structure of the poem whether it follows older metrical prosodic models or more recent types of breath-line notation' (1992: 60–1). However, the visible difference between prose and poetry is one of degree, as Roger Fowler reminds us: 'Novels are generally more continuous, less punctuated by space; the printed lines reach regularly to the margin, encouraging fast and unbroken reading. But it is clear that the conventions of spatio-temporal attention and reading speed, applied to the two genres, differ *relatively*, not absolutely' (1989: 51). In other words, although automatised by comparison to poetry, the function of the graphic surface *is* noticeable in prose, and has an influence on how a text is read. The reader of this text, for example, would undoubtedly be irritated to find it either entirely unparagraphed or in verse.

The marked difference between our responses to poetry and prose is an issue of interest. Genette points out:

> No reader can be completely indifferent to a poem's arrangement on the page – to the fact, for example, that it is presented in isolation on the otherwise blank page ... or that it must share the page with one or two other poems or, indeed, with notes at the bottom of the page. Nor can a reader be indifferent to the fact that, in general, notes are arranged at the bottom of the page, in the margin, at the end of the chapter, or at the end of the volume; or indifferent to the presence or absence of running heads and to their connection with the text below them; and so on. (1997: 34)

Such awareness of the graphic surface ultimately applies equally to prose. The initial categorisation of a text is in fact likely to be conditioned by our recognition of different forms of graphic surface. Our response to form at the level of the page may thus be described as automatised, yet this should not be allowed to disguise the extent to which our approach to reading is prompted by the graphic surface. One effect of this differentiation is that, as Dick Higgins states, 'The poem tends to be treated as a poem regardless of how prosy its actual text may be' (1977: 3).

Shklovsky, in going on to discuss the psychology behind the automatising process in reading prose, offers a principle for readerly decisions about whether, for example, rhythm is going to be an issue in the text presented: 'The process of "algebrization", the over-automatization of an object, permits the greatest economy of perceptive effort' (1988: 20). This principle may be applied directly to the way that the mechanically reproduced conventional layout of a page of prose allows (or encourages) the reader to ignore the graphic surface, so economising on 'perceptual effort'. This economy of effort is fundamental to the way we experience reality and what is habitual, in terms of perception, is generally economical. Thus when difficulties arise in perception they are generally solved through this principle of economy: we deal with disruptions to the flow of automatised perception by translating them into terms which are familiar to us and thus easily assimilated (see Berger and Luckmann (1967: 68) for example).

In 'Art as Technique' Shklovsky confines his subject matter to ways of producing 'unique *semantic* modification', but he provides some important pointers to ways in which the artistic process challenges this minimisation of perceptual effort. In the most famous portion of the essay Shklovsky says: 'The purpose of art is to impart the sensation of things as they are perceived and not as they are known. The technique of art is to make objects "unfamiliar", to make forms difficult, to increase the difficulty and length of perception because the process of perception is an aesthetic end in itself and must be prolonged' (1988: 20). In this quotation automatised perception is no longer perception; it is 'knowing', or, to be more specific, perception has been replaced by habitualised conditioned response based on the already known. Shklovsky shows how, in order to escape such automatisation, literary texts employ *ostranenie*, making strange, or defamiliarisation.[3]

I believe it is possible, however, to shift Shklovsky's concept of defamiliarisation easily from the language used in the text to the material text itself. For the reader the process of using and interpreting grammar and syntax is essentially automatised too, so that our responses to the graphic surface and the syntactic aspects of printed language are both habitualised. Instances where the graphic surface of the page does become apparent to the reader, through alteration of the conventional uniformity of the text, are those points

---

3 Defamiliarisation is Shklovsky's term but Shelley enthuses over the same process in *A Defence of Poetry*: 'Poetry lifts the veil from the world, and makes familiar objects be as if they were not familiar' (1958: 21).

at which the appearance of the page is 'defamiliarised'. However, we need to look a little more closely at what the implications of this process of defamiliarisation are. What I particularly wish to avoid implying is that disruptions of the conventional graphic surface which de-automatize reading merely serve to remind us that we are reading a book. By increasing the difficulty of perception, and enforcing the expenditure of extra time in order to understand a passage, texts can produce numerous very different effects that do not necessarily simply expose the normal reading process; they may also supplement, broaden and multiply it, as in Shklovsky's original, linguistic, meaning.

Convention, redundancy, noise

Literary texts repeatedly problematise the conventional use of language for their readers, defamiliarising the image or object described, but there are bounds within which this happens; the device of defamiliarisation can work only in a situation which is 'familiar'. Patricia Waugh argues: 'If literature deviates from a norm in order to renew perception, and has therefore continually to change its structures, then the older literary norm necessarily constitutes the "background" against which the new textual innovations foreground themselves and can be understood' (1984: 66).

This necessity of 'background' holds true for the graphic devices in all the texts we shall be examining. Waugh also points out: 'Literary texts tend to function by preserving a balance between the unfamiliar (the innovatory) and the familiar (the conventional or traditional). Both are necessary because some degree of redundancy is essential for any message to be committed to memory' (12). Implicit in Waugh's discussion here is a linguistic model of communication. Speech usually contains some redundancy in order to guarantee its message is not lost. So too does literature, but literary texts don't need to be 'committed to memory' quite so urgently as speech because they exist on paper. Redundancy is also a term used in information theory, a mathematical approach to communication, to describe that which allows messages to function in imperfect conditions. In *The Noise of Culture: Literary Texts in a World of Information*, William R. Paulson, discussing literature in the light of information theory, has the following to say about redundancy:

> We tend to deplore redundancy in writing, considering it to be a sign of muddled thinking, or the refuge of those who have little original thought to express. And yet almost all our utterances are filled with   , as for example this sentence, whose context and syntax would enable the reader to supply the missing word *redundancy* if by some collusion of author and printer it should be missing. In this particular example, redundancy is realized in two ways: first, the sequence 'deplore redundancy ...

And yet ... filled with   ' leads the reader to expect a particular
word, which would thus be partially redundant if and when it appeared;
second, and more heavy-handedly, there is what one might call a very
crude error-correcting code at work in the second part of the sentence, an
explanatory statement to the effect that 'in case there was a word missing
back there it was *redundancy*.' We can relate this example of redundancy
directly to the concept of information as a message that solves, for its
receiver, an uncertainty: since the reader can expect to find the word
redundancy in what turns out to be a blank space, its presence there would
have resolved very little uncertainty and provided very little information –
less certainly than the word *sex* ('our utterances are filled with sex') which
would have signalled a surprising change in the thematics of the chapter.
(1988: 58)

I have quoted this at length because, firstly, it illustrates how redundancy works
in text, and, secondly, it is an excellent example of how a minor disruption of
the graphic surface can be used to defamiliarise text productively. In this
instance, the absence of a word, or rather a space interpreted as an absence of
a word by our automatised familiarity with the way a paragraph 'should'
proceed, allows a rhetorical effect which ultimately enhances rather than disrupts the normal process of comprehending meaning in this non-fictional text.

The space in Paulson's paragraph generates graphic disruption in the
sense I wish to use this term because we do not immediately, at the point of
reading it within the sentence, understand it. Yet if the absent word was
signalled by a dash or a series of asterisks we may have been able to take it as
a convention for a guarded or censored piece of information and may have
instantly begun doing our best to supply its absence in a much more calm
(and much less memorable) way. The gap is not such a convention (precisely
because it is indistinguishable from an error) and thus what initially seems
odd, or defamiliarising, is a new way of offering information (or an absence of
information that calls on the reader to synthesise other information) to the
reader's perception. Yet the space device works only within the conventional
context of the paragraph.

Understanding the importance of context as a factor mediating between
defamiliarisation and redundancy, we can begin to question Paulson's information theory model of literature. The model itself may be briefly sketched as:

source > channel > receiver

As such this model parallels all communication models of literature,
including the linguistic-based structuralist model, and Roman Jakobson's
well known Addresser/Message/Addressee scheme (see Jakobson 1988: 32–
57). In the mathematical theory of information the key concept is that of
'noise'. With reference to the model sketched above, 'noise is defined as whatever enters a message *in transmission* and alters it so that whenever messages

do not arrive as sent, we can speak of noise in the channel' (Paulson 1988: 88, my italics).[4] On this basis Paulson argues that:

> language used as a pure instrument of efficient communication should be as free from noise as possible; thus if literature is to deviate from the utilitarian task of communication, it must be an imperfect process of communication, an act of communication in which what is received is not exactly what was sent. Rather than attempting to reduce noise to a minimum, literary communication *assumes* its noise as a constitutive factor of itself. (83)

In this reversal of the information theory model, literature declares its status as an intentional source of noise. This realisation and its implications for theoretical models of communication are significant, as Jerome McGann points out: 'Poetical texts must be ... sharply distinguished from texts that have imagined themselves as informational – texts that have been constructed on a sender/receiver, or transmissional model' (1991: 12). Critical approaches to literature with conventional communicative models too often have as their ideal linguistic models or information channels which relate only partially to the actual functioning of fictional texts.[5] The information theory model (and those views of literature that see it as pure communication) are clearly inadequate because:

> texts are always full of noise, and the age-old struggle with the ambiguities and paradoxes of texts registers the unhappiness of information transmitters with a medium not ideally suited to their purpose. Poets understand texts better than most information technologists. Poetical texts make a virtue of the necessity of textual noise by exploiting textual redundancy. (McGann 1991: 14)

At this point we might begin to see 'noise' in literature as the contextual interaction of textual elements held, subjectively, in the mind of the reader. In order to accommodate literature within his information theory model, Paulson has to broaden the concept of receiver, i.e. the reader, expanding into an area left vague by Shklovsky:

> the artistic text arises when its reader encounters elements for which the ordinary codes of language possessed by him are not adequate, elements, in other words, which are foreign to his reading process ... Of course the appearance of phenomena that cannot be accounted for by existing schemas of understanding is not unique to art or literature, so that what

---

4 I believe that noise must be ever-present in the actual use of language, whether the channel is spoken or written, differing only in the degree of its effect.

5 Transmissional models of literature lend themselves to author-based study in which the object of criticism is to cut through noise and discover what the sender 'really' meant. One result of such attitudes is that print becomes problematic 'noise'. See Chapter 2.

---

really constitutes the artistic text is the reader's decision to consider the elements hitherto unencountered as part of a new level of signifying structure. (89)

At this point Paulson moves beyond the Shklovskian model; noise is no longer his equivalent of Shklovskian defamiliarisation but is expanded to include more than just the simply verbal as potentially meaningful signification. This version of reading literature will be useful to us for the simple reason that it allows us to engage with 'elements hitherto unencountered as part of a new level of signifying structure', a description which can adequately encompass the graphic surface.

Levels, space, metatexts

We have to be careful about terming the graphic surface 'a new *level* of signifying structure' because the unqualified use of 'level' in literary study is liable to open the way for misinterpretation. In this section I want to draw on a number of critical responses to this concept (and related concepts) and plot a way through them with reference to how the reader deals with the text.

The idea of levels is a common critical device, as Umberto Eco notes: 'When trying to propose a model for an ideal text, current theories tend to represent its structure in terms of levels – variously conceived as ideal steps of a process of generation or of a process of interpretation (or both)' (1979: 12). Eco himself realises the inadequacy of the application of levels to texts, and that it bears no relation to the actual text: 'The notion of textual level is a very embarrassing one. Such as it appears, in its linear manifestation, a text has no levels at all … Therefore the notion of textual level is merely theoretical; it belongs to semiotic metalanguage' (13). In practice Eco uses a diagrammatic form and 'boxes' instead of levels, i.e. alternative spatial conceptions of text. But it needs to be made clear that there are NO LEVELS in literature itself, nor any other non-textual spatial reconfigurations of text, there is only text: 'Levels do not exist: our sense of them is the result of an allusive juxtaposition of registers' (Sage 1989: 38).

Levels operate as an alternative to a naive response that equates textual reality with external reality, or which, put another way, translates text on the principle of perceptual economy. At its most basic the concept of levels offers the possibility of literal *and* allegorical readings of the same text. The words on the page generate multiple possible readings that operate in or occupy different conceptual spaces for the reader.

The concept of levels enables critics to reconfigure text spatially in order to track reading but it needs to be made clear that the space in which this is done is not (in this instance) graphic. I will now paraphrase a particular example of spatial reconfiguration. Joseph Frank's 1945 essay 'Spatial Form in Modern Literature' (1963) develops Wilhelm Worringer's *Abstraction and Empathy: A Contribution to the Psychology of Style* (1953). Worringer sees that the urge to abstraction throughout the history of art is tied to the level of anxiety about the world. Frank equates the portrayal of pictorial space in painting with the portrayal of chronology in narrative, comparing Proust to the Impressionists, and Djuna Barnes to Cézanne. He sees that modernist fracturing of time in narrative springs from the modernists' contemporary angst. Thus their literature can be defined by the way the reader has to assemble information from the text into a totality: 'The reader is intended to acquire this sense as he progresses through the novel, connecting allusions and references spatially and gradually becoming aware of the pattern of relationships' (Frank 1963: 18).

Frank argues that in modernist works 'Time is no longer felt as an objective, causal progression with clearly marked out differences between periods; now it has become a continuum in which distinctions between past and present are wiped out' (1963: 59). However, this does not hold up when put into practice because what Frank describes is the new way the reader is asked to assemble information presented *without* a clear chronology of events because of a fragmented time scheme. This does not have to be apprehended spatially, as Frank accepts in his 1963 revisions. In fact the reader logically, and habitually, deals with this kind of 'noise' and assembles the information in chronological order (or makes story from plot) as best he or she can because his or her own life develops in that order and it involves less perceptual effort to hold events in such a framework. The phenomena Frank deals with are connections made (or not made) by the individual reader, according to his or her memory and understanding of the internal context, between points of information located at various places in the text. It is hardly worth speculating on how memories might actually be arranged in the reader's mind; the only space we can be sure the elements of these connections do inhabit is the pages of the text, i.e. the graphic surface from which the reader extracts them.

It is only from a reader's point of view that we may construct levels, recognising that they are a subjective device for dealing with text. In *Rhetoric of the Unreal* Christine Brooke-Rose dismisses narrative grammar, but states: 'I shall however retain the notion of levels of structure, for they seem indispensable' (1981: 189). Although Brooke-Rose does not go on to explain why this is so it seems to me that Italo Calvino sums it up succinctly: 'literature does not recognise Reality as such, but only levels' (1989: 120). This suggests why this concept of levels arises and why it is so prevalent as to be almost unavoidable. It will not, therefore, be necessary (or possible) to discard narrative levels entirely, but it will be necessary to develop our own conception of them. I believe it will be helpful to think of these features as 'contexts', a term that does not necessarily involve a spatial reconceptualisation of text.

Confronted with the potential subjectivity of any individual reading, criticism cannot track the generation of meaning from text and introduces rather more prosaic and two-dimensional models such as the communication model, spatial form, rigid levels or Eco's metalinguistic boxes; meanwhile the text continues to operate through a sense of productive textual noise, insubstantial levels and allusive contexts which are only 'unified' in the reader's metatext.

We derive the term 'metatext' from Christine Brooke-Rose's work on *The Turn of the Screw* in *Rhetoric of the Unreal* in which she rejects the grammatologists' concept of 'deep structure' in narrative and goes on to discuss 'surface structure' exclusively. One of the objections to 'deep structure', apart from any link to a 'false analogy' with sentence grammar, is that 'deep' somehow implies it is 'more profound in an evaluative sense'. In practice the four levels Brooke-Rose uses are *fabula* (story), *sjuzhet* (plot), text (surface structure) and metatexts. The last of these is divided into authorial and narratorial metatexts:

> Although the surface structure is the narrator's (fictional) responsibility, there will naturally be an author's metatext (AM), which indirectly tells the reader things the narrator does not state directly. And in the case of a dramatised and self-conscious narrator like the governess, there will also be a narrator's metatext (NM) on her own narrative. (1981: 191)

In practice, however, it proves difficult to distinguish between AM and NM. Later, Brooke-Rose offers an insightful answer to this problem: 'For metatext is always essentially the reader's text; it depends on the reader's attention ... and can therefore vary a good deal, not only in degree, but in specific judgements as to whether information implied comes direct from the author or is filtered through the narrator's consciousness' (1981: 208). Brooke-Rose's metatexts are difficult to distinguish because the text leaves the distinction to the reader. Barthes would argue that the reader is the creator of meaning in the text and the whole text is 'the reader's', but Brooke-Rose is defining particular textual features that work by *implying* information. Properly these metatexts are a complex function of the language of a particular text which, though only *implied* textually, goes directly to the reader's hypothesising activity. In other words, they are a particular kind of subjective context generated by the text during reading.

I would like to place these 'metatexts' on a 'high' *level* of hypothesis in a sense that *is* evaluative. In other words, in my admittedly subjective reading, a certain piece of textual information, implied or stated, can be regarded during hypothesising while reading as of greater significance than another such piece of information. I have thus found it helpful occasionally to discuss 'metatextual levels' during my analyses, and I suggest that 'levels' can be used in this way, without recourse to a problematic spatial reconfiguration of information, if we allow the reader's evaluation of information during the hypothesising process to carry some weight. Even so, this is done with the awareness that levels are wholly subjective reader constructs which are definitely not *in* the text; they are metatexts generated by the reader's hypothesising within the context created by the text.

Having established our reservations about the role of the term 'level' in textual interpretation, it remains to clarify the situation with regard to the graphic surface. Clearly the graphic surface is present at some 'level' of reading, even when that reading is wholly automatised. Unlike conceptual levels, the graphic surface is not put in place by readers or critics. Like the model page of text with which we began, the graphic surface has no imaginary depth. But this does not mean it is necessarily shallow. Restored to the reader's awareness, it can be seen to contribute to the reading process which involves the generation of contexts and metatextual levels.

A full understanding of the process of defamiliarisation shows us that it takes place against a background of familiar devices recognised and understood within internal or external conventions. This relationship is comparable to that between the familiar graphic surface, which is the background for all texts, and 'defamiliarising' elements on the graphic surface. Such devices cannot simply be regarded as adverting to the physical form of the book, reduced to a single possible effect. To paraphrase Nurse Edith Cavell: 'Defamiliarisation is not enough', at least not if the concept is used so generally as to obscure or disregard the important issue of context.

Why defamiliarisation is not enough

In order to explain why defamiliarisation alone is an inadequate concept with which to deal with graphic disruption, and before we can discuss a literary example, we must first outline a particular critical account of the stylistic armoury of postmodernism which includes an influential but inadequate response to the use of graphic devices.

When the subject of the use of the graphic surface is raised in Brian McHale's *Postmodernist Fiction* it is regarded as a way of defamiliarising the text as a whole (see 1987: 190–3). Or, put another way, McHale argues that graphic devices in narrative texts raise ontological problems for the reader by foregrounding the book as object. The disruption of the graphic surface becomes, for him, a signifier of postmodernism indicating the authorial intention of jolting readers into an awareness that they hold a product of pigment and paper in their hands. McHale demonstrates a number of ways in which this occurs (which we shall be returning to in our detailed analyses of particular texts), but let us take, for example, the problems of a text which appears in two non-sequential columns within a linear narrative.[6]

The example which follows (Figure 1.2) comes from Brigid Brophy's *In Transit* (1969), set in the transit lounge, and other areas of international limbo, at an unspecified airport. The narrating central character, consciously speaking to an interlocutor in the first person present, is more than simply between *places*. With a partly damaged passport Evelyn Hilary O'Rooley, known as Pat, has lost track of his or her gender. Unisex clothing, social embarrassment and uncertainty as to which toilets to use conspire to sustain this ambiguity. The example comes from a sequence where alternative ways to solve this problem are being considered, and is introduced by the words 'my mind was set on by two simultaneous trains of idea' (Figure 1.2).

McHale correctly identifies the question asked of the reader by the text; 'In what order should the parallel columns or blocks be read?' By the conventions of reading the left-hand column is read before the right-hand column and numerically (ii) follows (i), but we find that (i) is soon overcome by (ii) and thus our normal principles in reading fail us here. In these circumstances we might initially agree with McHale that 'the reader, forced to *improvise* an order of reading, since none is unequivocally imposed upon him or her as would be the case in a conventional prose format, remains constantly aware of the spatiality and materiality of the page and the book'. However, having gone this far with McHale I would like to point out the fragility of his conclusion: 'This awareness tends to eclipse, if only sporadically, the projected fictional world' (1987: 192). It seems odd that, while McHale capably exposes how texts featuring graphic disruptions of conventional layout demonstrate their materiality, he can imply no more than the idea that this necessarily invokes a sporadic ontological awareness of text in the reader. This is directly at odds with the 'constantly aware' of his reading.

I feel McHale struggles here because he fails to take into account the economy of perceptual effort we have noted, and the normalising impulse that attempts to assimilate what does not initially fit into an established pattern. Clearly this impulse dominates any sporadic awareness of the text as text. By his disregard for the normalising impulse of the reader, McHale sets out on a line

---

6 Although McHale does not discuss the particular example which follows, we can see it paralleled by those others which he does acknowledge (1987: 190–3). Other examples of such a device appear in B. S. Johnson's *Albert Angelo*, Alasdair Gray's *Lanark* and 'Logopandocy' in *Unlikely Stories, Mostly*, fragmentarily in Christine Brooke-Rose's *Thru* and Ronald Sukenick's *98.6* (1975). The earliest example I have found is in Ramón Pérez de Ayala's *El Curandero de su Honra* (1926). Gabriel Josipovici's short story *Mobius the Stripper* (1974) employs a similar principle of parallel interlinked sequences but divides its pages horizontally.

my mind was set on by two simultaneous trains of idea.

(i) edged me again towards the books I'd bought. Perhaps I had not exhausted documentary evidence when I had discovered the uselessness of my passport.

However, (i) was coming to me out of the weaker speaker.

Technology errs, I contrived to think just before fadeout supervened, in propping up our bifocalism: wasteful to direct the two speakers of a stereophonic system, or the two lenses of a pair of spectacles, to helping two sense organs to focus on a single object.

The true advance of civilisation will come when science enables a human being to see two Veroneses, one out of each eye, at once or to lend each of his ears to a different opera at the same time.

My own intellectual stereophony was, however, so little perfected that at that point (i) was, for the time being, drowned out by (ii).

(ii), meanwhile, put it interestingly to me that there was a secondary sex characteristic which I had so far completely ignored.

It was, moreover, the very one you would have expected to jump first to my mind, given my passion for opera and my even having received, somewhere in my child-hinter-hood, the elements of a vocal-musical education.

At that point I set my mark on a theme (ii)(a) to be resumed later, if need be.

In some hope that, as a result, need would not be, I rushed on to (ii)'s main burden.

Idiot, negligent idiot, I had not tested the pitch of my voice.

The speaking voice I discounted, that mere internal turning over of a gravelly mechanism, pitchless, claimed not by the external ear as notes but by inner, prior knowledge as, simply, *mine*.

I meant (*of course* operatic I meant) the singing voice, which you loose onto and can retrieve from the surrounding air, and which you can then examine as though you were hearing it objectively and notice in which register you have naturally pitched it.

Figure 1.2: Extract from Brigid Brophy's *In Transit* (1969: 90–1).

of argument that ultimately suggests that every text should seem like a first text for its readers, in which we ought to be alarmed by every chapter heading, and where every divergence from a line of text is a partial eclipse of the fictional world leaving no possibility of *ostranenie* or defamiliarisation since the 'projected fictional world' would be too flickering to establish any continuity.

Another problem for McHale's general interpretation of graphic devices is that an ontological awareness of texts that do not make an issue of their graphic surface is quite possible. McHale's book is full of examples that achieve this in other ways. I believe it is possible to argue that an ontological awareness is implicit in virtually all texts for the reader.

Returning to our example from *In Transit*, we see that the text is split into columns, in a way that is alien to normal conventions, because the columns are not sequential, as they are in newspapers for example, but simultaneous. Since we cannot read the two columns at the same time we *do* become aware of the 'external' world of the book, but I submit that the reaction of most readers will be to deal with this difficulty. Despite the fact there is no way for us to experience simultaneity in the linear process of reading, the double-columned arrangement of this page maps simultaneity for us in graphic space. Thus what seems to be a defamiliarising graphic device allows us to under-stand the internal functioning of the character's mind which it delivers.[7]

I suggest there is a useful principle here. Disruptions of the conventional graphic surface are soon assimilated into the fictional world. *In Transit* is self-consciously aware of it: 'An alienation effect may be a fiction within a fiction, purporting to thrust the spectator back into the real world outside the frame but in practice drawing him deeper into the fictitious perspective' (1969: 70). The outcome of this is to place the accuracy of the term 'alienation effect' in doubt. The reader will attempt to adapt his reading to understand a graphic device. If utilisation of the graphic surface offers a different or enhanced version of mimesis then, I would suggest, the reader is entitled to absorb it in this way, as part of the internal reality of the text, rather than as an example of the external reality of the book. Conversely, while the graphic surface is a physical level more easily defined than the non-existent levels within the text, interpreters should not adopt that visible level as a fall-back position when they are confronted with graphic disruption. In order for us, as readers, to create the internal world in the text, we have to enter the graphic surface. As

---

7 The sequence continues until p. 98. This is not the only double-columned sequence that could be taken from *In Transit*. See also the simultaneous translation Italian/English of the opera 'Alitalia' (50–8), reading the pornographic 'L'HISTOIRE DE LA LANGUE D'OC (THE STORY OF OC'S TONGUE)' with accompanying internal commentary (99–102), the parallel investigations of detective O'Rooley and his other half, Patricia (163–74), 'Stereo-Sci-Fi' (218–21), and, finally, mutually exclusive alternative endings in two columns with the central character as Patricia or Patrick (229–30).

Stephen Ross emphasises: 'A thoroughgoing poetics must confront literature as inscribed object and recognise that it can be engaged only through an act of reading' (1979: 307).

As the vehicle for the text the graphic surface may be anonymous and its role may often be only that of a reference point but when it is de-automatized the graphic surface does not only make us aware of its presence; it may also interact crucially with the text. Once again, the location for the interpretation of levels and/or metatexts operating within the text is the reader, who assimilates each and relates it back to prior knowledge. This includes the recognition and assimilation of graphic devices into reading strategies for specific texts where 'the reader is forced to move to a *new level* of understanding in order to integrate features which at a simplistic *level* seemed merely interference in a message' (Paulson 1988: 90, my emphases). The 'simplistic level' of reading is that in which the graphic disruption is an unacknowledged or unassimilated element. The graphic devices of any particular book have to be read simultaneously with the semantic context of the text. The graphic surface cannot be divorced from the syntactic capabilities of language that allow it to function as fiction and the graphic surface and the text which it mediates can produce meaning concurrently.

Any approach, such as McHale's, which places emphasis on defamiliarisation as an intention in itself is questionable. Instead of an attempt to defamiliarise the text and so show the non-mimesis of the physical form of narrative fiction such disruptions *may* be the result of efforts to make the text function in a *more* mimetic manner. McHale subsumes texts to his argument regardless of authorial intent and takes technique for the subject when, in most of the cases I have studied, technique is effectively at the service of the text itself in order to help it convey or represent information.

I am not seeking to reinstate authorial intent as the guiding factor in interpretation, but to point to it as a necessary factor in the creation of the text. Even so, this importance is strictly limited by the central role of the reader. As C. Kanaganayakam says in his essay on B. S. Johnson's *Travelling People*:

> whatever mode the author adopts to destroy conventional patterns of reading and interpretation, the reader chooses to make up his own pattern to suit his expectations. The ontological framework the reader brings to the text often overrides authorial intention and imposes its own angle of perception. (1985: 88 (see Eco (1992:78) for a limiting of this freedom))

Such angles of perception are usually concerned with continuing progress from the beginning to the end of the book at whatever pace the reader feels comfortable. Disruptions and difficulties at the level of graphic surface which require special negotiation are part of the process of reading the text in which they appear and, we must remember, cannot be abstracted from it. When the conventional graphic surface is disrupted, the reader responds to it in a very similar way to the way in which he or she responds to difficulties in the purely semantic message, by taking context and metatext into account. And, ultimately, the challenge to the reader is always finite and manageable since the coherence of the text, however much it is defamiliarised, is guaranteed by the presence of the physical book in the reader's hands.

References

Barthes, Roland (1986) *The Rustle of Language*, London: Blackwell

Berger, Peter L. and Luckmann, Thomas (1967) *The Social Construction of Reality: A Treatise in the Sociology of Knowledge*, London: Allen Lane

Brooke-Rose, Christine (1975) *Thru*, London: Hamish Hamilton

Brooke-Rose, Christine (1981) *Rhetoric of the Unreal: Studies in Narrative and Structure, Especially of the Fantastic*, Cambridge: Cambridge University Press

Brophy, Brigid (1969) *In Transit*, London: Macdonald

Calvino, Italo (1989) *The Literature Machine*, London: Picador

Eco, Umberto (1979) *The Role of the Reader*, Bloomington: Indiana University Press

Eco, Umberto (1992) *Interpretation and Overinterpretation*, Cambridge: Cambridge University Press

Fowler, Roger (1989) *Linguistics and the Novel*, London: Routledge

Frank, Joseph (1963) *The Widening Gyre*, New Brunswick: Rutgers University Press

Genette, Gérard (1997) *Paratexts: Thresholds of Interpretation*, Cambridge: Cambridge University Press

Gray, Alasdair (1981) *Lanark: A Life in Four Books*, Edinburgh: Canongate

Gray, Alasdair (1984) *Unlikely Stories, Mostly*, London: Penguin

Harris, Roy (1995) *Signs of Writing*, London: Routledge

Higgins, Dick (1977) *George Herbert's Pattern Poems in Their Tradition*, West Glover, Vermont: Unpublished Editions

Jakobson, Roman (1988) 'Linguistics and Poetics' in D. Lodge (ed.), *Modern Criticism and Theory: A Reader*, London: Longman: 32–57

Johnson, B. S. (1964) *Albert Angelo*, London: Constable

Josipovici, Gabriel (1974) *Mobius the Stripper*, London: Gollancz

Kanaganayakam, C. (1985) 'Artifice and Paradise in B. S. Johnson's *Travelling People*', Review of Contemporary Fiction 5 (2): 87–93

McCaffery, Steve and Nichol, B. P. (1992) *Rational Geomancy: The Kids of the Book Machine: The Collected Research Reports of the Toronto Research Group 1973–1982*, Vancouver: Talon

McGann, Jerome (1991) *The Textual Condition*, Princeton: Princeton University Press

McHale, Brian (1987) *Postmodernist Fiction*, New York: Methuen

Manguel, Alberto (1997) *A History of Reading*, London: Flamingo

Paulson, William R. (1988) *The Noise of Culture: Literary Texts in a World of Information*, Ithaca and London: Cornell University Press

Pérez de Ayala, Ramón (1926) *El Curandero de su Honra*, Madrid: Pueyo

Ross, Stephen M. (1979) '"Voice" in Narrative Texts: the Example of *As I Lay Dying*', PMLA Journal 94: 300–10

Sage, Victor (1989) 'The Art of Sinking in Prose' in Sue Vice (ed.), *Malcolm Lowry Eighty Years On*, London: Macmillan: 35–50

Shelley, Percy Bysshe (1958) *A Defence of Poetry & A Letter to Lord Ellenborough*, London: Porcupine Press

Shklovsky, Viktor (1988) 'Art as Technique' in D. Lodge (ed.), *Modern Criticism and Theory: A Reader*, London: Longman: 16–30

Sukenick, Ronald (1975) *98.6*, New York: Fiction Collective

Waugh, Patricia (1984) *Metafiction: A Theory and Practice of Self-Conscious Fiction*, London: Methuen

Worringer, Wilhelm (1953) *Abstraction and Empathy: A Contribution to the Psychology of Style*, New York: International University Press

CHAPTER 2

The presence of the book

Literature has a physical context which criticism should not ignore: the printed book. Assumptions about literature which entirely neglect the vehicle for the text must be dealt with before we can see our way clearly to the graphic surface. While examining such attitudes, we will be using examples from Laurence Sterne's *The Life and Opinions of Tristram Shandy, Gentleman* (1759–67).

The manuscript is not the real work

> What a pity it is not possible for you all to read the ms! (Johnson 1975: 28)

This quotation from B. S. Johnson – ironically lamenting that he cannot show us the butter stains which would demonstrate that his writing was indeed interrupted by his daughter bearing a freshly baked roll – satirises two ideas that I would like to begin to discuss here: (1) that the manuscript is the 'real' work; (2) that interpretation begins from the manuscript. In fact, I want to problematise and ultimately disagree with both of these ideas, and others which might be seen to follow from them.

In considering the status of the written manuscript Walter Benjamin's 'The Work of Art in the Age of Mechanical Reproduction' (1970) is useful. Benjamin refers to the loss of 'aura', or authentic and unique value, of the work of art around 1900 with improved modes of mechanical reproduction (largely referring to photography and film). However, the medium of print is inherently mechanically reproducible and had been in widespread use for three centuries when Benjamin was writing (as he knew well). The novel, which developed as a printed form, has thus never held the same type of aura as a painting, a fresco or a sculpture, because by its very nature it is not unique. The loss of aura from the work of the author begins with publication, and thus only original manuscripts may be invested with this quality.[1]

However, while we may still recognise the aura of a manuscript, to see the manuscript as the 'true' work is an act of folly in our typographic culture. In *A*

---

1 And even manuscripts may be copied from other sources, as, for example, is often the case in the medieval period.

Critique of Modern Textual Criticism, Jerome McGann identifies a prevailing critical practice that has been influential within literary studies in the past and, for some time, went unquestioned. This practice is grounded in the exigencies of editing Shakespeare, but possesses an essentially romantic conception of the creative autonomy of the author (see McGann 1983: 40–2). Such practice returns to the last copy of the manuscript from the author's hand where possible, or does its best to approach this as an ideal if manuscripts are lost (as in the case of Shakespeare). Clearly, editing different copy texts will produce different texts for different editions – we have no problem with that – but when an actual manuscript is used as a standard, rather than a first or corrected edition, editorial attitudes towards print itself come to the fore.

McGann points out the incongruities which the privileging of the authorial manuscript creates for textual scholars, and argues that this approach fails, firstly, in theoretical terms, to understand that authority and authorship are not solitary activities but part of a social nexus, and, secondly, in practical terms, to realise that the first published edition may be a better standard especially when the author has seen it through the press (as is the case more often than not after 1800). McGann summarises: 'an author's work possesses autonomy only when it remains an unheard melody. As soon as it begins its passage to publication it undergoes a series of interventions which some textual critics see as a process of contamination, but which may equally well be seen as a process of training the poem for its appearance in the world' (1983: 51).

Print is a necessity as much as it is a contamination.[2] The idea of authorial autonomy and 'pure' manuscripts, free of the contaminations of mass production and compositors' hands remains, however, sometimes leading to a misguided view which regards the task of editorship to 'restore the lost manuscript as we strip away some of the veil of print' (Bowers 1959: 81). Such attitudes imply that textual study should not consider print as 'part of' texts at all. Our purpose is to develop an approach to fiction which recognises such an attitude as bizarre. Quite simply, without print there is no 'text', only manuscripts.

This is not to diminish the importance of manuscripts, only to suggest that behind the editorial attitude which treats the manuscript as 'the best' example of the text lies another which essentially rejects the material text altogether. Roy Harris identifies this attitude in his introduction to *Signs of Writing*, giving reasons why specialists in different disciplines have not made efforts to understand writing in a comprehensive way. The quotation generalises, but also provides a plausible account of anti-textual critical attitudes:

> For students of literature and music, however, the material manifestations of writing are of only marginal importance. Writing for them is the process of composition, rather than the setting out of the results in a legible form. A 'writer'

---

2   There are exceptions to this; Blake is the outstanding example, but see also Jerome McGann on Emily Dickinson (1993: 27–30) and Kate Bennett's work on Aubrey (2000).

is a creative artist, whose function is not to be confused with that of a mere amanuensis, secretary or printer, and the literary critic is rarely concerned with the actual manuscript or book, any more than the music critic is interested in the score, except as a document recording 'the work' to be studied. But the work itself is not the written document. (Harris 1995: 15)

This attitude can be seen in the Shakespearean study of A. C. Bradley, for whom the task of criticism, or 'dramatic appreciation', is 'to learn to apprehend the action and some of the personages of each [play] with a somewhat greater truth and intensity, so that they may assume in our imaginations a shape a little less unlike the shape they wore in the imagination of their creator' (1961 [1904]: xiii). The effect of this attitude is to rob the physical text of all significance and thus render it 'invisible'.

By contrast we take the view that the ideal is inaccessible to readers and critics and any hierarchy based on divine creative imagination is simply not viable. The printed text is equally as valid and actual as manuscript and in most cases the printed text not only reflects the writer's intent but *is* the writer's intention. What we really have in cases where manuscripts are still extant is two versions of the same text.[3]

This is not to say that manuscripts do not still have aura, or hold a vast amount of interest for literary historians, but that the priestly critical role of such historians comes with some responsibility. In much editorial and critical work involving manuscripts the critic has the manuscript to herself or himself and we readers have no knowledge about it other than what he or she tells us.[4] But what manuscripts can say about authorial intentions is limited, since the product of these intentions should be, at least in principle, what ends up on the printed page. Manuscripts may be valued for what they show of authorial working methods and thought processes, but this must always be related back to the end result on the printed page.

It is only while dealing with a printed text (and one that has not become a rarity) that a literary critic can reasonably expect to share knowledge of that text with readers. The mechanical reproduction of the text allows you to check your own copy, and for us to discuss the novel. Without print the usefulness of that which the scholar discovers in the manuscript, and indeed that which creates an environment in which there is interest in the manuscript, would disappear.

McGann's concept of print as the 'training of the manuscript' for its appearance in the world is appropriate. The 'training' or translation into printed text would seem to confer two things on the manuscript as a whole (apart from commercial viability, at least in potential). The first of these is *fixity*; the end of revision of the manuscript; the printing of the approved words, the deletion of deletions, the insertion of

---

3 See Philip Gaskell (1972: 336–57) for a summary of the limits of textual bibliography, and Gaskell (1978) for a discusson, with many interesting case studies, of the progress from literary manuscripts to printed editions and the question of which version to choose as copy text for editing.

4 We often rely on another graphic device – this one, the footnote – to assure us of the location of rare documents consulted.

insertions, everything made final.[5] The second is *uniformity*, in which instead of manuscript variants we have a situation in which all copies of the text are the same. These two statements seem fairly sound, but we can question the extent to which they are true with reference to *Tristram Shandy*.

Fixity

After the alterable manuscript, the text is finally 'settled' in print: 'For the author ... there is a certain message for which she ... chooses words (... manuscript variants), but for the reader, each word on the printed page has become a necessity, inseparable from the message, since the reader does not [generally] consider the possibility that another word might have been selected in its place' (Paulson 1988: 63).[6] The contrast with the spoken word is even more decisive, as Walter Ong states: 'Print situates words in space more relentlessly than writing ever did. Writing moves words from the sound world to a world of visual space, but print locks words into this position in space' (1982: 121).

Nevertheless text is set in type, not in stone, and may alter over time, circumstance and reproduction. We should not consider the printing of a text as a one-off. Any decent bibliography will list previous, different, editions and will describe the differences between these editions. The influence of the history of texts should not be underestimated and demonstrates the complexity of such multiple appearances.

The difficulty of variation between editions exposes the lack of fixity in what Bowers and other textual critics call 'accidentals' and raises the question of what actually constitutes the text. To take *Tristram Shandy* for example: although no manuscript survives we know the original editions were overseen, quite exactingly, by the author. In fact, in response to forgeries inspired by the success of the novel, Sterne personally signed every first edition of volumes five and six, the inscription by the author, theoretically at least, guaranteeing authenticity.[7] Unfortunately, even in a case of such individual authorial approval of the text on the page, the fixity of the text proved to be only temporary. Sterne's choices of format (page size), typeface (and deviations from it), and design (margins) were idiosyncratic, and a personal response to the publishing conventions of his time. Since then there have been many editions (and many translations (see Portela 2000)) and these later editions, for one reason or

---

5 This finality may be supplemented by errata slips. Their lifespan is, however, generally shorter than that which is printed on the graphic surface. The spoof erratum slip in Alasdair Gray's *Unlikely Stories, Mostly* ('This slip has been inserted by mistake') reverses this logic and the slip's insertion becomes the inevitable thing about it.

6 This may not be true for the critic, depending on how he or she sees their role.

7 See Monkman 1970: 26. The late Mr Monkman demonstrated this to me personally from his library of original editions at Shandy Hall, Coxwold, North Yorkshire.

another (fashion, cost, lack of ingenuity (see below)), have altered the original layout. There are a number of examples of how this affects the text, of which I shall give only a sample.

The address to the reader at the beginning of Volume Six is somewhat exposed by modern single-volume editions. It reads: '– We'll not stop two moments, my dear Sir, – only, as we have got through these five volumes, (do, Sir, sit down on a set – they are better than nothing) let us look back on the country we have just passed through' (Sterne 1985: 397 and 1997: 339). We cannot mistake the single volume of today's editions for a set and thus the statement is at odds with the original joke which depends on the humorous, but at least plausible, possibility of sitting on a stack of rather small volumes reading another.[8]

Other more visual graphic devices also suffer. Trim's famous flourish of his stick, while reproduced at approximately original size in the modern editions, is hemmed in with text, above and below, not given the bottom two-thirds of the page as it is in the original.[9] The effect of this is to proportionally diminish the impact of this graphic summary of what is another recurrent theme of the text: the eloquence of the gesture.[10]

At other times the condensation of the text, both in size and time of publication, is more disruptive. When, in volume three, we are referred back 'to the word *Crevice* in the fifty-second page of the second volume of this book of books' (Sterne 1985: 225) the advice leads us astray since, in the 1985 Penguin edition, it is the eighteenth page of the second volume, numbered 121, that carries the requisite word.[11] There has, we might say, in this instance been a condensation of thirty-four pages.[12] The occasion of the reference is Tristram, as fully grown author, walking with Eugenius and referring directly to the volume in question: '– Here are two senses, cried Eugenius, as we walked along, pointing with the forefinger of his right hand to the word ...' This sequence generates a bawdy suggestion; an innuendo (incited by 'two senses') upon the interaction between reader and text, finger and word. The original edition thus has the author and his companion referring to a part of the text that has already been printed, and may be referred to by the reader separately, as compared with the modern editions in which the same characters refer to another part of the same text as that in which they appear, and thus theoretically not available for them to refer to. This creates a paradox that might not, ultimately, have displeased Sterne but which was

---

8 The 1997 editors acknowledge this in 'A Note on the Text' (xlvi–xlvii).

9 Compare Sterne, 1985: 576 and 1997: 506. The former version is also rather more vertical than the latter which follows the original edition in a more slanted orientation for the flourish.

10 This theme may be seen, perhaps most famously, in the elaborate description of Trim's pose while reading the sermon, in vol. II, ch. 17, but see also Trim's devastating representations of death by means of dropping his hat, vol. V, ch. 7, and by clicking his fingers (rendered as two dots '..') vol. V, ch. 10.

11 For the 1997 edition see page 178 and the seventeenth page of vol. II (83).

12 Or 35 for the 1997 edition.

certainly no part of his original intention. However, what in fact spoils this internal reference is a scholarly reverence for the text that *does* fix it, but only as written, *not as designed*. The edited text attempts to be faithful to the original edition but modernisation does not allow it. The text of *Tristram Shandy* is regarded as a long concertina of words to be squeezed or stretched as required and not, as it was originally planned, related to pages. By what logic may we treat the text in this way but scruple at altering 'fifty-second' to 'eighteenth'? I am not necessarily advocating the latter course, since there are alternatives, but the comparison is a useful one.

(a)

—ſo that from the *manner of it*, it ſtands half excuſed; and being wrote moreover with very pale ink, diluted almoſt to nothing,—'tis more like a *ritratto* of the ſhadow of vanity, than of VANITY herſelf—of the two; reſembling rather a faint thought of tranſient applauſe, ſecretly ſtirring up in the heart of the compoſer, than a groſs mark of it, coarſely obtruded upon the world.

(b)

—so that from the *manner* of it, it stands half excused; and being wrote moreover with very pale ink, diluted almost to nothing,—'tis more like a *ritratto* of the shadow of vanity, than of VANITY herself—of the two; resembling rather a faint thought of transient applause, secretly stirring up in the heart of the composer; than a gross mark of it, coarsely obtruded upon the world.

(c)

—so that from the *manner of it*, it stands half excused; and being wrote moreover with very pale ink, diluted almost to nothing,—'tis more like a *ritratto*[9] of the shadow of vanity, than of VANITY herself—of the two, resembling rather a faint thought of transient applause, secretly stirring up in the heart of the composer, than a gross mark of it, coarsely obtruded upon the world.

Figure 2.1 (a–c): Different punctuation (and appearance) of the same passage from vol. 6, ch. 11 of *The Life and Opinions of Tristram Shandy, Gentleman* in: (a) the first edition (1761); (b) Penguin Classics edition (1985); and (c) Penguin Classics edition (1997)

As a result of such concertinaing, some items have dropped out of the text altogether. The convention of Sterne's day most obviously missing is the 'catchword'. This was the placement on the right of the lower margin providing the word or part of a word that would begin the next page. This convention, for the convenience of the reader and the printer, was one Sterne sometimes resisted and at other times played with.[13] In the first edition there is an instance where the catchword device is doubled for main text and long footnote, both strands of which then converge into the long quotation from the doctors of the Sorbonne on baptism before birth. The loose ends of this can be seen in the 1985 Penguin Classics edition: the footnote on page 83 and the English text of page 84 both ended on page 132 of the first edition and the French 'quotation' began, overleaf, on page 133.[14] Sterne's play with this contemporary device explains why the modern editions' footnote ends on a hanging 'as follows'.

Paradoxically, this situation is partly a symptom of critical reverence for text at a verbal, orthographic level. It seems impossible for editors to change a word in order to retain an intended effect, despite relative freedom with other aspects of the text. For example, compare the original edition and the two Penguin Classics editions for three different punctuations of sentences from *Tristram Shandy* (Figure 2.1). In such minutiae of editing careful consideration has clearly been given to the 'accidentals' of punctuation. The neglect of elements of the graphic surface, all far more significant than the difference between semicolon and comma, makes a stark comparison.

These examples seem to demonstrate that the text is not fixed at all: I am not, however, going to suggest that modern editions of *Tristram Shandy* are travesties. This would be like claiming that any of Shakespeare's plays could not be performed without Elizabethan costume. Modern editions do not lose anything more than a fraction of Sterne's intent, but they do leave something behind and the evidence is at hand, unlike information about Shakespearean theatrical costume. A facsimile edition of *Tristram Shandy* would be a worthy enterprise. Until then we must be careful not to imagine that a text is a text is a text when it appears in more than one edition.

Uniformity and individual reading

The result of mechanical reproduction is, indeed, the reproduction of a uniform text; one copy being functionally the same as the next. It may be suggested that every individual copy is different, but without obvious damage or marks this is not a functional difference: the uniformity of mechanical reproduction holds good. However, as the previous section shows, using the example of *Tristram Shandy*, this uniformity may exist only within individual editions.

Even so, while we may rationally recognise this, an awareness of the uniformity

---

13 For information on catchwords see De Voogd 1988: 387–90 and Portela 2000: 296–303.
14 The 1997 Penguin edition fails less spectacularly on page 49.

of one text with the next does not always impinge upon the individual reader's relationship with the book, as Alberto Manguel suggests: 'Even today, submerged as we are by dozens of editions and thousands of identical copies of the same title, I know that the book I hold in my hands, that volume and no other, becomes the Book. Annotations, stains, marks of one kind or another, a certain moment or place, charac-terize that one volume as surely as if it were a priceless manuscript' (1997: 245 (see also Gass 1996: 340)). Individual copies of printed texts may thus still retain an aura of sorts, of individuality if not of uniqueness, linked to our own subjectivity, individuality or egocentricity. Yet it is clear that *Tristram Shandy* exists as an identifiable entity because of standard editions which offer uniformity.

I think that there is, perhaps, a way to accommodate these contradictions around the presence of the book if we scrutinise the idea that material uniformity is the unbreakable rule of printed text. In fact *Tristram Shandy* comes into play once again as one of the few texts that has managed to defeat the rule of uniformity within editions, and then only in volume three of the first edition.[15] It is a graphic device that does this: the marbled page in chapter 37 (1985: 233–4 and 1997: 185–6).

In the original edition each side of the marbled page was individually produced (non-mechanically) in colour. The page margins were folded to protect them from picking up colour, the page was lain over pigment floating on water, then lifted off. Once dry, the folding was reversed and the process repeated. The marbled pattern of each side of each page was, by the nature of the process, random and thus every copy was different. No later editions seem to have been able to cope with this. Later eighteenth-century editions simply indicated that a marbled page had been inserted. Most twentieth-century editions supply a photographically reproduced marbled page in black and white (as do the Penguin Classics editions). The Japanese translation and the Florida edition of 1978 may be praised for their colour reproductions, but in every copy the same marbled page is reproduced. Some editions stuck marbled sections on to the page, others cut marbled pages from larger sheets and inserted them (e.g. Folio Society (London, 1970), achieving the goal of making every copy different but ignoring the original layout which, very carefully, had the marbled surface fit the size of the text on the page.[16]

What makes Sterne's marbled page a blow against uniformity that is far more than just a bibliographical anecdote, or a challenge to the art of publishers and printers, is the context within which it appears. Perhaps the most surprising feature

---

15 Another significant example would be William Blake's own editions of his works. Ackroyd (1995) argues that by combining engraved images and poetry in individually hand-coloured copies Blake achieved 'works of art that resist conventional interpretations' (122).

16 Day (1972: 143–5) gives a full account of the expedients used by printers and bookbinders to confront or avoid this challenge. Thompson (1973) suggests that the George Macy's Limited Editions Club edition, New York (1935), laboriously fulfilled the original conditions for (inferring from the advertising material quoted) seven hundred copies.

of the first and second volumes (Vols I–VIII were published in pairs) is the black page which mourns, figuratively, 'Alas, poor YORICK!' This earlier device which the marbled page consciously tops is explicitly referred to in the text that introduces the latter. The following quotation begins with the use of a more usual device within the text, that of the insertion of a supposed question from the (implied) reader:

> Who was Tickletoby's mare! – Read, read, read, read, my unlearned reader! read, – or by the knowledge of the great saint Paraleipomenon – I tell you beforehand, you had better throw down the book at once; for without *much reading*, by which your reverence knows, I mean *much knowledge*, you will no more be able to penetrate the moral of the next marbled page (motley emblem of my work!) than the world with all its sagacity has been able to unravel the many opinions, transactions, and truths which lie mystically hid under the dark veil of the black one. (1985: 232 and 1997: 184)

This direct challenge to the textualised reader by the often muddle-headed Tristram, who may not have as much to hide as he boasts, carries with it a challenge to the actual reader. Because the 'motley emblem' will be different in each case the challenge is also something in the nature of a riddle. The quotation is not really about *much reading* in the sense of esoteric knowledge and obscure learning because, as we know, reading and knowledge are not synonymous. The contrast of Walter Shandy's great reading for its own sake with Uncle Toby's mixture of book-learned obsession with fortifications and natural innocence points to what is a constant theme of *Tristram Shandy*: the difference between wit and understanding.[17] To penetrate the marbled page itself – which is not anchored to the fate of a character like the black page – is impossible, whatever sources we may be able to bring to bear. Like the black page, the marbled page cannot be read, but it is infinitely more subtle. Its role as emblem of the work, its moral, seems to me to be simply the exhortation to more reading in a deeper, metatextual, sense, and in particular of *Tristram Shandy*. I believe the emblem is addressed to the individual reader whose reading is assumed to be as individual as the marbled page in his or her individual copy of *Tristram Shandy*. As Peter de Voogd says (imagining that we all have original copies): 'Each marbling is unique, as is each reading of *Tristram Shandy*. It is fitting that your copy of *Tristram Shandy* is different from mine, since your subjective experience of the book is different. And when you turn the page, the design is different again' (1985: 287).

I would suggest that, if each understanding of a text will be unique and individual, then what Benjamin calls aura does not reside with manuscript but with the text and in the reader. Most texts do not make such efforts but they feel none the less unique and individual and this to some extent explains and justifies the perceived pseudo-aura of individual copies described by Manguel. Reading requires entering the

---

17 See the Author's Preface (naturally in the middle of vol. III) on wit and judgement (1985: 202–11 or 1997: 157–65).

text through the graphic surface. Uniformity is a quality only of the inert, unread text. Harris has suggested that writing and reading are 'linked semiologically by a relationship of reciprocal presupposition' (1995: 6). The graphic surface is the medium by which such reciprocity operates. The automatisation of the process of reading tempts us to treat narratives as divorced from the physical means of their telling, yet the separation of text and reading, of content and the graphic surface, does not hold up to scrutiny. To give another example from *Tristram Shandy*, a graphic device such as the black page can live in the memory quite as well as any purely verbal sequence in the novel.

The book as codex form

Having discussed ways in which the printing of texts gives rise to variance (fixing and not fixing text, uniformity and individual readings) we must now consider the nature of the book form itself. Our chosen units of the graphic surface, pages, are conventionally bound into a book, a codex form, and numbered in sequence. This generally functions as a given for the Western reader, but the codex form is not the only alternative for presenting text. It predominates as a form in the present because it is much easier to use than the scroll, much less cumbersome than the tablet, actually much less fragile than wax tablets and slates. It also has advantages over modern technological forms, such as computer-stored text. Editing this manuscript on screen one can only *scroll* up and down, and there is no device for moving between 'pages' quite so 'user-friendly' as flipping between the pages of a book.[18] For ease of reading, and editing, text becomes much clearer on a printed-out page. Quite simply, the most convenient form for reading pages of text is this codex form.

The issue of how the codex form influences the reading of narrative texts was identified and used by Jane Austen, who notes in the last chapter of *Northanger Abbey* that 'my readers ... will see in the tell-tale compression of the pages before them that we are hastening together to perfect felicity' (1950 [1818]: 209). It was addressed theoretically, in a late nineteenth- and twentieth-century context, by Hugh Kenner in *The Stoic Comedians*. Kenner, following the work of Walter Ong on the influence of text on our way of approaching the world, has an awareness of the materiality of the book which allows him to see its significance for narrative. When we make a comparison between a novel and a different kind of text the nature of the book as object

---

18 Though often suggested as the ultimate replacement for books, computers in their present form seem unlikely to achieve an equivalent role. Bookshops often have rather large computer sections providing conventional texts through which potential users are to learn the new technology, and the medium itself is saturated with vocabulary borrowed from literary usage, for example, one *browses* the internet and *bookmarks* those *pages* of interest. Much of the fiction being 'published' on the internet is quite experimental in graphic terms, and the effects this medium is able to achieve are worth studying, but the presence of the book remains our concern here.

becomes immediately apparent: 'The only advantage the physical format of the book confers on a novel like *Great Expectations* is its portability and convenience of manufacture ... It is the books of reference that think to make use of leaves, sheets, numbered pages, and the fact that all pages of all copies are identical' (Kenner 1974: 59). The novel, which tells a story without reference to the physical vehicle of its telling, needs to provide the reader with none of the conveniences of the medium utilised by the dictionary, the scholarly tome, the manual, but nevertheless the novel still has the potential to access them since it appears in the same form.

Kenner refers specifically to the work of Flaubert, Joyce and Beckett, in whose work an awareness of the potentialities (and limitations) of the codex form can be seen to develop. These potentialities may be exploited to extend the range of narrative, and Kenner makes the following point with reference to *Ulysses*:

> the demands Joyce makes on the reader would be impossible ones if the reader did not have his hands on the book, in which he can turn to and fro at his pleasure. And more than that: the whole conception of *Ulysses* depends on the existence of something former writers took for granted as simply the envelope for their wares: a printed book whose pages are numbered. (34)

Kenner continues his argument in this way: 'the text of *Ulysses* is not organised in memory and unfolded in time [like oral narrative], but both organized and unfolded in what we may call *technological space*: on printed pages for which it was designed from the beginning' (35).[19] The same applies to *Tristram Shandy*. 'Technological' space is an important aspect of the texts we shall be examining in detail, one which they share with *Ulysses*, but which all of them also go further in exploiting.

As he follows the very logical progression from Joyce to Beckett, in whose work issues of the stripped-down mise-en-scène and debilitated narratorial competence come to the fore, Kenner's vision of the graphic surface becomes more entropic.[20] Ultimately he suggests that the three authors he calls 'Stoic Comedians' know they are working in a closed system, an impasse involving the 'arrangement and rearrangement of twenty-six bits of type' (74). This sounds somewhat like the premise of Borges's 'The Library of Babel' in which 'all the books, no matter how diverse they might be, are made up of the same elements: the space, the period, the comma, the twenty-two letters of the alphabet' (1970: 81).[21] However, as Kenner admits, there is the possibility of 'something utterly unforeseen' (1974: 107).

We might find the library expanding dramatically if the variables of typeface, layout, orientation, linelength, potential division into two, three or more columns, and

---

19 This quotation may remind us of Frank's concept of spatial form, but Kenner's version is grounded in the materiality of the book.
20 Beckett's use of graphic devices in narrative tends to belong to his early English texts (see Chapter 5) although some of his late plays are almost entirely diagrammatic.
21 Borges's alphabet is, of course, Spanish, hence its twenty-two letters (an example of literal translation).

sudden interruption by space, table and illustration – in short, a full range of graphic devices – are taken into account. These are significant elements of the use of text on the graphic surface with signifying potential which have been staring writers and critics in the face as long as there have been printed texts. The following two chapters attempt to identify how and why the graphic surface has evaded serious critical attention. Readers impatient with theory may take advantage of the technological space of this book to turn to later chapters that again engage with actual novels.

References

Ackroyd, Peter (1995) *Blake*, London: Sinclair-Stevenson
Austen, Jane (1950 [1818]) *Northanger Abbey*, London: Dent
Benjamin, Walter (1970) *Illuminations*, London: Cape
Bennett, Kate (2000) 'Editing Aubrey' in Joe Bray, Miriam Handley and Anne C. Henry (eds), *Ma(r)king the Text: The Presentation of Meaning on the Literary Page*, Aldershot: Ashgate: 271–90
Borges, Jorge Luis (1970) *Labyrinths*, London: Penguin
Bowers, Fredson (1959) *Textual and Literary Criticism*, Cambridge: Cambridge University Press
Bradley, A. C. (1961 [1904]) *Shakespearean Tragedy: Lectures on* Hamlet, Othello, King Lear *and* Macbeth, London: Macmillan
Day, W. G. (1972) '*Tristram Shandy*: The Marbled Leaf', *The Library*, 27: 143–5
Gass, William H. (1996) *Finding a Form*, New York: Knopf
Gaskell, Philip (1972) *A New Introduction to Bibliography*, Oxford: Clarendon.
Gaskell, Philip (1978) *From Writer to Reader: Studies in Editorial Method*, Oxford: Clarendon.
Harris, Roy (1995) *Signs of Writing*, London: Routledge
Johnson, B. S. (1975) *See the Old Lady Decently*, London: Hutchinson
Kenner, Hugh (1974) *The Stoic Comedians*, London: University of California Press
McGann, Jerome (1983) *A Critique of Modern Textual Criticism*, Chicago: University of Chicago Press
McGann, Jerome (1993) *Black Riders: The Visible Language of Modernism*, New Jersey: Princeton University Press
Manguel, Alberto (1997) *A History of Reading*, London: Flamingo
Monkman, Kenneth (1970) 'The Bibliography of the Early Editions of *Tristram Shandy*', *The Library* 25: 11–39
Ong, Walter (1982) *Orality and Literacy*, London: Methuen
Paulson, William R. (1988) *The Noise of Culture: Literary Texts in a World of Information*, Ithaca: Cornell University Press
Portela, Manuel 'Typographic Translation: The Portuguese Edition of *Tristram Shandy* (1997–98)' in Joe Bray, Miriam Handley and Anne C. Henry (eds), *Ma(r)king the Text: The Presentation of Meaning on the Literary Page*, Aldershot: Ashgate: 291–308
Sterne, Laurence (1985) *The Life and Opinions of Tristram Shandy, Gentleman*, London: Penguin Classics
Sterne, Laurence (1997) *The Life and Opinions of Tristram Shandy, Gentleman*, London: Penguin Classics
Thompson, Susan Otis (1973) 'Correspondence', *The Library* 28: 160–1
de Voogd, Peter (1985) 'Laurence Sterne, the Marbled Page, and the Use of Accidents', *Word and Image* 1 (3): 279–87
de Voogd, Peter J. (1988) '*Tristram Shandy* as Aesthetic Object', *Word and Image* 4 (1): 383–92

CHAPTER 3

The graphic surface in theory

In this chapter we shall be examining a series of linguistics-based concepts of literary forms, including the post-structuralist concepts of 'the text' and 'writing'. The critical work of Roland Barthes will be particularly useful to us in demonstrating the assumptions which underlie structuralist and post-structuralist work, though we shall be looking these ideas across their chronological development.

The idealised text

Barthes states, 'We know that a text is not a line of words … but a multi-dimensional space' (1977: 146). When this is put into practice, as it is in his textual analyses of some of the various codes operating in Balzac's *Sarrasine* and Poe's *The Case of M. Valdemar* for example, it is quite clear that Barthes's interest is in the field of meanings thrown up by the text. He has stepped through the graphic surface of the page into the conceptual space within text to examine linguistic signifiers and what they signify. In so doing he privileges the text as sign while the medium of print itself 'is treated as a mere technical device' (Culler 1988: 222). But Barthes's 'multi-dimensional space' *does* emerge from the physical text, as is tacitly acknowledged in the following quotation: 'The plurality of the text depends, as a matter of fact, not on the ambiguity of its contents but on what we might call the stereographic plurality of the signifiers which weave it (etymologically the text is a fabric)' (1986: 59–60). Here 'the text', ambiguous and plural, is the product of its signifying 'fabric': the print on the page. This acknowledgement of the dependence of 'the text' on its graphic surface does not alter Barthes's approach, but it does allow us an insight into the post-structuralists' construction of the relationship between their idealised textual space and the physical graphic surface. As we have reminded ourselves in the foregoing chapters, the reader must access the text through the graphic surface, and this relationship may be usefully kept in mind when we examine the way structuralism and post-structuralism treat the plurality of their idealised text.

What Jacques Derrida says of Philippe Sollers's *Numbers* (an untranslated French novel that makes full use of its graphic surface) seems to demonstrate the lengths to which the text extends itself in post-structuralist thought:

The geometry of this text's grid has the means, within itself, of extending and complicating itself beyond measure, of its own accord, taking its place, each time within a set that comprehends it, situates it, and regularly goes beyond its bounds after first being reflected in it. The history of the text's geometries is a history of irrefutable reinscriptions and generalizations. (1981: 337)

How, then, is the reader to respond to the text? According to Barthes, 'To read is to find meanings'. It is not to reduce the text to one meaning, 'a truth', but to emphasise the plurality of the text. Hypothesising about the text, accumulating metatexts during reading, produces a lot of 'wastage'. Under the subtitle 'Reading, forgetting' Barthes describes the process: 'I pass, I intersect, I articulate, I release, I do not count. Forgetting meanings is not a matter for excuses, an unfortunate defect in performance; it is an affirmative value, a way of asserting the irresponsibility of the text' (1975: 11). But although we cannot fix any definitive meaning to the endless signification of 'the text' in theory, in practice – as readers – we do. Christine Brooke-Rose expresses it: 'meaning is an illusion, absolutely necessary to us but an illusion' (1981: 46). This necessity of making meaning is forced upon us by the very nature of text which is, as Derrida and Barthes have it, theoretically unlimited: 'a true reading ... would be a mad reading ... because it would perceive the simultaneous multiplicity of meanings, of points of view, of structures, a space extended outside the laws which proscribe contradiction ("Text" is the very postulation of such a space)' (Barthes 1986: 42). The reader, then, must limit his or her reading whether it is to retain his or her sanity or simply to contain the multiplicity of potential meanings in such text.

Barthes also suggests that the plurality of meaning varies from text to text on the principle: 'The more plural the text, the less it is written before I read it' (1975: 11). The conventional 'realist' text (which Barthes terms 'readerly') attempts to make the reader's life easy by lessening plurality and therefore making reading more economical. The de-automatised text (the 'writerly' text) offers various challenges to the reader's ability to limit or contain the text and therefore requires more hypothesising, more forgetting.

But ultimately post-structuralism and deconstruction are intent on exposing the fiction of any attempt to bound or enclose the signification of the text, even in terms of the reader. In his essay 'On Reading' Barthes argues:

This imagination of a total – i.e., totally multiple, paragrammatic – reader may be useful in that it permits us to glimpse the Paradox of the reader: it is commonly admitted that to read is to decode: letters, words, meanings, structures, and this is incontestable; but by accumulating decodings ..., by removing the *safety catch of meaning*, by putting reading into freewheeling (which is its structural vocation), the reader is caught up in a dialectical reversal: finally he does not decode, he overcodes; so he does not decipher, he produces, he accumulates languages, he lets himself be infinitely and tirelessly traversed by them: he is that traversal. (1986: 42, my italics)

Similarly Derrida, again inspired by Numbers, argues that the reader may be read by the text:

> The text is remarkable in that the reader (here in exemplary fashion) can never choose his place in it ... There is at any rate no tenable place for him opposite the text, outside the text, no spot where he might get away with not writing what, in the reading, would seem to him to be given, past; no spot, in other words, where he would stand before an already written text. Because his job is to put things on stage, he is on stage himself, he puts himself on stage. The tale is thereby addressed to the reader's body, which is put by things on stage, itself. The moment 'therefore' is written, the spectator is less capable than ever of choosing his place. This impossibility – and this potency, too, of the reader writing himself – has from time immemorial been at work in the text in general. (1981: 290, Derrida's italics)

I would prefer a reader not so passive as Barthes's, one who actually makes the traversal of the physical text, and one less helpless than Derrida's, one who is not compelled to create himself or herself from text. But both these quotations portray an 'ideal' reader, ideal in the sense of being a correct counterpart to the ideal text. Our reader, we have to admit, is less than ideal; his (or her) relationship to 'the text' is external, subjective, limiting. Similarly our 'text' is defined as actual, physical print which is the essential component of the actual, specific texts which our reader encounters.

Our approach will depend on a concept of an active, determined and adaptable actual reader. This reader is implied and encoded in the text but at the same time actual and external to it, with other thoughts and the ability to walk away. Perhaps he or she is best positioned hovering at the nebulous inside/outside edge of 'the text', the region where the graphic surface mediates specific texts. The reader, so positioned, deciphers, hypothesises about and limits individual texts. This is what reading is.

There are difficulties inherent in a reader-oriented approach, perhaps the most problematical being around the issue of subjectivity. Critics are required, if they aim to do anything more than make an empirical description of their own reading, to create their own (as opposed to the author's) fictional reader. We cannot avoid this difficulty but, like Barthes, we will pass this off in the first person plural and 'We shall take the text as it is, as we read it' (1988: 174). It is in fact the subjectivity of any reading, the individuality of reader response and its independence from the intentions of the author, that makes examination of the graphic surface important.

The 'text' of structuralism is idealised text, intertextually limitless, whereas specific actual texts must be created and limited by their readers. We began the first chapter with the concept of a model page showing the weave of the graphic surface, the texture of text, and we began this section with Barthes's tacit acknowledgement of its necessary role in the creation of 'the text'. Ultimately the concept of the ideal text can be seen to be a metaphorical expansion of the actual graphic surface of text which, while seemingly finite, intertextually calls up the whole of printed language and which, as such, signifies at a variety of 'levels' of the kind Barthes acknowledges in the indented quotation above; page, paragraph, sentence, word, letter. But the relationship of the graphic surface to understanding and interpretation is not purely metaphorical. The graphic surface of the page must be processed for us to engage with the text at all. Without it we would be unable to arrive at the ideal text of structuralist and post-structuralist work.

It is not my intention to invoke the graphic surface to install another level of complexity to interpretation (after all, it has always already been there). Instead I am seeking to supply an approach to the vital actual text which will allow the elucidation of its intersection with more idealised forms. My overall intention is to examine the creation of meaning at this point of interaction between text and 'the text' without soaring into abstraction, or forgetting that the text can only signify in interaction with a reader, or neglecting the fact that, as words on paper, text is a very special form of communication.

The linguistic model

The basic premise on which the structuralist approach to literature is founded is succinctly summed up in Barthes's 'Introduction to the Structural Analysis of Narratives': 'discourse must be studied from the basis of linguistics' (1977: 83). Thus Barthes and other structuralists approach literary study with the advantages of a science of language, but at the same time they import the flaws and prejudices of that discipline. Stated simply, linguistic analysis is only one way to respond to the complexity of narrative, and, from some angles, a bad one. Linguistics-based analysis routinely ignores the material aspect of any text, despite the fact that it is this materiality, the process of publication, that gives the text its communicative power through distance and time and allows it to be discussed by critics. The reasoning behind this attitude appears to emerge from an interdisciplinary dispute between linguists, whose interest in language lies in phonology and speech, and historical grammarians, whose approach depends on etymology and written sources (see Harris 1981: 50–1).

The linguistic side of the argument begins, in the twentieth century, with Ferdinand de Saussure. Saussure insists upon the primacy of speech, speaks of 'the tyranny of writing' and baldly states: 'writing obscures language; it is not a guise for language but a disguise' (1960 [1922]: 30, 31). The term 'language' itself is an unhelpfully broad term, which by covering both speech and writing sets up the conflict, but this attempt to appropriate it for speech is clearly problematic. However, this claim has proved more than superficially plausible to many linguists following Saussure, and must stand as an example of the phonocentrism of linguistics (see Derrida 1976: 29).

In *Signs of Writing* Roy Harris studies the implications of Saussure's approach to the graphic form of language: 'For Saussure, writing systems, although semiologically separate are not semiologically *independent*: the written sign presupposes the spoken sign, but not vice versa' (1995: 31). This version of the relationship between speech and the graphic form of writing will not, however, hold up to scrutiny.

The reason that writing is not subservient to speech (and vice versa) depends on the fact that they work in totally different media. Speech operates through sound while writing and other graphic forms depend on the utilisation of a surface: 'Functionally, it is true that writing may become an extension of speech; but technically it is not. From a technical point of view writing is an extension of drawing, or more generally of graphic art' (Harris 1986: 25–6). In other words, the linguistics-based attitude to the graphic form of language neglects its totally separate physical context.

Harris argues that virtually anything is possible for graphic communication: 'The idea of genius behind the great invention of writing was an intuitive grasp of the principle that graphic signs have no limitations for purposes of human communication other than those which derive causally from their primary parameters as visible marks. *They have no other semiological constraints*' (1986: 155, emphasis in original). Semiology itself, the study of sign systems, need not be tied to language, but what is suggested here is that the signifying potential of the graphic surface is a resource only partly tapped by the system of written language, and by no means tied to sound. The effect of this is that graphic space can be seen as a powerful medium for communication in its own right and not simply as a way to record a supposedly prior form such as speech: 'To see that graphic communication is a mode of communication *sui generis* is to see that graphic signs are free to be adapted – systematically or unsystematically – to any particular communicative purpose desired' (1986: 155). From this perspective written communication can include oral communication rather than vice versa, and the study of linguistics itself can be seen to depend on the written word: 'the history of Western linguistics suggests that without reference to an established tradition, it might be extremely difficult to grasp the general criteria of oral "sameness" which would ground any criteria of linguistic units at all' (ibid.).

The essential flaw in the linguistic approach is to regard the ephemerality of speech as an ideal, and thus install an unachievable goal for graphic communication. It would be wrong, however, to entirely 'write off' a linguistic basis for the study of graphic communication. Post-structuralist analysis sought to apply the rigour of linguistics and philosophy to *written* forms.

Writing

In *Of Grammatology* Derrida argues that 'the concept of writing … [is] no longer … a particular, derivative, auxiliary form of language in general' (1976: 6–7). Or, as Geoffrey Hartman puts it, writing should no longer be 'reductively conceived as stored speech' (1981: 43) 'or, more exactly, as the (graphic) signifier of the (phonic) signifier' (Bennington 1993: 42). A positive awareness of the signifying power of writing led Derrida to write about a novel that utilised its graphic surface (as we have already noted), Philippe Sollers's *Numbers* (1981), and to write *Glas* (1975). Strictly speaking *Glas* is a critical work, not prose fiction, but in terms of the use of the graphic surface it dramatically extends the academic conventions of footnotes and references by conducting two different analyses side by side on the page. It was translated into English in 1986. Both editions of *Glas* are presented in a square page format allowing two columns per page, but the two columns are not continuous. Instead they offer separate arguments, the left hand focusing on Hegel and the right on Genet. As Bennington (1993: 6) points out, 'almost the whole of what Derrida has written consists in "readings" ... of literary and philosophical texts'. *Glas* puts examples of both types of reading side by side, but the two columns are visually distinct, none the less. The text of each column is presented in a different typeface and size and both columns are at points inset with sans-serif quotations and clarifications (for example there is a definition of Gladioli running from page 45 to page 52 in the Genet column). On a smaller scale words are fragmented for effect and the prose is full of puns and double meanings.

Hartman (1981) analyses *Glas* in some depth and sees the two columns as 'a structural or architectonic metaphor' (7) with fixed and unfixed meanings – 'distinct symbols' and 'confused words' (72) – which operates as a reminder of prior readings by Derrida:

> The disjunct or aleatory form, which includes variable spacing of paragraphs within columns as well as the insert[ion] of new columns or columnar boxes ..., is soon perceived to be less an experiment than a deliberate technique underwritten by concepts developed previously. It inscribes the theory of ecriture, differance, dissemination, deconstruction, freeplay. (24–5)

Overall, Hartman sees the columns' interpenetrating allusions to their subjects, to each other and to Derrida's prior work as an exercise in 'echo-montage' (61) but he discusses *Glas* as though it were literature rather than theory and compares it explicitly to Joyce's *Finnegans Wake* (79) as a text which also poses the question: 'How many dimensions does writing have?' (85). Hartman is conscious that *Glas*'s multidimensional complexity may be seen to exhibit a 'disregard for the reader' (72) that asks the question but ultimately describes *Glas* as 'a piece of non-representational art, with glimpses of historical or natural reference' (86).

This is a significant point and reminds us that we might compare the two columns of *Glas* with the two columned sequences in *In Transit* that we discussed in Chapter 1. Both are certainly writing but there is an important distinction between them, between the metatexts that they generate; Derrida's two columns offer viably independent contributions to theory; Brophy's columns offer fictional alternative trains of thought within a fictional consciousness. In the non-fiction text there is less room for the reader to escape the problematic juxtaposition of alternatives because, not only are they equal in terms of graphic surface covered, but their relationship is conceptual and less subject to readerly prioritisation on the grounds of relevance. But Derrida's ideal (i.e theoretical) text is not presented here; ultimately, judgements are made: the reader more familiar with Hegel than with Genet will be more engaged with the left-hand column than the right and vice versa. What the literary and theoretical two-columned texts have in common is that their reader will find a way to negotiate them. Defamiliarisation is achieved, to a degree, in theoretical and fictional cases, but there is more here.

Readers, particularly literarily oriented readers, look to limit, contain, make coherent and, in short, *read* even when Derrida makes it difficult. The double-columned form gives each column a very specific context, determines that we must seek connections in both argument and allusion. *Glas* is a metatext of its two columns. For Hartman this makes it a thrilling *literary* experience through which Derrida by his wit, puns and wordplay (i.e. the qualities of a skilful writer) is redeemed. Derrida for his part uses the graphic surface to make his philosophy sing in a different register. He has subsequently returned to the two-columned form (this time splitting pages horizontally) in his collaboration with Geoffrey Bennington, *Jacques Derrida* (1993), a work which also makes use of personal photographs and reproductions. Hélène Cixous, with the help of Mireille Calle-Gruber, has produced a similar volume (*Rootprints* 1997) to which Derrida contributed. The inclusion of extracts, fragments and pictorial material co-opts, a dimension of life writing, just as *Glas* destabilises monological philosophical discourse through its two-columned form.

Other theorists have been much more cautious in their use of such possibilities. A rather more common feature of critical works is to fix ideas by presenting them as diagrams, attempting to use the graphic surface to impose a hierarchical order on language, communication, literature and psychology. Theorists who have used diagrams include Saussure, Jakobson, Barthes and Lacan and these have been highly influential in literary studies but, as Bennington argues, the ultimate effect of such diagrams is to acknowledge that 'one cannot formulate everything in a logic but at most in a graphic' (1993: 287). When the graphic surface is used as a theoretical limit, an anchoring device, it is not surprising that some critics fail to see its possibilities in fiction.[1]

Critics less hostile than Derrida to the linguistic model still see it as a basis from which to approach writing. Jonathan Culler, in his essay 'Towards a Linguistics of Writing', argues for 'a linguistics that would attend seriously to the structures, strategies and effects of writing' (1988: 216). Like Harris, Culler refers to phonocentrically-prejudiced Saussurean linguistics' methodological dependence on the written word, by which some kind of fixed context for study can be established. He then goes on to argue that such linguistics actually relates to text better than to the spoken word, since

---

1 We shall have more to say about particular critical diagrams when discussing Christine Brooke-Rose's *Thru* in Chapter 7.

it excludes such matters as volume, phonetics, timing and gesture that are vital parts of the speech act: 'When discussions of language claim to focus on speech and set aside writing as unimportant, what they in fact do is set aside certain features of language or aspects of its functioning' (222). Culler's 'linguistics of writing' 'would be one that gives a central place to those aspects set aside by this model, whether they are associated with the written character or with the features of speech neglected by linguistic idealization' (ibid.). Culler's argument is interesting, particularly where he refers to 'the written character', but his own grounding in post-structuralism causes some problems.

The first problem is that Culler, again like Harris, uses the term 'writing' in its post-structural usage, i.e. as 'extended metonymically to include, besides the merely graphic, all forms of printed matter, as well as the products of the new and ever-expanding electronic media' (Sage 1994: 5033). The term 'writing', first expanded beyond the written to include the printed, is expanded again, through post-structuralist thought, to the extent that 'it becomes an infinite transgressing of all boundaries' (ibid.: 5035). This usage will 'allow a critic to analyze cultural phenomena of great diversity within a single frame' (ibid.: 5034) as Culler does in *Framing the Sign*, but the term 'writing' now encompasses too much for it to be of use to us. Harris, for example, includes mathematics and music under the term.[2] Thus the study of 'writing' goes beyond the printed literary narrative which we are concerned with into other areas, just as the idealised text escapes the specific, actual text we wish to preserve. It is important to emphasise that what we wish to examine is not ideal, abstract or transcendent but something quite specific: the printed novel.

The second problem with Culler's 'linguistics of writing' occurs because he wants to enlarge (or restructure) linguistics to deal with speech *and* writing more fully than the Saussurean/structuralist model is able to. This means he is asking for the current science of linguistics to expand in two directions at once: (1) to encompass those aspects of speech currently regarded as paralinguistic; and (2) to develop a critical vocabulary to deal with 'writing', in all of its manifestations, as a separate phenomenon. These demands are unified under the call for a development of linguistics that will deal with the problematic 'materiality of language':

> A linguistics of writing ... must address a textuality linked to the materiality of language, which necessarily gets misread when transformed into signs, as it must be by our semiotic drive. Such a linguistics can work on [the] materiality of the spoken word as well as the written – 'the huuuuge fish' that gets away from the

---

2 This broadening of 'writing' brings mixed returns. Harris's argument that numeracy is necessary for the development of writing is persuasive (1986: 133), but his bracketing of writing and musical notation is clearly flawed (1986: 146). If every example of musical notation we have is 'contaminated by pre-existing forms of writing' it seems rash to suggest that an independent notation could be conceived when the evidence seems to imply that in all cases the urge or need to write music down only follows literacy.

fisherman, or such matters of tone and emphasis that are crucial to good storytelling and thus to language in its most decisive manifestations. (1988: 230)

Our aim is to look at 'the materiality of language' solely in its textual form and search out the textual equivalents of the 'paralinguistic features' of spoken language. Thus Culler's example ('the *huuuuge* fish') interests us as a fragment of text differentiated from the text which surrounds it by *visual* means, rather than as an example of speech differentiated by vocal emphasis. But, as perhaps befits Culler's dual aims for his second linguistics, there is another aspect to this device. As a piece of printed dialogue, the textual emphasis given to it by the use of italics seemingly *represents* the spoken emphasis of an imaginary speaker (the fisherman) and thus the simple graphic device assists in creating a brief suggestion of mimesis.

Textual voice

An important step towards understanding the dual nature of the way dialogue functions within text (as, for example, in the above extract from Culler) is made in Stephen M. Ross's essay '"Voice" in Narrative Texts: the Example of *As I Lay Dying*'. In this article Ross outlines and separates two kinds of voice in narrative texts: 'mimetic voice' and 'textual voice'. He defines the former straightforwardly enough as 'that collection of features in a work's discourse which prompts readers to regard a particular portion of the work's total discourse as the utterance of an imagined person (character, narrator, "author")' (1979: 305). 'Mimetic voice' benefits from the suggestion of an extra-textual referent which is made by the use of speech marks.

But it is the term 'textual voice' that holds the most interest for us. Ross is aware of structuralist approaches to narrative, but dealing with the difficulties of Faulkner's text requires him to give some consideration to the visual and material nature of the text. He argues that there is a parallel materiality between speech and text: 'In any discourse, whether speech or literary text, some portion (however small) of the discursive signification arises from a paralinguistic context' (306). This leads Ross to claim that textual voice is the *parole* (performed linguistic instance) of a literary text, though he notes: 'the felt participation of the text may be close to nil, however; if all conventions of print (typography, punctuation, etc.) are strictly adhered to, readers are oblivious of the text as object' (ibid.). Ultimately Ross defines his new term in a way that depends upon its materiality: 'Textual voice is the result of elements in the physical text that signify without necessary dependence on language and that prompt or allow the reader to regard the printed text as a source of signification' (ibid.).

'Textual voice' is close to what we have described as graphic disruption, but Ross's term still carries the accompanying baggage of the first part of his essay in which textualised speech is termed 'mimetic voice'. Though the parallel between speech and text may be a helpful comparison in some cases, for example in relating the way textual voice exchanges audible for visible, I feel the terms 'mimetic voice' and 'textual voice' do not sufficiently differentiate the very different phenomena they cover and may in fact confuse them since what Ross defines as mimetic voice is also clearly textual, and what he terms textual voice (operating on our graphic surface) may also be mimetic. To divide the mimetic and the textual in this way seriously inhibits our ability to interpret the graphic surface of the page.

This problem spoils the advances that Ross's insights make, rather as Culler's inclusion of paralinguistic features with the materiality of written language unhelpfully obscures the important distinction between the functioning of spoken and printed language. In both cases, attempts to deal with what occurs on the graphic surface are hampered by the inability to leave speech out of the equation. The printed word may offer a distinctive voice but it is totally unlike a spoken voice in its silence, its visual form, its physical nature, its relative permanence and its portability. Speech and print should not be considered as two manifestations of an ideal but abstract message. The graphic surface may convey the illusion that what it presents is speech or is from a spoken source but this is only one aspect of its mimetic potential.

The important lesson here is that the graphic surface can contribute to signification in tandem with conventional linguistic signifiers and that this signification can be mimetic. This realisation is obscured, as we have seen, in the post-structural project. Barthes's concentration on the 'weave' of text and intertext allows him to regard bourgeois realism as an inoperable convention, and leads him to produce a dichotomy between 'realism' and the text, mimesis merely being a 'reality-effect' of language (see Barthes 1986: 141–8). In so doing, Barthes has in effect abstracted the idea of the text from the medium of print to produce this polemical opposition. In our view, text, the medium of print itself, *is* compatible with some forms of mimesis. Just how this is possible will be one of the ongoing themes of our analyses, and its absence from critical formulations will be the particular subject of the next chapter.

References

Barthes, Roland (1975) *S/Z*, London: Jonathan Cape (translated by Richard Miller)

Barthes, Roland (1977) *Image Music Text*, London: Fontana (translated by Stephen Heath)

Barthes, Roland (1986) *The Rustle of Language*, Oxford: Blackwell (translated by Richard Howard)

Barthes, Roland (1988) 'Textual Analysis: Poe's "Valdemar"' in D. Lodge (ed.), *Modern Criticism and Theory: A Reader*, London: Longman: 172–95

Bennington, Geoffrey and Derrida, Jacques (1993) *Jacques Derrida*, Chicago: University of Chicago Press

Brooke-Rose, Christine (1981) *Rhetoric of the Unreal: Studies in Narrative and Structure, Especially of the Fantastic*, Cambridge: Cambridge University Press

Cixous, Hélène and Calle-Gruber, Mireille (1997) *Rootprints: Memory and Life Writing*, London: Routledge

Culler, Jonathan (1988) *Framing the Sign*, Oxford: Blackwell

Derrida, Jacques, (1975) *Glas*, Paris: Editions Galilée

Derrida, Jacques (1976) *Of Grammatology*, Baltimore: Johns Hopkins University Press (translated by Gayatri Chakravorty Spivak)

Derrida, Jacques (1981) *Dissemination*, Chicago: University of Chicago Press (translated by Barbara Johnson)

Derrida, Jacques (1986) *Glas*, Lincoln: University of Nebraska Press (translated by John P. Leavey Jr and Richard Rand)

Harris, Roy (1981) *The Language Myth*, London: Duckworth

Harris, Roy (1986) *The Origin of Writing*, London: Duckworth

Harris, Roy (1995) *Signs of Writing*, London: Routledge

Hartman, Geoffrey H. (1981) *Saving the Text: Literature/Derrida/Philosophy*, Baltimore: Johns Hopkins University Press

Ross, Stephen M. (1979) '"Voice" in Narrative Texts: The Example of *As I Lay Dying*', *PMLA Journal* 94: 300–10

Sage, V. R. L. (1994) 'Writing: Literary Criticism' in R. E. Asher (ed.), *The Encyclopaedia of Language and Linguistics*, Oxford: Pergamon: 5033–7

de Saussure, Ferdinand (1960) *Course in General Linguistics*, London: Peter Owen

CHAPTER 4

Mimesis and the graphic surface: a critical blindspot

Fiction, representation and mimesis

Across all the following chapters the relationship between fiction and literary representation will be prominent. In order to shorten our discussion of this issue, I would like to summarise the limits of this relationship. All kinds of literary fiction take place between the opposing – but equally unreachable – poles of reality and abstraction.[1] This is not intended to oversimplify for there is clearly scope for enormous variety in this scheme, even within one novel. The basic implications are, however, twofold:

(1) Written narrative cannot escape fictionality; even documentary or journalistic reportage is a version of, or a re-presentation of, a reality which is not text.

(2) No narrative can escape reference to reality, however fantastic, disrupted or fragmented the text might be, because language is innately referential.

Because representation is inherent in language (2), there is a tendency in reading towards the opposite of 1. Ultimately it leads to the Lockean atomic version of language (one word = one thing) convincingly discredited by I. A. Richards in *The Philosophy of Rhetoric* as the 'Only One True Meaning Superstition' (1965 [1936]: 39). The relationship of language and the world is much more complex than that. Any relationship between words, any series of pieces of language, continues, extends and complicates the process of understanding language so that even ungrammatical sentences demand subjects.[2] In our discussion of defamiliarisation and automatisation we have already dealt with the perceptual mechanisms which mean that in reading a text there might

---

1 Northrop Frye (1990 [1957]: 51) offers a similar opposition. His poles are of 'the mimetic tendency' and of 'myth' but both are contained within literature rather than ultimately inaccessible to it.

2 Harris (1981: 81) argues that Chomsky's example of a grammatical and nonsensical sentence, 'Colourless green ideas sleep furiously', cannot possess both these qualities simultaneously since incompleteness of context and the referentiality of language lead us to conclude that either the sentence's grammar is inadequate or that there *is* a way to make sense to the sentence. In my view we are simply capable, if required, of reading – of making sense of – this statement, helped by the presence of functional grammar, however paradoxical the result might be.

---

be several degrees of awareness of the relationship between the world and the book; automatised, defamiliarised, intertextual, subjective.

In what follows I will be using 'representation' and 'mimesis' rather than 'realism', for reasons of precision and clarity. In his essay 'On Realism in Art', written in 1921, Roman Jakobson suggests that the term 'realism' has become so widely used as to be critically useless. He points out that it is used for the author's conception of reality *and* the reader's, while they may well be different, and has been used by radical and conservative writers time and time again to refer to very different conceptions, once again, both authorial and readerly. He also points out the twentieth-century historical conception of certain nineteenth-century writers as 'realists': 'Hence one specific case, one separate artistic movement, was identified as the ultimate manifestation of realism in art and was made the standard by which to measure the degree of realism in preceding and succeeding artistic movements' (1962: 31). We shall avoid the overused non-specific term, as Jakobson suggests. At the very least it implies rather too direct and unproblematic a link between textual representation and the real.[3]

The term 'mimesis' has its own history. The original use of 'mimesis' appears in Plato. David Lodge has called the presence of this word, as an alternative to 'realism', in contemporary theory 'confusing' (Lodge 1977: 65), probably because Plato uses the term in seemingly contradictory ways (see Lodge 1990: 6, 28–9), but I believe it can be a useful companion to 'representation'. In the first usage, book 4 of *Republic*, Plato discusses the morality of 'poetry' (epic poetry or drama) and finds it wanting, but in so doing defines the nature of that poetry as a combination of 'pure' narrative, that coming from the narrator, which he calls diegesis, and imitative narrative in which the voice of a character is represented by the author, which he calls mimesis and disapproves of (1993: 87–9).[4] Plato's second use of the term, in book 13, via a painting metaphor, has mimesis standing for representation as a whole (diegetic *and* mimetic) and this is the more commonly accepted usage.[5] Once again 'mimesis' is found to be morally wanting, being only the two-dimensional representation of a representation of a divine ideal (Plato's example is a prosaic bed of which there are divine, actual and represented types).

---

3 Not everyone agrees with Jakobson. Stern (1973: 31) is enthusiastic about the 'double life of the word [realism]'.

4 Lodge (1990) latches on to this dual idea of narrative because he sees in it a functional parallel with Bakhtin's concept of the dialogic novel. The idea that postmodern writing may be defined as more diegetic than its modernist predecessors is plausible, but this book will show three 'postmodern' texts either without diegesis (*Thru*), or with it reserved to special sections of the text (*Albert Angelo*, *Lanark*).

5 It is worth noting that Plato's idea of 'holding a mirror up to nature' does not advocate realistic attention to detail but is another way of demonstrating the distance of representation from reality, i.e. it is a metaphor *against* mimesis.

It strikes me that it might be useful to retain the 'impure' imitation usage of mimesis from book 4, not for dialogue alone but for any literary device which acts through imitation on the representational efficacy of the text. For the larger 'mimesis' of book 13, which would include the innate referentiality of language (2, above), it seems adequate to substitute 'representation'. In making this distinction between representation and mimesis no moral advantage is assigned to one or the other; mimesis is simply a more focused kind of representation.

Literary criticism has always tended to interpret texts diegetically, either as an acknowledged fiction presented by an author, or against a particular standard of representation (e.g. the realists). In my sense mimesis is neither of these, but more closely resembles what it was for Plato: the new device, the 'unacceptable' imitative device for representation; the device which seeks to represent directly, rather than through the status of an author figure or via dependence on tradition. Whatever particular label is given to the new device at the time in which it appears is useful only historically. The whole history of literature may then be seen as the recurrent assimilation of mimesis to representation.

The novel and mimesis

The critical history of the novel beginning from Defoe, Richardson and Fielding, had a conception of mimesis which, though ultimately based on classical models, was much more specific in terms of time, place and character, or, in short, detail. As Ian Watt puts it in *The Rise of the Novel*: 'Modern realism ... begins from the position that truth can be discovered by the *individual* through his senses: it has its origins in Descartes and Locke' (1987 [1957]: 13, my italics). The developing methods of representing through character provided an emphasis on originality and, in this way, the source of the name of the form.

However, these early novels do have one further thing in common: in order to support the conception of an interaction between individual and world they often appear as artifacts which are the direct, rather than the mediated, products of that interaction; for example, journals and letters. Thus, significantly, the contribution of the graphic surface, through mimesis of epistolary and journal forms, is the attempted elision of the artifice of the book. Encouraged by the Aristotelian line on mimesis which required artifice to be hidden: 'From the start [Defoe, Richardson] the writers of novels seem determined to pretend that their work is not *made*, but that it simply exists ... The effect is to divert attention from the fact that a novel, like a poem, is a made thing, a book, an object' (Josipovici 1971: 148). Even if we were to question how accurate a judgement of the early novelists' intentions the above quotation offers, it is a fact that critical attention has been almost wholly diverted from the fact that the novel is an object and, equally, from the graphic surface which represents itself to be something other than what it is (see Lennard J. Davis (1983)). However, when we acknowledge this and bear these facts in mind, Watt's discussion of the difficulty of criticising novels can be seen in a slightly different light:

> When we judge a work in another genre [of literature], a recognition of its literary models is often important and sometimes essential; our evaluation depends to a large extent on our analyses of the author's skill in handling the *appropriate formal conventions*. On the other hand, it is surely very damaging for a novel to be in any sense an imitation of another literary work: and the reason for this seems to be that since *the novelist's primary task is to convey the impression of fidelity to human experience, attention to any pre-established formal conventions can only endanger his success.*
> (13, my italics)

Here, in the origins of the novel in English, we have the urge to convey individual human experience placed alongside a sense that new literature must develop different strategies from those which have gone before. These are two impulses which pervade the history of the novel, but which are seldom seen expressed in such a unified way as in these early novels. This is largely because, as Bernard Bergonzi states: 'During the nineteenth century the relations between the writer, the book and the world seem to have stabilised' (1970: 194). However, in the late nineteenth century the tensions between representation and the urge towards new forms within fiction come to the fore more explicitly. The works of modernists and the works of realists share both impulses but differ in the emphasis which they give to each. In modernism the emphasis falls on the different strategies: in traditional realism the emphasis falls on conveying human experience. Neither wholly excludes the other, but the definite sense of increasing divergence at the turn of the nineteenth century may be related to historical considerations outside literature.

Walter Benjamin's 'The Work of Art in the Age of Mechanical Reproduction' describes the advent of a new awareness of the mediation of works of art: 'Around 1900 technical reproduction had reached a standard that ... permitted it to reproduce all transmitted works of art and thus to cause the most profound changes in their impact upon the public' (1970: 221). Since the novel was intended to be mass produced, or at least to circulate in some numbers, reproduction was not a new issue for a writer, but, nevertheless, in the period Benjamin is discussing, the writer, like the painter, was confronted by new technology *of representation* – particularly in the forms of cinema and reproduced photography. And some writers, equally concerned as painters and performers by the implications of these new developments, sought to expand the scope of their medium for representing the world. For example, Benjamin himself expanded his philosophical writing into cultural analysis through the use of pictorial montage (see Buck-Morss 1991).

Thus, while practitioners of conventional realism simply ignored the presence of new forms of representation, and carried on in the fashion of their nineteenth-century realist ancestors without any great anxiety about their medium, those who would eventually be called modernists felt compelled to reject the conventions of literary realism without renouncing its aspirations to the truthful depiction of the world. As Eric Auerbach says in his analysis of Woolf's *To the Lighthouse*: 'We are dealing with attempts to fathom a more genuine, a deeper, and indeed a more real reality' (1971: 540). The opposition between modernism and conventional, nineteenth-century realism in the novel ultimately brought about an opposition in critical perception between modernist texts (with the possible awareness of the book as a printed medium) and realist texts (which did not exhibit this awareness).

As the twentieth century developed, what had become traditional realism (though at one time itself innovative) tended to appropriate a broader 'realism' (which would include some modernist forms of mimesis). As a consequence of this, conventional criticism began to set itself against any kind of experimentation, dismissing divergence from traditional (but broadening) forms of representation as a rejection of a rather narrowly conceived version of literary tradition. The major exponent of this branch of criticism for some time was F. R. Leavis, whose criteria for valuing writers were ostensibly those of moral responsibility. His chosen 'Great Tradition' excluded Sterne for 'irresponsible (and nasty) trifling', Dickens because he was 'an entertainer ... [of] no profounder responsibility as a creative artist than this description suggests' and Joyce, whose work was seen to contain 'no organic principle' and be 'a dead end' (1967 [1948]: 11, 29, 36).

The divisions in literature and literary criticism became strongly polarised in Britain after the Second World War. The nineteenth century, an age of (apparent) formal orthodoxy, was the model for most writers, and all ostensible influence of modernism was rejected; so much so that this literary consensus was called 'The Victorian Revival' by some.[6] From extensive research into this postwar period Rubin Rabinovitz concludes: 'By the early 1950s the dominant critical attitude had become anti-experimental, and very soon afterwards this attitude also predominated among most English novelists' (1967: 37). This produced 'a climate in which traditional novels can flourish and anything out of the ordinary is given the denigrating label 'experimental' and neglected' (ibid.: 168).

---

6 See Evans (1948: 20): 'those years of hostile criticism and dreary vituperation are passed. The Victorian Age has come into its own again.'

Largely as a response to this critical stasis, new, less literary-historical ways of approaching text developed. We might argue that Russian formalist, linguistic, structuralist and New Critical approaches are all responses to the limitations of conventional criticism.[7] They might also all be included under the general heading of formalism (see Waugh 1992). The impetus within this arm of criticism, in attempting to establish itself against entrenched attitudes, is to concentrate on texts themselves and not on literary influence, historical context or authorial intention ('the intentional fallacy'): 'Literary formalists attempt to make the organization of an autonomous text into an object of enquiry in its own terms' (Paulson 1988: 119). As the side of criticism associated with newer forms it thus fell to formalists to define modernism, and consequently the interpretation of modernist texts has tended to drift this way.[8]

When an issue such as the use of the graphic surface in novels is offered to a criticism riven by these biases the flaws in the critical edifice become apparent. By being associated with newer developments in literature, and supposedly therefore leaving convention and representation behind, graphic devices were seen to be mere formal play. The (mistaken) idea that the use of the graphic surface must be anti-representational springs from this fissure.

To be relatively simplistic about it, it seems to me that the divisions within literary criticism can be reduced to secondary fractures from one major schism between the humanist and the formalist, neither of which is entirely adequate for contemporary literary study, nor, to acknowledge my own subjectivity, to carry out the intentions of this project. The former tends towards the author and authorial intention, the latter towards the text and its internal language. Paulson attempts to define these two strands around the issue of representation:

> Literary historical, biographical, psychological, or sociological approaches take the text to be in some sense a vehicle of transmission, something to be described as a representation of a reality external to it. New Critical and structural approaches, on the other hand, consider the text as referring ultimately to itself, as an autonomous entity whose organisational principles must be sought within it and not in some external, referential domain. (1988: 124)

Ultimately this opposition produces a rigid critical convention in which the concept of representation (property of traditional criticism) is incompatible with textual self-awareness (property of 'formalist' criticism). This might be more succinctly formulated for our purposes as the axiom: *any text aware of*

---

7 Although it flowered early in the century, Russian formalism was not to be available to Western criticism until after the Second World War.

8 T. S. Eliot, a leading modernist, became a leading Anglo-American 'formalist' critic, against both intentional and reader-based analysis. Waugh (1992: 136–47) attempts to retrieve his actual ideas from later condensations.

its printed status cannot offer mimesis. This critical convention will be seen, more or less obviously, in the majority of the criticism we shall be drawing on, whichever side of the realist/modernist, humanist/formalist, tradition/experiment and (particularly difficult) postmodernist versus postmodernist opposition the particular critic comes from. Yet it is clearly flawed.

It is too general to say that humanism is in favour of art as reality (and thus against art) and that formalism is in favour of art as art (and thus against reality) but the gist of this helps us to use Raymond Williams's argument against the contrast made between art and reality by most critical schemes:

> High theory and low prejudice share this position equally. Plato or a Puritan or a modern Practical Man can dismiss art as inferior. Aristotle or a Renaissance theorist or a modern Romantic or aesthete can praise art as superior. Yet the long and often bitter dialogue between these contrasted positions leads now, not to a taking of sides, but to a rejection of the premises which both parties share. The contrast between art and reality can be seen, finally, as a false meaning. (1961: 19)

This applies extremely well to the history of literary criticism and theory. We have seen that representation in narrative cannot be escaped or fiction avoided. The impulses that strive towards each of these poles cannot isolate themselves from the other and to respond as if they can is wholly unhelpful to the interpretation and appreciation of literature. However, the point at which reality and fiction are bound together is that of the graphic surface of the page: it forms both the text's grounding in the world and the jumping off point for fiction. Unfortunately, this means that the graphic surface *must* be an interpretative blindspot for any critical scheme that includes the idea of an antagonism between art and reality.

Mimesis and postmodern criticism

The effect of modernism distancing itself from realism and thus, somehow, from reality, seems to have been encouraged by favourable as well as hostile criticism and this has its legacy today in the postwar/postmodern period. The schism is now a contemporary problem for which Patricia Waugh takes formalist criticism, in particular New Criticism, to task:

> Despite the new perspectivism which enters literary history in the early part of the [twentieth] century, [with] the potential for the re-evaluation of the relations between subjectivity and objectivity, so many of the aesthetic manifestos of the time and later critical accounts of the period emphasise 'impersonality', 'autonomy', 'objectivity', universal 'significant form', 'spatial form', 'objective correlative' even when most of the artifacts, such

as *Ulysses*, clearly problematise such notions. The New Critical theorisa-
tion of literature, in particular the modernist text, as an autonomous
linguistic structure, reinforced these ideas. Since then the increasing
professionalism of literature has extended the vocabulary of form and
structure: defamiliarisation, systems of signs, the death of the author, the
free play of the signifier, simulations. (1992: 131)

This last sentence, a polemical summing up of 'formalism' from Shklovsky to
Baudrillard, shows how general our discussion is at the moment. It does, however, suggest that these two camps are still functional in the postmodernist
debate, though some traditional allegiances have shifted and the lack of
historical perspective on our own times makes the situation within criticism
seem much more obscure and complex.[9]

Waugh herself seems to exemplify a more conservative form of postmodernist literary criticism (in fact tentatively claiming a 'New Humanist'
position), which, while accepting there has been a break with traditional
concepts, carries over into postmodernist literary study a distaste for certain
texts regarded as extreme. In *Practising Postmodernism, Reading Modernism*
Waugh expresses this idea: 'The postmodern concept of language games ... is
one postmodern discourse often naively appropriated by an avant-garde
desire to conflate artistic textual disruption with political subversion. Analogy
may be confused with causality in order to claim a massive political significance for formally innovative writing' (1992: 127). In a sense this is a strike
against the devil having all the good tunes. While Waugh stands up for and
accepts postmodernism as a valid field of study against those who regard it
wholly as a corrupt political form (Fredric Jameson, for example), she is still
inclined to view some areas of postmodern experiment as sheer stylistic decadence (*Thru*, for example: see Chapter 7). I would suggest that this judgement
is a rhetorical device which, while it claims there are areas in the postmodern
wilderness to fence off and cultivate, relies on a false perception of 'formally
innovative writing'. It is not possible for any text to dismiss representation.[10]

The graphic surface, often utilised in 'formally innovative writing', is not
to be dismissed as corrupt or meaningless. In fact I would like to suggest it has
a good deal in common with metafiction, the subject of Waugh's first book,
which she defines thus: '*Metafiction* is a term given to fictional writing which
self-consciously and systematically draws attention to its status as an artefact
in order to pose questions about the relationship between fiction and reality'

---

9 Kermode's essay 'Modernisms' (1968) suggests that (what will be called) postmodernism is only neo-
   modernism. In terms of fictional texts this seems highly plausible. Perhaps the greatest difference
   between postmodernism and modernism is that the former comes with a strongly anti-mimetic theory,
   which has become anti-realist rather than the modernist anti-Realist equivalent.
10 Even practitioners of 'surfiction' (an early term for postmodern literature) realise this. See John Barth
   and Raymond Federman (Federman 1981: 8, 26).

(Waugh 1984: 2). And I believe that the awareness and exploitation of the graphic surface, like metafiction, 'is a tendency or function inherent in *all* novels' (ibid.: 5).

In this context it is hard to see how literary works which utilise the graphic surface are 'an abandonment of traditional forms of thought or aesthetic expression' (Waugh 1992: 63). As Lodge says, 'it would be false to oppose metafiction to realism; rather metafiction makes explicit the implicit problematic of realism' (1990: 19).[11] But critical errors over the role of the graphic surface still occur because of the convention, noted earlier, which assumes that an awareness of the physical medium cannot be representational, and which means, in its postmodern formulation, that *texts featuring graphic devices cannot be regarded as anything other than self-reflexive.*

I want to stress that the graphic surface *can* be used to represent in other ways than simply bearing the representational sense of prose. As we have seen with the brief example from *In Transit*, the graphic surface can contribute to reading and most importantly, can represent, though in ways not wholly accounted for by language alone.[12] Furthermore, as the study of specific texts will show us, the graphic surface can determine how we read particular sections of a novel, can problematise reading and represent the difficulties of interpreting experience by mimetically representing of the complexity of thought.

The world and the book

We have seen the opposing influences within criticism which determine that any unconventional utilisation of the physical form which mediates text is seen either as a betrayal of representation or a celebration of its flaws. A more sympathetic attitude to the graphic surface is called for, and we find the beginnings of it in *The World and the Book* by Gabriel Josipovici. He argues that literary study needs 'an awareness of the *double* nature of written words: they are black marks on a white page and they are utterances of a person' (1971: 149, italics in original).[13] This is true, though, from the point of view of the reader, books are the source in themselves; Foucault's author function (1984) details those things we habitually construct around the author figure,

---

11 It might be objected that 'metafiction' does not necessarily include everything that could be placed under the postmodern label. However, if we bear in mind the two statements made at the beginning of this chapter, the scope of the group of texts seen as potentially opposing 'realism' is largely irrelevant. It is the opposition itself that doesn't work.

12 Pols (1992) effectively argues that language is not our only way of knowing 'the real'.

13 Josipovici tries to attach the importance of reading to the utterance of author. In one sense I totally concur but I believe this emphasis to be limiting from a literary critical (rather than a biographical or historical) approach.

but they all come from the text. This is (implicitly) what Josipovici is saying when he argues that the author *is* a book: 'Having made his work, the author is now both the book and outside the book' (1971: 308). There is a real author outside the text and an implied one encoded within it. These can be separated, though very often they overlap. Authors may put any amount of themselves 'into' the text but all this is absorbed by the implied author. However, jacket photos, biographical notes, advertising material, reviews and other paratexts add information about the real author to the implied author generated by the text even though these sources are often unreliable and may contain their own fictions.

Josipovici suggests that 'The modern writer ... makes his art out of the exploration of the relation between his unique life and the body of literature, his book and the world' (291). Instead of maintaining the distinction between art and reality from earlier criticism Josipovici has unified them: world and book interact vitally. Josipovici suggests that this idea is present in modernism to the extent that 'the final meaning of the work is one which it is itself powerless to say, and this is *that it has been made*' (288).

Bringing his argument up to the time of writing Josipovici argues that modern fiction (the term 'postmodernism' was not in common use in 1971) has a different approach from earlier modernism. Such works neither retain the realist pretence that they are not made nor adopt the modernist's absent author consistency. Through the use of destabilising devices predicated on representational (realist) conventions, postmodernist works are able to use the awareness that the text is a physical object to project readers into reality (see Josipovici 1971: 298). In this way Josipovici actually suggests an alternative to McHale's scenario, in which the text simply dumps readers into reality, because in Josipovici's version the movement towards external reality is not to the detriment of the text; the effect is on the reader in the context of continuing reading. In this way such texts can make us realise things about reality, the unexpected, intractable nature of it: 'To make us recognise the boundary of *our* world' (299).

The outcome of this line of argument is that Josipovici suggests that 'the modern novel ... reveals itself as process and not as meaning' (310). Modern fiction is governed not by content but by the process which allows the experience of reading (not what is read) to represent (see also Frye 1990: 66-7 and Hutcheon 1980: 5). The reader must reconstitute a comprehensible world from the text, and this *process* involves creativity and struggle. The problem of interpreting is thus included within the text. Reading may create an imitation not simply of a character's voice but of a situation, realisation, mental state or reaction.

We shall see this mimesis of process, particularly in relation to the use of the graphic surface, in the texts we examine in detail in subsequent chapters.

All these texts are conscious of their status as artefacts, conscious of the mediation of content and language by print on the graphic surface. Josipovici concludes: 'the point about a work of modern art is that it insists on its own status as an artefact and that it cannot therefore be treated like a piece of language or an aspect of society' (300). The specific literary works we shall be studying are all works of 'modern art', called eventually, if not originally, 'postmodern', but their status as artefacts is one they hold in common with earlier works. In agreeing with Josipovici that literary works ought not to be treated primarily as 'pieces of language', i.e. as linguistic, pure messages, rather than visual, physical objects, I feel them to be nevertheless, and perhaps all the more, part of society. Josipovici rejects this latter phrase because he wants to move on to examine the *private* experience of reading. The concept of the reader is something which will be very important to what follows too, but reader and text depend on each other. If a text is not read it does nothing, it is only an artefact; but when it is engaged by the reader, through language, their relationship's external context should not be forgotten.

While most critics conspire either to ignore the material book or over-emphasise defamiliarising elements I suggest that actual readers don't divorce their readings from the book that they read. Only critics tend to have, or rather to theorise, such an 'ideal' or 'pure' relationships with texts. What I wish to examine is not the imagined response of the canon-cultured reader of literature, nor of the idealised reader of *the* text, but the reading of actual physical texts, in a way that does not exclude the possible influence of this materiality.

What is needed to clear the way for this to take place is quite simple: an awareness, without making any judgement as to whether this is a good or a bad thing, that *the use of the graphic surface of the page is not only or necessarily self-reflexive.* The marginalisation of works which utilise the graphic surface depends on graphic devices and mimesis being seen as inherently hostile. Because graphic devices are habitually perceived as anti-representational, modes of criticism inherently inimical to innovation reject them, and modes of criticism resistant to representation and reference claim them, but only to interpret them as autonomous and self-reflexive.

I believe that the task in hand requires us to fall into neither of the above tendencies but to adopt what may appear to be a motley costume of both. In this study we know that it is authorial intention, in combination with publishing and printing considerations, that shapes the graphic surface. Yet it is not these considerations that interest us but the text itself, and the relevance of the text lies in the reader's interaction with it within the larger context of the world. As Paulson suggests: 'Once cast, the text becomes the stuff of dissemination, never again subject to the mastery of he or she who brought it forth in language. The responsibility to make the texts mean something, to use the texts, now belongs to us, who encounter them' (1988: 185). And in that encounter, a mental engagement with a physical object, we already have a microcosm, a mimesis, of our own experience of the world. For this reason engaging with the graphic surface as readers, once our automatised, conventional expectations have been laid aside, should be unproblematic, and with experience there is every chance that graphic devices can become increasingly familiar and acceptable to readers. I offer a brief historical overview of experimentation with the graphic surface in prose below, indicating its frequency and changing critical fortunes, and, perhaps, pointing to its increasing acceptance.

A brief historical overview

The graphic surface has been part of the medium of the printed book throughout its history and thus the utilisation of the graphic surface for effect has been potentially available in all periods since Gutenberg's system of movable type was developed (c.1447). For example, early printed editions of ancient treatises were edited and surrounded by commentary creating a hierarchy on the page which has stayed with us in the reduced form of the modern academic footnote. Another example can be seen in Renaissance poetry: George Herbert's shaped poems, such as 'Easter Wings',[14] go back to classical models, and lead forward to Apollinaire, Marinetti, Cummings, Mallarmé, and from them to the more widespread concrete poetry of the 1970s. The continual availability of the graphic surface for innovation should be kept in mind during this brief (and by no means comprehensive) historical outline.

We can see the use of the graphic space begin to develop beyond straightforward functionality when Spenser provides his own elaborate critical apparatus for *The Shepheardes Calendar* (1991 [1579]), or Pope encrusts *The Dunciad* with the comments of Martin Scriblerus (1990 [1728]). In prose, experimentation with the graphic surface begins with Swift's *Tale of a Tub* (1989 [1704]) which plays up its paratexts: offering lengthy Analytical Tables, Author's Apology with postscript and a list of other works by its anonymous author (including *A General History of Ears*), The Bookseller's Dedication, The Bookseller to the Reader, The Epistle Dedicatory, and the Author's Preface before finally reaching the Introductory chapter of a fifteen-sectioned text, six sections of which are labelled as digressions.

---

14 For the context to Herbert's 'graphic' works see Higgins (1977). The standard version of this poem appears in Herbert (1991: 38). However, the 1633 original edition placed the text over two pages to produce a much stronger impact. See facsimiles such as in Herbert (1968), (1876) or (1885). Warne's edition (Herbert 1878: 88) tries to go one better than the usual compromise by enclosing the text in drawn, horizontal angel wings. The role of graphic space in this poem is discussed by Harris (1995: 60–2).

As we have seen, the graphic surface of the novel received its first major exploration in Sterne's *Tristram Shandy*. But we might also point to the earlier work of Richardson in which we find printer's ornaments used to suggest both the passing of time and the particular character of the epistolator (Barchas 1996: 1–20), and, in *Clarissa* (Richardson 1985 [1747-8]: 893), the surprisingly direct representation of mental anguish by graphic disruption. I refer specifically to 'Lovelace to Belford', Letter 261, which contains 'reproductions' of Clarissa's writings after this introduction: 'some of the scraps and fragments, as either torn through or flung aside, I will copy for the novelty of the thing, and to show thee how her mind works now she is in this whimsical way'.

The nineteenth century does not, as a whole, show many examples of the use of the graphic surface. This seems to have been because of the development of conventional forms through a combination of publishing considerations (for example, novels going through periodical and then volume publication) and a certain utilitarian outlook that, in combination, meant that the novel's form was less susceptible to satire and play unless, perhaps, the work was for children. We can also point to the close collaborations between authors and illustrators in many novels that kept visual and verbal duties distinct (e.g. Ainsworth and Cruikshank, Dickens and Phiz, Dickens and Cruikshank). Nevertheless, there are examples of playful use of the graphic surface in some editions of Thackeray, an enemy to Sterne's work, in which illustrations are directly introduced, standing in for verbal description, or archaic typefaces are chosen appropriate to the subject period.[15] Then there are the significant works of Machado de Assis in Brazil, such as *The Posthumous Memoirs of Brás Cubas* inspired by Sterne. We may also note the mysterious antarctic cryptograms 'reproduced' in Edgar Allan Poe's *The Narrative of Arthur Gordon Pym of Nantucket*, the diagrams of class differences in G. M. W. Reynolds's *The Mysteries of London*, Lewis Carroll's 'concrete' poetry of 'The mouse's tail' in *Alice in Wonderland* and his small type for the flea's voice in *Through the Looking Glass*.

Another limiting factor in the nineteenth century was the sheer volume of public appetite for the written word and the relative cost of paper. These are the circumstances which kept rag-pickers busy for much of the century. Wood pulp did not really replace rags in paper production until around 1875 but rag paper then became a signal of quality which we can see being utilised in William Morris's elaborately designed Kelmscott Press works, and in the extraordinary predatory margins of Whistler's *The Gentle Art of Making Enemies*.[16] These high-quality, small-run publications carried the taint of aestheticism in Britain at the turn of the century (Lodge 1977: 42), but this

---

15 On Thackeray see De Voogd 1988: 384, 389 and Genette 1997: 34.
16 McGann (1993: 6) discusses paper. Frankel (2000) discusses Whistler's publications.

tradition is closely linked to the small press publications which were the first home of the works of many early twentieth-century modernists.

Poets of the modernist period (Mallarmé in *Un coup de dés*, Marinetti in *Words in Freedom*, Apollinaire in *Calligrams*, Pound in *The Cantos*) used the graphic surface of their poems in very distinctive ways, and some modernist novelists of this time were also to experiment with the use of the graphic surface of the page, including Joyce in *Ulysses* and *Finnegans Wake*, Faulkner in *As I Lay Dying* and *The Sound and the Fury*,[17] and Flann O'Brien in *At Swim-Two-Birds* and *The Third Policeman*.

In the two decades following the Second World War the use of the graphic surface seems only to have had novelty value. We can find it occasionally, however, as in Patrick Hamilton's *The West Pier* (1953: 109, 147, 195, 212) where the obscenity of Gorse's collaged poison-pen letters is contrasted with urbanity of Hamilton's prose, but such relatively straightforward mimetic usage went unnoticed. It was left to the 'sub-literary' genre of science fiction to take the opportunity to use graphic devices. The most exciting examples are Alfred Bester's representations of the telepathic society of *The Demolished Man* (1966 [1953]), including abbreviated nomenclature like @kins, Wyg&, and 1/4main, and his ambitious typographic representation of plasmodia in *Tiger, Tiger!* (1956).[18]

It is, however, from the works of modernists that writers interested in the graphic surface in the second half of the twentieth century take their cue. To varying degrees American novelists of the 1960s and 1970s such as John Barth, Richard Brautigan, Raymond Federman, William Gass, Ronald Sukenick and Kurt Vonnegut used the graphic surface to different ends in their works. Contemporary writers such as Kathy Acker, Martin Amis, Paul Auster, Mark Danielewski, David Eggers, Lucy Ellmann, Richard Flanagan, Janice Galloway, Alex Garland, Stephen Knight, Michael Ondaatje, W. G. Sebald, Ray Shell and Irvine Welsh have all made varied or significant use of the graphic surface of their texts.[19]

Between the 1960s and the present there seems to have been a mellowing of critical reaction to the use of graphic surface. Disruption of the conventional graphic surface is becoming more common in literature, though almost without comment as readers accept it. Indeed there is no reason why they shouldn't. The form of the book hasn't dramatically altered and there has

---

17 Faulkner (1987 [1929]) renders temporal shifts in Benjy's consciousness by means of Italics but would have liked to have been able to use type of different colours. See Wasson 1983: 84.

18 Bester returned to fiction late (1980) and contributed a visually psychedelic trip (illustrated by Jack Gaughan).

19 This is an eclectic list and, I believe, far from exhaustive. Relevant works by these and other authors are referenced in Further Reading.

been little as radical as artist Tom Phillips's project *A Humument: A Treated Victorian Novel*, begun in the early 1970s, in which Victorian author W. H. Mallock's *A Human Document* is treated to real deconstruction, with all but selected words on every page blotted out by paint, illustration or collage (1980/1987/1997). The effect of this work is not to demonstrate the destruction of the novel but to celebrate the seemingly limitless potency of just one text. Nevertheless the novel still appears essentially in a form that would have been recognisable to Defoe.

The muffled and sporadic history of the use of the graphic surface in literature, especially within the twentieth century, is the result of its being at once strikingly new and old hat. The graphic surface is everpresent. It may be used in new ways, but graphic disruption has been seen before and, as a result, shallow criticism can always dismiss graphic devices as unoriginal. It is not, however, originality in *discovering* the graphic surface that attracts us to our chosen texts, but the enquiry into how these elements are put to use, and how the arrangement of printed text can contribute directly to the meaning of the narrative that it mediates.

For this reason I will not attempt to deal with all authors with an interest in using the graphic surface or to survey the field in a general fashion. Instead I have chosen to focus on a small number of British exponents: ground-breaking writers whose bodies of work show serious and significant commitment to exploiting the possibilities of the graphic surface during some part of their careers. Specific works studied range in date from the mid-1930s to the end of the century. Their authors are Samuel Beckett, B. S. Johnson, Christine Brooke-Rose and Alasdair Gray, and chapters on each follow in roughly chronological sequence.

References

Auerbach, Eric (1971) *Mimesis*, Princeton: Princeton University Press

Barchas, Janine (1996) 'The Engraved Score in *Clarissa*: An intersection of Music, Narrative, and Graphic Design', *Eighteenth Century Life* 20 (2): 1–20

Benjamin, Walter (1970) *Illuminations*, London: Cape

Bergonzi, Bernard (1970) *The Situation of the Novel*, London: Macmillan

Bester, Alfred (1956) *Tiger, Tiger*, London: Sidgwick and Jackson

Bester, Alfred (1966 [1953]) *The Demolished Man*, London: Penguin

Bester, Alfred (1980) *Golem 100*, London: Pan

Buck-Morss, Susan (1991) *The Dialectics of Seeing: Walter Benjamin and the Arcades Project*, Cambridge, Massachusetts, M.I.T. Press

Davis, Lennard J. (1983) *Factual Fictions: The Origins of the English Novel*, New York, Columbia University Press

Evans, B. Ifor (1948) 'The Victorian Revival', *Britain Today*, February, p. 28

Faulkner, William (1987 [1929]) *The Sound and the Fury*, New York: Norton

Federman, Raymond (ed.) (1981) *Surfiction: Fiction Now ... and Tomorrow*, Chicago: Swallow Press

Foucault, Michel (1984) *The Foucault Reader*, London: Penguin

Frankel, Nick (2000) 'The Meaning of Margin; White Space and Disagreement in Whistler's *The Gentle Art of Making Enemies*' in Joe Bray, Miriam Handley and Anne C. Henry (eds), *Ma(r)king the Text: The Presentation of Meaning on the Literary Page*, Aldershot: Ashgate: 87–104

Frye, Northrop (1990) *Anatomy of Criticism*, London: Penguin

Genette, Gérard (1997) *Paratexts: Thresholds of Interpretation*, Cambridge: Cambridge University Press

Hamilton, Patrick (1953) *The West Pier*, London: Constable

Harris, Roy (1981) *The Language Myth*, London: Duckworth

Harris, Roy (1995) *Signs of Writing*, London: Routledge

Herbert, George (1876) *The Temple: Sacred Poems and Private Ejaculations*, London: Elliot Stack

Herbert, George (1878) *The Works of George Herbert from the Latest Editions*, London: Frederick Warne

Herbert, George (1885) *The Temple: Sacred Poems and Private Ejaculations*, London: Elliot Stack

Herbert, George (1968) *The Temple*, Menston: Scolar Press

Herbert, George (1991) *The Complete English Poems*, London: Penguin

Higgins, Dick (1977) *George Herbert's Pattern Poems in Their Tradition*, West Glover, Vermont: Unpublished Editions

Hutcheon, Linda (1980) *Narcissistic Narrative: The Metafictional Paradox*, Walterloo, Ontario: Wilfred Laurier University Press

Jakobson, Roman (1962) 'On Realism in Art', *Readings in Russian Poetics*, Ann Arbor: Michigan Slavic Materials 2: 30–6

Josipovici, Gabriel (1971) *The World and the Book*, London: Macmillan

Kermode, Frank (1968) 'Modernisms' in Bernard Bergonzi (ed.) (1968), *Innovations*, London: Macmillan: 66–92

Leavis, F. R. (1967 [1948]) *The Great Tradition*, Harmondsworth: Peregrine

Lodge, David (1977) *The Novelist at the Crossroads*, London: Routledge and Kegan Paul

Lodge, David (1990) *After Bakhtin*, London: Routledge

McGann, Jerome (1993) *Black Riders: The Visible Language of Modernism*, Princeton: Princeton University Press

Paulson, William R. (1988) *The Noise of Culture: Literary Texts in a World of Information*, Ithaca: Cornell University Press

Phillips, Tom (1980/1987/1997) *A Humument: A Treated Victorian Novel*, London: Thames & Hudson

Plato, (1993) *Republic*, Oxford: Oxford University Press (translated by Robin Waterfield)

Pols, Edward (1992) *Radical Realism: Direct Knowing in Science and Philosophy*, Ithaca: Cornell University Press

Pope, Alexander (1990) *Poetical Works*, Oxford: Oxford University Press

Rabinovitz, Rubin (1967) *The Reaction Against Experiment in the English Novel 1950-1960*, New York: Columbia University Press

Richards, I. A. (1965 [1936]) *The Philosophy of Rhetoric*, New York: Galaxy

Richardson, Samuel (1985) *Clarissa*, London: Viking

Spenser, Edmund (1991) *Poetical Works*, Oxford: Oxford University Press

Stern, J. P. (1973) *On Realism*, London: Routledge and Kegan Paul

Swift, Jonathan (1989) *Jonathan Swift*, Oxford: Oxford University Press

Voogd, Peter J. de (1988) 'Tristram Shandy as Aesthetic Object', *Word and Image* 4 (1): 383–92

Wasson, Ben (1983) *Count No 'Count: Flashbacks to Faulkner*, Jackson: University Press of Mississippi

Watt, Ian (1987 [1957]) *The Rise of the Novel*, London: Hogarth Press

Waugh, Patricia (1984) *Metafiction: A Theory and Practice of Self-Conscious Fiction*, London: Methuen

Waugh, Patricia (1992) *Practising Postmodernism, Reading Modernism*, London: Edward Arnold

Williams, Raymond (1961) *The Long Revolution*, London: Chatto and Windus

'If the gentle compositor would be so friendly': Samuel Beckett's *Murphy* and *Watt*

Murphy and *Watt* are Samuel Beckett's first two completed novels. They were written in English, unlike the majority of his later writings, and are also unusual in Beckett's prose in that they engage with the possibilities of the graphic surface. This chapter considers the ways in which these novels and particularly their graphic devices have been critically interpreted.

Beckett's work is attractive from the perspective of this study in that his novels address the relationship between the physical and mental worlds – the world in which the book exists and the arena in which its reading takes place. Writing on early Beckett, Anthony Farrow is prompted to say:

> We readers of Beckett often find ourselves confronted with an admittedly problematic object – a novel or play – which occupies space but does not seem entirely like other objects, since its existence suggests various rapports with the non-object world of meaning and mental events. Of course it would be procedurally simpler to treat the problematic object as an object pure and simple like a sausage or an inkwell, or on the contrary regard it as a purely mental event, independent of the world of ordinary objects. But to do so is to miss the point – and this is true of all fiction and all drama of course – that books seem to belong to some area between, or including, both mental events and objects. (1991: viii)

As explained in the introductory chapters I believe the presence of the book is an important consideration for criticism, but one which is all too easily overlooked. Despite the passage quoted above Farrow does not examine the physical book's role in creating mental events for the reader. Though there is good deal of other published criticism of Beckett's earlier works, the particular features of their graphic surfaces have not been coherently explored. Particularly detailed work on *Murphy* has been undertaken, such as Michele Aina Barale and Rubin Rabinovitz's *A KWIC Concordance to Samuel Beckett's Murphy* (1990) and C. J. Ackerly's *Demented Particulars: The Annotated Murphy* (1998) in the *Journal of Beckett Studies*, but in both cases the work is so detailed that it cannot acknowledge graphic devices or accumulated features of this type.

My point is not to diminish such concentrated and useful work but to remember that the words of any given novel are arranged in a certain way on the pages of the book and that this, too, can signify. It should also be stressed that I am not offering a new key to Beckett's work, invisible to his numerous foregoing critics, but merely expanding on an indicative, but by no means governing, aspect of these two particular novels that seems to me revealing within the context of Beckett's prose work. My aim is not to fetishise the graphic surface but to include it as a legitimate feature to be considered within the literary criticism of a well known author's work. I do so by asking what its devices contribute to the reader's experience of the texts in question.

Murphy (1938)

Murphy is Beckett's first published novel and his most conventional since, as Hugh Kenner says, '*Murphy* is at least something like a novel' (1974: 77). Its impact when published was small, and criticism has only returned to it in the light of Beckett's later success. As Rupert Wood suggests; 'With the benefit of hindsight, we can see that *Murphy* ... sets out a sort of logical field for his sub-sequent writing. It is a testing ground for various stylistic devices, for various philosophical ideas, most of which do not re-appear in later works' (1993: 27). This is an accurate assessment but indicates the nature of the temptation to explicate *Murphy* in the light of later work. Restraining the tendency towards hindsight, and leaving aside Beckett's engagement with philosophy, I would like to look at *Murphy* as a self-contained text, a book, an artefact, trying to make its way in the world. This approach is, I believe, well justified by the text since *Murphy*'s narrator possesses a self-reflexive awareness that he is writing for publication (and the readers that this process will bring). As Richard Begam says: 'the novel refers us to almost every stage of its production and consumption' (1996: 61). This may in itself have contributed to the numerous rejections which the manuscript received before its eventual acceptance (forty-two in all (Bair 1978: 269)). Begam ticks off the incidents and graphic devices (which I will discuss in detail) as designed to erode 'the realist intentions of the nineteenth century novel' and 'break aesthetic distance and remind the reader that the book is a published artefact and not a window on reality' (1996: 61). Certainly *Murphy* is not a realist novel but its graphic devices and narrative asides do more than remind us that this is so; they discuss the relationship between text and book and expose the position of the novel's unnamed narrator to be one that lacks any control over the text he appears to mediate. Beckett's later narrators entirely lose any sense of being involved in such a formal arrangement – the publishing process – for reasons we will demonstrate.

Murphy has a number of significant graphic set pieces. One of these is the astrological reading Celia has obtained for Murphy from the Suk and which she rings him about in chapter 1. It is finally delivered in chapter 3 and presented in full, marked off with blank lines and headed by its title in CAPS, author's name in SMALL CAPS and introductory matter centred in *italics* (*Murphy* (hereafter *M*) 22–3). This divergence from the typographical norm is easily ignored because it is representational in form. Nevertheless it does more than fulfil a convention: the Suk's 'Thema Coeli' is a key text within the novel which is quoted on numerous occasions as a guide by Murphy and as a goad by Celia. In mapping out Murphy's life it functions as a cartoon for the plot of *Murphy* and, since the distinctive layout helps the reader to refer back to it, the 'Thema Coeli' plays its part in mapping the graphic surface of the novel too.

There is another shorter document similarly embedded in the narrative, distinctively centred: Austin Ticklepenny's card (*M* 51). The card is itself physically the means by which Ticklepenny attracts Murphy's attention in what is a key encounter within the plot of the novel. The change of layout momentarily arrests the reader's attention as it does Murphy's. The appearance of Ticklepenny's card also links back to the Suk's reading because the astrological concerns that appear to govern the plot are foregrounded immediately following:

> This creature does not merit any particular description. The merest pawn in the game between Murphy and his stars, he makes his little move, engages an issue and is swept from the board. Further use may be conceivably found for Austin Ticklepenny in a child's halma or a book-reviewer's snakes and ladders, but his chess days are over. There is no return game between a man and his stars. (*M* 51).

The closing line of this paragraph is prophetic since it refers to Murphy's demise. When *Murphy* casts off the Suk's influence in chapter 9, again referring back to the content of the 'Thema Coeli', he is not long for the book's fictional world (though he will have time to take part in the chess game that forms the graphic climax of the book, as we shall see later).

A more frequently recognised and remarked graphic device is the statistical presentation of Celia at the beginning of chapter 2. Nevertheless this 'particular description' is seldom given full weight critically. John Pilling's reading offers a good example:

> Ironically, one of the most obviously innovative features in *Murphy* (and rendered the more obvious by appearing at the head of chapter 2) – the dismissal of several categories of Celia's physiognomy as 'unimportant' ... – proves in the event to have been merely local in effect. Our impression of her as immensely important in areas far more crucial than those which this narrator documents grows stronger as the novel unfolds. (1994: 34).

I agree that Celia is immensely important to the novel, increasingly so as it develops, and may be, as Pilling suggests, its 'still centre'. But this ought to provoke us to look more closely at her physical introduction rather than discard it as a doubly obvious gesture only 'local in effect'.[1] Of the two entries which are 'Unimportant', 'Age' and 'Instep', one seems genuinely unimportant and the other much less clearly so.[2] While there is humour in the list ('Head: Small and round / Features: Mobile') it seems to be unlikely that these two unimportants form 'the joke' since it would have worked much better with the genuinely unimportant 'Instep' setting up 'Age: Unimportant'.

The real joke comes when this unnamed list of statistics is brought into the narrative with 'She stormed away from the callbox accompanied delightedly by her hips etc.' (M 10). This is a wonderful sentence that does a number of things simultaneously, rather like Celia's walk. Firstly 'the callbox' allows us to place the statistically described figure plausibly as the Celia who has telephoned Murphy in the previous chapter. Secondly, it individuates the statistics, as though Celia could walk away from the callbox without her hips etc. Thirdly it uses the pathetic fallacy attributing agency and enjoyment to the hips in what is apparently a very distinctive walk and a badge of occupation that turns public parks into places of work for Celia since, however melancholy her mood, 'she could not disguise her gait' (M 42).

As Ackerly (1998: 18) suggests, the list parodies itemised literary descriptions of female characters' characteristics (her eyes …, her lips …), but the list also goes further than poetic references and ridicules measured physical descriptions in general because they tell us so little.[3] The list's obsession with attributes nevertheless has a particular, significant and lasting effect: it serves to divorce the mental Celia from the physical Celia.

Celia's physical attractiveness, emphasised throughout, is first intimated in the telephone conversation between her and Murphy:

> 'I have it,' she said.
> 'Don't I know,' said Murphy.
> 'I don't mean that,' she said.

And it is confirmed, as far as possible, in the statistics themselves, reinforced by the pools collectors who follow her, and again later when she effortlessly draws the amorous Wylie's attention from the 'exceptionally anthropoid' 'beautiful Irish girl' (M 69) Miss Counihan (see M 130–1). The non-physical Celia is

---

1 The list of statistics is a one-off in this novel, clearly not schematised in the manner of the Ithaca section of *Ulysses*. The one-off use of this descriptive form also misses an opportunity to compare characters in the narrative in the way Vonnegut (1974: 137–9) reveals his characters' intimate measurements.

2 How old is Celia? The statistics indicate physical maturity but the death of her parents in the *Morro Castle* disaster (1934) give her only a few years to grow up in Mr Kelly's 'care' and, as Ackerly points out, a relatively brief career on the street pre-Murphy (1998: 21).

3 Amongst such systems we might include the Bertillon system for recording the physical measurements of criminals as a means of identification prior to fingerprint records and theories that physical characteristics could identify criminal types first advocated by Cesare Lombroso in 1876.

presented in the phone call and in her dialogue with Mr Kelly and as she meditates during Murphy's absences. The awareness generated of exterior and interior Celias both engages us and emphasises Murphy's folly in abandoning her.[4] If not bound up in his own seedy solipsism Murphy might have accessed Celia's hidden depths instead of fatally pursuing the pathological independence of certain inmates of the Magdalen Mental Mercyseat, particularly Mr Endon (Gk. within).

The climax of *Murphy* also modifies the use of the graphic surface of the book (136–8). The chess match between Murphy and Mr Endon is rendered in the conventional form for recording chess matches on pages 136–7 and is annotated, keyed by letter, on pages 137–8. The chess form is not very readable alone and a board set up alongside tends to enforce its own logic over the printed code.[5] The keyed commentary on the game forms a substitute summary (or match report) but does not make clear the insane schizophrenic solipsism of Mr Endon's play, leaving Murphy's and Endon's non-communicative butterfly kiss to make the point emphatically.

If the layout of the game on the page is visually striking, it assumes readers' familiarity with chess and the ability to set it up in three dimensions. In presenting the game in this way *Murphy* appeals to another code, specialist knowledge, while at the same time emphasising a precision in the text's analysis and implying a significance to the game that will justify the break with prose convention and reward the reader's indulgence of it. As Hugh Kenner suggests, without developing the possibilities any further, in this alone *Murphy* 'may be the first reader participation novel. Fully to get the hang of it, you must set pieces on a board when you are part the way through Chapter 11 and work out a chess game' (1973: 56). In this sense the chess game does appear to demand extra-textual participation though, as I've suggested, we may also read past it.[6] In any case, whether skimmed or enacted, the chess game shows *Murphy* shifting the goalposts, offering a key in another form (in two and three dimensions). The

---

4 There is one further sequence of the novel in which the graphic surface may be said to be used to develop our sympathy for Celia. At the end of chapter 10 (131), while Wylie 'glutted his eyes' on her, there are paragraphs in which Celia remembers snatches of songs (presented in indented italics) sung to her infant self by Mr Kelly. It may be that the seekers of Murphy who arrive from Ireland bring on 'a touching flashback to Celia's earliest years …' which will subsequently be undercut (Ackerly 1998: 184), but the scene might equally be described as Celia under the eyes of predatory males. This would place her memories in a more sinister light, with implications about Mr Kelly's 'care' for his niece. Either way in this scene the reflective Celia is emphatically the novel's 'still centre'. Beckett's later novels lack such sympathetic female characters.

5 As implied by Ackerly's confession about missing a typo present in editions of the novel since 1963 despite his prior studies of this aspect of the novel (1998: 192).

6 In prompting the reader to rely on materials outside the book the chess game resembles the fairly numerous examples of arcane etymology utilised in *Murphy* which invite the reader with less aptitude for languages than their author to turn to the dictionary (preferably a good one) or improvise a plausible reading from context as best they can.

chess game is a turning point in the plot in which Murphy is able to realise that he is not communicating with Mr Endon and that in this sense communication outside himself still motivates him.

This is an alteration of Murphy's desires as codified in chapter 6 of the book (*M* 63–6) wherein Murphy's psychology is dealt with. Chapter 6 is referred to in advance (6, 8, 9) and thus *Murphy* makes use of what Kenner calls the 'technological space' of the book (see 1974: 35). To do so is, as Ackerly says, 'an affront to the conventions of [twentieth century] realism' (1998: 4). The narrator ostensibly regards the provision of chapter 6 as a 'painful duty' (*M* 66) to be discharged with apologetic concern ('It is most unfortunate' (63)). But, so introduced and emphasised by him, the attempt to shepherd such considerations into one chapter is a measure of the narrator's controlling influence. While economically efficient, in theory, chapter 6 seems to appear at exactly the moment least convenient for the reader concerned to find out about the 'shocking thing' announced at the end of chapter 5 (*M* 62) and which revelation is further delayed by chapter 7. Thus apparent concern for the reader's ease actually plays upon the reader's curiosity in a stratagem that demonstrates narratorial power.

The odd dialectic of power over and concern for the reader comes together repeatedly in the text's internal awareness of the book form. Figured in the narrator's awareness of the process of publication, and of his potential readers, it manifests in his attention on impediments to and opportunities for communication between himself and readers. For example, the reader is buttonholed in the sequence in the cornerhouse where Murphy's method for regularly defrauding such establishments is elucidated with the following invitation in its own paragraph: 'Try it sometime, gentle skimmer' (*M* 51). This invitation could be read as an unflattering assumption about the reader's financial bracket or as a booby-trap for the bookshop skim-reader, but I suggest the most natural reading is collusive; assuming and emphasising a bond between narrator and reader. Once again an 'affront to the conventions of realism' reminds readers of their relationship to the text.

A potential impediment to the narrator's communication with the reader, referred to several times, is 'the censor':

> Celia said that if he did not find work at once she would have to go back to hers. Murphy knew what that meant. No more music.
> This phrase is chosen with care, lest the filthy censors should lack an occasion to commit their filthy synecdoche. (*M* 47)

This passage insults the potential interloper and flaunts a code between a narrator and reader. Music means sex, and 'serenade, nocturne and albada' (*M* 46, 141) describes Murphy and Celia's lovemaking. In establishing this transparent code, or his own synecdoche, the narrator challenges the censors to censor music itself. This idea is developed further in the following passage about two of the novel's other lovers which uses more musical terminology and the legal language of libel and pornography prosecutions:

> Miss Counihan sat on Wylie's knees, *not* in Wynn's Hotel lest an action for libel should lie, and oyster kisses passed between them. Wylie did not often kiss, but when he did it was a serious matter. He was not one of those lugubrious persons who insist on removing the clapper from the bell of passion. A kiss from Wylie was like a breve tied, in a long slow amorous phrase, over bars' times its equivalent in demi-semiquavers. Miss Counihan had never enjoyed anything quite so much as this slow-motion osmosis of love's spittle.
> The above passage is carefully calculated to deprave the cultivated reader.
> (*M* 69)

The first joke in this passage turns on the emphatically italicised '*not*', suggesting a litigious hotel too scrupulous to allow unmarried couples to meet. The remainder of the passage which confronts the potential censor with an intention to deprave is distinctly defamiliarising, summoning the censor to read over the reader's shoulder and asking the reader to consider what type of reader they might be. The cultivated reader is certainly no better off than the uncultivated one (since music cannot be sexually explicit) and the joke appears to be on any reader as much as the thwarted censor. Apparent concern for the experience of readers again becomes an exercise of power over them.

The equation of sex and music is tied once again to the awareness of the book-making process when, at the beginning of chapter 11, Murphy begins to miss Celia strongly:

> Late that afternoon after many fruitless hours in the chair, it would be just-about the time Celia was telling her story, MMM stood suddenly for music, MUSIC, MUSIC, in brilliant, brevier and canon, or some such typographical scream, if the gentle compositor would be so friendly (*M* 132)

The issues raised by this sentence are numerous, but two things are particularly striking. Firstly the narratorial awareness of the compositor (composing the text, letter by letter, in the lead type used at the time (and into the 1970s)) and, secondly, the typographical deviation itself. The same 'music, MUSIC, MUSIC' appears also on page 141 and the progression in type is used for 'all, ALL, ALL' on page 134. The effect is to make the reader especially aware of the device and how it has been achieved (by the intervention of a compositor). But, in addition to this act of defamiliarisation – Murphy's mental scream as a typographical device mediated by a narrator and a compositor (at least) – there is an alternative avenue of interpretation opened up; a hypothesis that this instruction was not meant to be revealed at all; that the appeal to the compositor remains only because of authorial (or editorial or compositorial) incompetence: the instruction has been confused with part of the text and so hasn't been edited out and has been typeset.

Furthermore, if we track down the typographical meanings of 'brilliant, brevier and canon' we see the typographical device – as printed – falls far short of the narrator's intentions (though 'some such' allows the compositor a certain amount of leeway). According to Ackerly(1998: 184), the size of the sequence should vary between 3.5 and 48 point, i.e.

much smaller than presented $_{\text{music}}$

approximately the size of normal type music

and much larger **music**

What is actually composited is the word in lower case, SMALL CAPS (as used for the telegrams sent by Cooper (*M* 36)) and upper case (CAPS).[7] The effect provides increasing emphasis but hardly a 'scream' since in *Murphy* it does not break from the conventional size of type within the font that is used for this typesetting.

It may be interesting to speculate that Beckett was in no position to insist on the extra expense for his publisher in this instance after struggling for so long to find one, but the relative fizzling of the device, as it appears, is (1) indicative, in a subdued way, of Murphy's state of mind; (2) suggestive this could be, ought to be, further emphasised, and (3) nevertheless quite fitting with the way in which the text frequently adverts to the process of book production. If, as readers, we take up any part of the 'blunder' hypothesis, I suggest that blame does not accrue to the author but to the authorial narrator we have been aware of as involved in the production of the book ever since we were first forewarned of the contents of chapter 6 on the novel's second page. What is most striking about this device, and this is highly significant for the development of Beckett's fiction, is the erosion of the status of the narrator that the appeal to the compositor effects. Within this novel, as Pilling suggests, we have an active narrator and a relatively passive central character (1994: 30); a narrator who is prone to making proleptic statements ('His rattle will make amends' (*M* 44)) and capable of responding to potential disbelief in his reader ('yes, really lost in the shadows' (*M* 40)). Paul Davies has said: 'This doubting comment, qualification, review, built into the story, is … endemic to his prose' (1994: 59). However, for most of *Murphy* such commentary is made from a position of narratorial strength and control. We need to adopt a note of caution about how we conceive of the narrator and what Victor Sage says about the narrator of *Watt* applies equally here: 'to think of the narrator as a person is an oversimplification, for this is to assign "him" one of the many simultaneous functions that he has' (1971: 53). Nevertheless, it is with this

---

7 The upper and lower cases were originally literally the containers used by compositors.

graphic device that we see the illusion of a narratorial entity with power and control over the text begin to crumble.

The effect of this 'failure' is worth considering. As Joe Brooker has argued, in an article on *Malone Dies*, statements emphasising the boredom of their narratives, like 'What tedium', short-circuit the tedium they target. To put it another way, apparent statements of provisionality such as this shift register from readerly hypothesising about the characters to hypothesising about the narrator that inscribes them. This 'marks a kind of excitement, a shift between narrative levels sufficiently sudden to constitute a major event in the book's act of voicing' (Brooker 2001: 35). We have already seen several such moments in *Murphy*, for example the references to chapter 6 and to the censor, but not all such shifts in *Murphy* relate to the graphic surface. A short paragraph such as: 'All the puppets in this book whinge sooner or later, except Murphy, who is not a puppet' (*M* 71) cannot help but attract critical attention, encouraging us (perhaps) to see the central character as an objective correlative for the author, but such a reaction is not viable. Although the statement refers to 'this book' it comes from inside the text where narrator, part of 'the book's act of voicing', belongs and the author doesn't. The narrator's function is to mediate the text: a role which is not, as he appears to envision, control of the book itself.

The narrator's relationship with the text strikingly resembles the relationship of Murphy's mind to his world and chapter 6 to the book as a whole. We are told that Murphy's mind 'excluded nothing that it did not itself contain'. But the narrator's account of Murphy's mind goes on: 'Nothing ever had been, was or would be in the universe outside it but was already present as virtual, or actual, or virtual rising into actual, or actual falling into virtual, in the universe inside it' (*M* 63). This quotation exhibits an attempt at inclusiveness that spirals into complexity, a literary phenomena that characterises *Watt*. The essential point is that, in *Murphy*, the possibilities are held, under control, even as the language hints that the attempt of the text to master itself is a difficult one.

I have argued that prior examples of such 'shifts', for example the announcements in preparation for chapter 6, relate to the apparent power of the narrator over the narrative. In the address to the compositor the narrator tries to take control beyond his narrative and into its physical mediation but fails. The failure of narrator is the failure of the text itself as it attempts to master the physical presence of the book. The appeal to the compositor is a moment which engages our interest as the limits on the text's struggle to master itself becomes apparent. When it overreaches itself the narratorial function that breaks down may be said to be one of competence. Narratorial competence will be seen to be in very short supply throughout the novel Beckett composed next.

Watt (1953)

Written largely in hiding in France during the Second World War *Watt* was published only much later, after the success of *Waiting for Godot* on the stage, in 1953. *Watt* is a very different novel from *Murphy* and also from the first two volumes of the Trilogy (*Malloy, Malone Dies, The Unnamable*) which had already appeared in print in French. Reactions to *Watt* vary: even individual commentators are divided in their opinions, so that it has been described as 'the most irritating as well as the most beautiful of Beckett's novels' (Sage 1971: 113) and 'by no means his best book, but arguably his funniest' (Pilling 1994: 39). This best and worst of books offers a number of challenges to the reader and interpreter.

By comparison with the overall coherence of *Murphy, Watt* appears to exclude things it could and, sometimes it seems, should contain. Use of the graphic surface in *Watt* is slightly less varied than that found in *Murphy*, but incidences are more numerous. There are threnes and songs, musical notation and indented, italicised lyrics and quotations, and footnotes (which we shall deal with in more depth later). Ineptitude within narration might be *Watt*'s watchword, and this characteristic is often demonstrated through graphic devices. Differentiated graphic presentation, such as that used in *Murphy* to display the Suk's document or Ticklepenny's card – both significant points within the plot of that novel – are lavished awkwardly in *Watt* just where they prove to be least relevant, for example, on the poem enclosed in Grehan's letter which Mr Hackett reads to the Nixons in the first section of the first chapter. It is given a capitalised title and italicised verse setting, but the graphic title appears twice, since Hackett is interrupted the first time, and the poem itself is bawdy and otherwise irrelevant to what follows. Similarly while Mr. Spiro's theological reading is italicised (*Watt* (hereafter *W*) 26–7) it introduces questions on whether transubstantiation happens for rats, an issue that remains unanswered when Watt's internal (schizophrenic) voices don't allow him to hear Spiro's response.

Yet this eccentric precedent for quoting the irrelevant isn't consistently followed through: when Mr. Case the signalman is reading A. E.'s *Songs by the Way* the short paragraph 'Mr. Case read:' is followed by a line which is blank except for a centred '?' (*W* 227). Quite likely this text was under copyright and permission to quote was not obtained or, perhaps more likely, was not sought. By the point at which this non-quotation occurs, the reader of Watt should be used to the manner in which question marks are employed to fill absences.

Other gaps in the text appear within paragraphs, noting missing words ('   ?   ') first on page 27, then twice on page 30, and on pages 233 and 236. There are other gaps occasionally throughout the novel, similarly marked but on a slightly larger scale: for example, Erskine's missing song is marked with a question mark and at least three blank lines on page 82. A similarly sized question-marked gap covers the absence of any information about one of the

Lynches: 'Tom's boy young Simon aged twenty, whose [sic] it is painful to relate' (*W* 99). Finally, four question marks, two per line, mark the absence of Sam's mental faculties on page 167. This strand of noted absences culminates in two very short '(Hiatus in MS)' on page 238 and on page 240, in a paragraph of its own, '(MS illegible)' obscuring a potentially rude word. The text thus marked appears to be from an incomplete manuscript, but, case by case, the missing material seems trifling. However, even when we are satisfied that the gaps are not crucial individually their recurrence must sap our confidence in the text and its editors or publishers. The absences are enough for the blurb to the current Calder edition of *Watt*, first published in 1976, to close the paragraph about the novel with the following comment: 'The typographical oddities and omissions are as Beckett left the text.' In the belief that these apparent omissions may dissuade a potential buyer, or dismay a reader, the Calder blurb writer is keen to disclaim them. The publishers do so by attributing these absences to the author, but they are really devices of the text, mediated by a narrator and/or editor handling the MS who is content to leave gaps and create ambiguities. This is entirely in keeping with the text as a whole.

As well as opening up these gaps the graphic surface is used to attempt to clarify the text's extensive considerations of possibilities and series. To an extent these devices echo the device of the chess game in *Murphy*, but *Watt*'s tabular and numbered sequences do not occupy the role of climax or an alternative to description of plot; they demonstrate little but further narratorial incompetence. For example, twelve numbered possibilities about Mr Knott's mealtime arrangements are recorded as occurring to Watt on pages 86–7. Of these it seems to me that 1 and 9 are functionally the same, and that, while 5 and 7 seem at least plausible, 11 and 12 are either logically impossible or imply Mr Knott is insane, an implication the text itself raises (*W* 120) and which, if adopted, would have saved Watt considerable effort. The list is followed by a paragraph noting that 'Other possibilities occurred to Watt' but that 'he put them quite out of his mind, and forgot them' (*W* 87). This undermines the list even more than its own inconsistencies as the attempt at enumeration is shown to be incomplete. Shortly afterwards there is a sequel to the matter of Mr Knott's meals as Watt obsessively considers ways in which his master's leavings might be consumed by a dog not of the household. There are four numbered options, over pages 91–4, followed by a table which permutes solutions and objections (*W* 95). Only having gone so far do we find out the actual situation whereby the task is accomplished with no reference back to which 'solution' the actual one most resembles. But this is not the least relevant of *Watt*'s more elaborate graphic devices: half of page 135, all of 136 and the top of 137 are taken up with a tabular representation of a sequence of croaking frogs that Watt remembers from *before* he entered Mr Knott's house. This detailed material has no relevance for his current situation except that it is (specifically labelled as) another 'series' (*W* 135). It has no sequel, however, as it is followed abruptly with the account of Watt's relations with Mrs Gorman, the fishwoman.

The emphasis on irrelevant details in *Watt* is striking, especially since so much other seemingly more relevant material seems to disappear without comment. To take one example of this, there is no description of Watt's departure (or non-departure) from the station at the end of the novel. A boy brings a message from the points operator about the waiting 5.57 and 6.06 trains (*W* 242–3) and subsequently we hear a train is arriving (*W* 244). Then on page 245, as soon as Mr Cox has asked for two tickets and his arrangement with Mr. Waller has been inconclusively explained, we hear 'Not many minutes later the six four entered the station. It did not take up a single passenger.' Passing reference to Watt occurs on the final page but what happened to him (after being the object of such attention for station staff and customers) is left hanging. We might be able to assume that he has boarded an intermediate train (the 5.57, unless this has become the 6.04) and left and the narrator has missed it. During the novel we are given a large amount of information without having any confidence that we are receiving the necessary information. Ambiguities and obscurities multiply in these ellipses.

Even at a micro level the text struggles to pin down certain events and facts. Frequently labouring syntax, e.g. 'Not that … for it would not' (*W* 81) has led to *Watt* being described by Kenner as 'a raid of syntax upon chaos' (1973: 77). But, if so, it is an action in which syntax does not escape unscathed and its injuries introduce further ambiguity into the text and induce frustration in the reader (see Sage 1977: 36).

The ineptitude of the narrator hinted at in *Murphy* has become complete in *Watt*, and, unlike the narrator of *Murphy*, the narrator of *Watt* has a name: Sam. As Sage has suggested, the narrator has multiple functions, and in his analysis of *Watt* Mathew Winston offers a range of these: 'We may distinguish four separable but inter related functions of Sam: he is a participant in Watt's experience, the recorder of Watt's story, the writer and arranger of a book, and a commentator on the action' (1977: 73). Following this scheme we may be tempted to say that Sam performs all except his participant function badly, but to sort out the various writing functions attributed to Sam here – recorder, writer, arranger and commentator – is difficult since, as Pilling suggests, what we have here is 'a narrator who is out of control' (1976: 41).

Sam only gradually becomes apparent in the text. Initially he is disguised by a narratorial convention, 'an expression that *we* shall not record' (*W* 15, my emphasis). Later, the narrator begins to mention himself as an individual ('me', 76). This comes just after he begins to be concerned about his shortcomings in transmitting information from his source (Watt) to the reader: he mentions his own 'scant aptitude' for the task (*W* 72) but soldiers on in the apparent belief that 'even there where there is no light for Watt, where there is none for his mouthpiece, there may be light for others' (W 66). The years that the process took are revealed later still (W 123), as is his total dependence on Watt (124, 126), and further reservations about his own ability follow including the fact he may have left out some of Watt's account and 'foisted in' other material (124–5).

This undermining of the source and process culminates in the beginning of the novel's third section where it becomes apparent that, like Watt, Sam is an institutionalised character. His first use of his own name is on page 151 and it is shortly clear that Watt and Sam are a deeply disturbed pair (W 153). They are separated but continue the latter part of their conversations through the use of holes in the fences around the respective grounds of their 'pavilions'. Pursuing his writerly functions Sam struggles to interpret second-hand 'information' during Watt's disjointed account which loses comprehensibility over time. Sam goes on to describe Watt's manner of communication and its stages of degeneration, giving examples in seven italicised pieces of monologue, but missing out any attempt at the final stage with 'I recall no example of this manner' (W 167).[8] But this is not the nadir of the state of Sam and Watt's communication because the text continues;

> Thus I missed I suppose much I presume of great interest touching I suspect the eighth or final stage of the second or closing period of Watt's stay in Mr. Knott's house.
> But soon I grew used to these sounds, and then I understood as well as ever, that is to say fully one half of what won its way past my tympan. (W 167)

The best, then, before this latest degeneration, was a 50 per cent maximum success rate which, as the last phrase suggests, is in itself limited by Sam's declining hearing and the paragraph immediately following with its graphic device caps even this:

> For my own hearing now began to fail, though my
> myopia remained stationary. My purely mental faculties
> on the other hand, the faculties properly so called of ?
>   ?   ?
>   ?   ?
> were if possible more vigorous than ever.

We can expect nothing of Sam because his mental faculties, as demonstrated on the graphic surface, are literally missing or at least his claims for them are given the lie by the fact he cannot remember to supply later the words he needs.

Given this level of ineptitude there are paradoxes in Sam's account where other more fluent sources appear to intervene. These interventions are of two types. The first has clear narrators embedded within the text; Arsene's 'short' statement (W 37–62) and Arthur's account of Louit's research and trial (W 168–96).

---

8 The extant examples of Watt's language are unravelled in Hesla (1971: 68).

Though they are quite different in content (one about Mr Knott's house, the other nothing to do with it) both these grow out of all proportion.

The second type is that found in the opening and closing sequences of the book: the conversation between Hackett and the Nixons and the railway station finale, which appear to be narrated from an eccentric but omniscient point of view. There may be some logic to their similarity in style in the statement, reminiscent of the narrator of *Murphy*'s claims for his section 6, which begins *Watt*'s fourth section: 'As Watt told the beginning of his story, not first, but second, so not fourth but third, now he told its end. Two, one, four, three, that was the order in which Watt told his story. Heroic quatrains are not otherwise elaborated' (*W* 214). Beyond the unlikely literary comparison for Watt's efforts, One and Four are temporally linked but this does little to explain the seeming omniscience of these passages which appear to show Sam warming to the task of fiction rather than reporting Watt's experiences.

In evaluating Sam's performance as writer and arranger there is a further aspect of the graphic surface of this text to explore; where attempts to clarify matters for the reader take place in a series of footnotes. Winston's article '*Watt*'s First Footnote' argues that 'Because it talks about saving space (rather than time or effort or eyestrain) it [the footnote, *W* 6] focuses our attention on the book as a physical product, which has been created by someone, and which is offered by another of the notes to "the attentive reader"' (1977: 72). In addition, if taken literally, the first footnote introduces ambiguity since its promise to exclude the 'plethoric reflexive pronoun after *say*' means, for example, we don't know if the passage that Mr. Spiro 'read' (*W* 26) is to himself, or to Watt, or meant to include Watt but without being understood as addressed to himself by Watt. Through the intervention of the footnote, hypotheses about the text are problematised, as the convolutions in my attempted explanation indicate. This echoes what goes on internally in the text as Watt's perceptions during his stay at Mr. Knott's house become increasingly unreliable. The footnotes, which logically exist at some intermediate point between text and reader ought, we may feel, to stabilise the situation. They do not. For example, on page 211:

> For the guidance of the attentive reader, at a loss to understand how these repeated investments, and divestments, of the night dress, did not finally reveal to Watt Mr. Knott's veritable aspect, it is perhaps not superfluous here to note, that Mr. Knott's attitude to his nightdress was not that generally in vogue. For Mr. Knott did not do as most men, and many women, do, who, before putting on their nightclothes, at night, take off their dayclothes, and again, when morning comes, once again, before they dream of putting on their dayclothes are careful to pull off their soiled nightclothes, no, but he went to bed with his nightclothes over his dayclothes, and he rose with his dayclothes under his nightclothes.

There is an explanation here but one that is exhaustingly verbose and, since it does not add or supplement a key point (only an evasion of one), wholly superfluous.[9] A similar example on page 79 offers a looping and inconclusive consideration of knowing whether Knott's house is a last refuge, or is understood as such, by Watt and Arsene respectively. By contrast, narratorial structuring in *Murphy*, like the placing of chapter 6, does offer to the reader a concise summary – even though it impedes progress in the plot. Footnotes such as the one quoted above impede a progress that is itself in doubt. What the reader achieves in reading through *Watt* is progress measured in pages rather than in enlightenment.

It seems clear that Sam is the inept author of footnotes such as the one on page 211, but a sharper waspish tone is occasionally present in some of the notes. One note which is regularly quoted is the concise: 'Haemophilia is, like enlargement of the prostate, an exclusively male disorder. But not in this work' (*W* 100). This note is of a different order from the ones which labour to explain the text in its own verbose idiom. The terseness here is reminiscent of the narrator of *Murphy*. 'But not in this work' deals critically with the text from a position apparently temporally displaced and exterior (the text is a 'work' rather than in composition). The content short circuits the device of the footnote as mere supplementary information (whether informative or not) and calls into question the status of the text and its relation to reality.

There are a number of similarly sharp notes (*W* 6, 32, 101).[10] The footnote on page 101 tells us that the calculations following from the incorrect sum total of generations of Lynches are 'doubly erroneous' but doesn't intervene and correct the confusion. The 'attentive reader' might have been provoked into mathematics (rather like *Murphy*'s chess game) except that the risks and rewards are once again of dubious value – a family myth of a horde of bit players whose sole function is to provide a dog to eat Mr Knott's leavings – and the briskness of this footnote encourages us to move on.

Another footnote in this tone is attached to the title of the 'Addenda' to the text which suggests: 'The following precious and illuminating material should be carefully studied. Only fatigue and disgust prevented its incorporation' (*W* 247). A considerable amount turns on how we interpret and attribute this footnote and the section it describes.

The additional matter of the 'Addenda' has been taken as somehow providing a key to the text as there is once again an apparent shift (authorwards) of narrative level. It appears all too easy to telescope these levels. For example, Pilling appears to read 'fatigue and disgust' as belonging to Beckett and his attitude to the

---

9 Connor (1988: 35) chooses to see the footnote's information as disturbing rather than redundant and banal. This turns on his reading of the last clause with 'under' instead of 'over', an alteration that makes the footnote in *Watt* function much more as a footnote should.

10 There is one note that might be fitted into either camp, the remarkably straight note on *ego autem* (181). Perhaps the fact that this note is tied to Arthur's narrative about Louit's academic trial argues for another annotator recording a verbal note made by Arthur for Mr Graves's benefit.

novel in question: 'The extrinsic conditions which summoned *Watt* from oblivion not unnaturally prompt the question why – given the mood of "fatigue and disgust" recorded in the footnote to the novel's "Addenda" … – it survived as an entity at all' (1994: 35). This is continued into his interpretation of the 'Addenda': 'Though there are indicators in the "Addenda" to *Watt* that Beckett considered reintroducing perspective later on – "Note that Arsene's declaration gradually came back to Watt" (*W* 248) – even these are submerged … when *Watt*'s author (or editor) casually neglects to elicit any significance from it [information in the "Addenda"]' (36). I agree that the material of the 'Addenda' is unilluminating as to the text that has preceded it but it is also unilluminating as to Beckett's attitude towards the novel and future plans for it.[11] The name Sam leads some scholars to see a strong link between him and the author, Samuel Beckett. Pilling suggests that '[Sam] is really only a persona for Beckett himself, an analogue, a creator like himself' (1976: 42). Similarly, Begam concludes: 'And so we call him, for the sake of convenience, Sam Beckett, the fictional author of an impossible joke' (1996: 96). For Begam *Watt* takes the 'autobiographical novel to its (il)logical conclusion' (97). But the 'author' that does nothing with the 'Addenda' is only provisionally Sam and is certainly not Samuel.

In her major essay on *Watt*, 'Watt, Knott and Beckett's Bilingualism', Ann Beer picks up on the problems in Beckett studies in dealing with this issue: 'Beckett never succeeded (if such was his aim) in imposing Sam as the overall narrator; this assumption can be exposed as absurd even without the support of the manuscript. Yet the few heavy-handed claims made by Sam have often been taken as transparently true' (1985: 73). I agree that Sam cannot be taken at face value, and we should not make him the subject of the text, as Winston appears to do: 'We are apt to suppose, as it has been convenient for me to do through most of this essay, that if *Watt* does not represent any objective reality then it must reveal the shape of Sam's mind or the nature of his psyche. We therefore try to understand the narrator, to see from his viewpoint, to test his veracity' (1977: 80). While aware of Sam's fictionality Winston is also capable of saying: 'Ultimately, Sam is the text, both because the book is inseparable from him and because he exists for us only as words on a page' (79). Apart from conflating text and book here, this kind of interpretation hangs on the importance of the narrators of later Beckett novels where they are indeed the key figures in focusing our interest, as Kenner suggests: 'For since someone else, a character, is responsible for the narration, we are not simply considering buttons, but attending to the intimate deliverances of a human mind, which in finding buttons of absorbing interest, proves to be itself of absorbing interest, to us' (1974: 84–5).

---

11 For this we must turn to the notebooks and holograph manuscript, 'the most fascinating single Beckett item to be found anywhere' (Admussen 1979: 7), held in Austin, Texas, studied by Coetzee (see Ackerly 1993: 175), Beer (1985), Ackerly (1993), Hayman (1997) and Pilling (1997).

In *Watt* this stage has not yet been reached. I have suggested an editor figure or some other intermediary, who waspishly critiques Sam's efforts even as he presents them unchanged. Even if we do not accept the presence of another 'editorial' narrator who handles Sam's MS, it would be necessary to see Sam at some stage editing his own work and giving up on the material contained in the 'Addenda'. In either scheme the presence of the 'Addenda' problematises the coherence of the text. Firstly, at a very basic level it suggests (as do the ostensible gaps in the graphic surface) that the novel is in some way unfinished. This ought, perhaps, not to come as a surprise for, as Connor (1988: 31) argues, 'There is no possibility of closure for such a book, only abandonment.' Secondly, the 'Addenda' appears to contain missing elements of what has gone before without supplying all the gaps, for example, the footnote on page 32 demands, in relation to the choir Watt hears in the ditch on the way from the station, what the soprano sang and the musical threne. The 'Addenda' supplies the latter but only announces the former (and in the difference between the two manages to have Watt travelling in both directions at once) (*W* 255). The 'Addenda' also supplies some non-gaps in the text, in effect inserting supplementary material, so that we find a description of a second picture in Erskine's room despite the main text's 'The only other object of note in Erskine's room was *a* picture, hanging from the wall, on a nail' (*W* 126). Thirdly, the 'Addenda' appears to be incomplete in itself with, for example, a '(Latin quote)' missing from the description of the second painting mentioned above (*W* 252) (possibly the one to be found on 254). What is the status of these fragmentary 'additions' and what can we do with them?

'Change all the names' (*W* 254) may indeed be a task Beckett performed on his text before publication, as Beer (1985: 57) reveals, and Ackerly, who has made specific study of the 'Addenda', sees this note as one which 'encapsulates a moment of metamorphosis in the history of the text' (1993: 81). Nevertheless as re-presented within the 'Addenda' this statement is highly problematic. There are the names of servants from Arsene to Arthur, usually first names, and non-servants from Hackett to Gorman. To alter their names, and nothing else, is a peculiarly meaningless exercise for the reader. Even if we wish to extrapolate an author figure addressing himself it becomes an issue of interest only if we know which names are being concealed and why. But in so doing we are once again led towards biographical criticism and away from the text. The text is not in the hands of author or editor any more, though to think oneself back to a point at which it was, and read it as such, seems a remarkably common critical manoeuvre. If we treat the 'Addenda' from the reader's position then this statement about names is destabilising, mischievously or incompetently introducing an element of provisionality to one of our fundamental bases for hypothesising (including the title, since 'all the names' includes Watt's).

The final fragment of the 'Addenda' prompts Pilling to argue calmly that: 'Almost every object in *Watt*, and almost every moment of narrative production, *could* be treated as symbolic, but need not be' (1994: 37). But the whole question of how we know whether a symbol is intended or not is agonisingly irresolvable. In fact 'no symbols where none intended' is a Canutian statement that cannot be enacted by writer or reader and through it the text prompts us to re-evaluate (again) our entire reading. As Ackerly states: 'This is indeed an Addendum, a final word, one that embodies both its origins [in MS] and its own contradictions, and this goes to the very heart of the novel' (1993: 187). Saddled with an incompetent narrator, writer and arranger interpreting an incoherent witness, the reader struggles to make sense of the novel. Philosophically and conventionally the novel refuses to co-operate. But this is not the end of it because we cannot be skewered on Watt's paradoxes, even though we cannot quite put the novel aside. Victor Sage argues:

> it is not the actuality of our reading that is being questioned, but the actuality of what it is about, what it refers to. If such a distinction were not possible, then the doubtful epistemology of the book would already be the orthodoxy of any reader's experience prior to reading it. Such is the book's power that it seems to override this distinction, but the process of reading is deeply and actively accretionary. (1971: 99)

Hugh Kenner in his *Reader's Guide to Samuel Beckett* suggests: 'the reader, coping with the book, finds his position to be not unlike that of the writer, writing it, and Watt experiencing it' (1973: 77). There are two possible reading positions here; a biographical one and one more empathic with the novels helpless and hapless central character. There are points, however, where both positions diverge from their models (i.e. writer and character respectively). Occupying the former position suggests the possibility of revision which can't be enacted and therefore turns our thoughts Beckettwards (as I have pointed out, a common critical response). Occupying the latter position is much more in keeping with Watt's powerlessness in the novel as it is, but while Winston (1977: 80) suggests that 'Watt's dilemma is that he is trapped in a novel' the reader is not. I believe this is the more fruitful approach but both options are essentially stymied by the book fixed and impenetrable as it is.

Winston concludes that '*Watt* affirms nothing' (ibid.) but there are two ways to take this statement, depending on whether we stress the second or third word. Sam, having got so far, hedges: 'But was that not something?' (*W* 147). In fact the novel tells us that 'the only way one can speak of nothing is to speak of it as if it were something' (*W* 74) and does offer some cues about adaptation to its pleasures: 'Watt learned towards the end of his stay in Mr Knott's house to accept that nothing had happened, that a nothing had happened, learned to bear it and even, in a shy way, to like it. But then it was too late' (*W* 77). One of the German fragments in the 'Addenda' also points this way: 'das fruchtbare Bathos der Erfahrung' ('the fruitful bathos of experience') (*W* 254). Bathos is bound to be our fate as long as we are determined to read in the same way that Watt initially tries to interpret his fictional world: 'he felt the need to think that such and such a thing had happened then, the need to be able to say, when the scene began to unroll its sequences, Yes, I remember, that is what happened then' (W 71). For readers, if they can adjust to the experience of the gallingly vague and drawn-out non-event of the visit of the Galls, there may be hope. The following sequence in particular draws attention to similarities in method between Watt and readers:

> if Watt was sometimes unsuccessful, and sometimes successful, as in the affair of the Galls father and son, in foisting a meaning there where no meaning appeared, he was most often neither the one, nor the other. For Watt considered, with reason, that he was successful, in this enterprise, when he could evolve, from the meticulous phantoms that beset him, a hypothesis proper to disperse them, as often as this might be found necessary. There was nothing, in this operation, at variance with Watt's habits of mind. For to explain had always been to exorcize, for Watt. And he considered that he was unsuccessful, when he failed to do so. (W 74–5)

In fact what Watt attempts to do throughout is to limit readings, foist meaning, make hypotheses concrete, but is unable to achieve any of these fully. Watt's weaknesses are those of the struggling reader: 'But there were many things Watt could not easily imagine' (W 118). To this extent Watt is a picture of the reader, foisting meaning, and symbols, where none are intended.

If the reader doesn't feel sufficiently attached to Watt this is not surprising. Unlike the statistical introduction of Celia in *Murphy*, descriptions of Watt in the novel are given gradually, but are sufficient to make him quite particular. His eccentric mode of walking is described in full on page 28 taking the example of Watt attempting to travel due east. It is not clear, however, that he can actually make progress in this way rather than simply rocking on the spot. It is easy to see this description as the sort of tantalising anomaly that appears in *Murphy* (where is his seventh scarf?) but difficulty in making progress will become familiar to the reader too. What I would like to suggest is that one may see the action of reading in Watt's walk; turning pages, eyes travelling from one side to the other. This may be fanciful but, on his journey to the station at the end, Watt sees an obscure figure following him who has 'his' own side to side gait, makes no progress and then fades away (W 224–7). Watt hypothesises at length about the type of person approaching and is positively enthusiastic about seeing them. Is this a literal portrait of *Watt's* reader or a symbol where none is intended?[12] At the very least, here is another incident that fails to resolve itself for Watt, for Sam, and for the reader, shedding no light at all, just where we would hope things might finally drop into place.[13]

---

12 Of course, one would like to have it both ways and have the unstable Mr Knott and his house be the person and building as imagined differently by each reader while appearing simultaneously to Watt.

13 Begam does use this passage to provide resolution by taking the italicised phrase which ends the paragraph 'the only cure is diet' (W 226) as 'an admission that all the characters in the novel are effectively emanations from one character ' (1996: 96) .

The process of trying and failing to understand is a constant in *Watt*, from Mr Hackett's attempts to find out about Watt to the enquiries made by the crowd at the railway station and at all points between as Watt tries to get to grips with Mr Knott's house or Sam struggles to follow Watt's account. In this way *Watt* offers a consistent representational parallel to the experience of the reader who time and time again finds the narrative offering only inconclusive experiences. Sam attracts critical attention because as narrator he, too, is conscious of the problematic nature of his account, but it is the overlapping and ambiguous culpability of failing character, failing narrator and failing reader that accounts for the varied reactions to this novel, and it is readers' and critics' inability to exorcise the ensuing indeterminacy that generates *Watt*'s extraordinary combination of insubstantiality and durability.

The graphic surface of *Watt*, like that of *Murphy* before it, is used to foreground instability and generate lack of faith in the text's mediators and ultimately the text itself. Through the use of the graphic surface in his early fiction Beckett has identified and drawn on a fundamental aspect of the codex form: text, no matter how it writhes, is subservient to the presence of the book. His use of the graphic surface depends on an awareness of the shaping of texts into print. None of Beckett's devices relies on specific changes to page layout, typographical choices or font. Instead they make use of paragraphing, line spacing and the normal characters of the typewriter; the tools which are easily to hand. Thus the devices of *Murphy* and *Watt* are all capable of surviving the concertina effect, noted in Chapter 2 with reference to modern editions of Sterne, intact. Nevertheless, they animate the texts and disconcert their readers and, through the increasing ineptitude of the narrators apparently trying to orchestrate them, point to Beckett's later works where the very idea of a printed text is beyond the narrating figures. By contrast the writers and texts I will go on to discuss make greater and more specific demands of their designers, typesetters and compositors, but the issues of stability and control raised for readers when devices exploit the graphic surface will continue to be vital consideration.

References

Ackerly, Chris (1993) 'Fatigue and Disgust: The Addenda to *Watt*', *Samuel Beckett Today* 2, Amsterdam: Rodopi: 175–88

Ackerly, C. J. (1998) *Demented Particulars: The Annotated Murphy* (*Journal of Beckett Studies* 7 (1–2))

Admussen, Richard L. (1979) *The Samuel Beckett Manuscripts: A Study*, Boston: G. K. Hall

Bair, Deidre (1978) *Samuel Beckett*, London: Cape

Barale, Michele Aina and Rabinovitz, Rubin (1990) *A KWIC Concordance to Samuel Beckett's Murphy*, New York: Garland

Beckett, Samuel (1973 [1938]) *Murphy*, London: Picador

Beckett, Samuel (1976 [1953]) *Watt*, London: John Calder

Beer, Anne (1985) 'Watt, Knott and Beckett's Bilingualism', *Journal of Beckett Studies* 10: 37–75

Begam, Richard (1996) *Samuel Beckett and the End of Modernity*, Stanford: Stanford University Press

Brooker, Joe (2001) 'What Tedium: Boredom in *Malone Dies*', *Journal of Beckett Studies* 10 (1–2): 29–39

Connor, Steven (1988) *Samuel Beckett: Repetition, Theory and Text*, London: Blackwell

Davies, Paul (1994) 'Three Novels and Four Nouvelles: Giving up the Ghost to be Born at Last' in John Pilling (ed.), *The Cambridge Companion to Beckett*, Cambridge: Cambridge University Press: 43–66

Farrow, Anthony (1991) *Early Beckett: Art and Allusion in More Pricks than Kicks and Murphy*, New York: Whitston

Hayman, David (1997) 'Beckett's *Watt* – The Graphic Accompaniment: Marginalia in the Manuscripts', *Word and Image* 13 (2): 172–82

Hesla, David (1971) *The Shape of Chaos: An Investigation of the Art of Samuel Beckett*, Minneapolis: University of Minnesota

Kenner, Hugh (1973) *A Reader's Guide to Samuel Beckett*, London: Thames & Hudson

Kenner, Hugh (1974) *The Stoic Comedians: Flaubert, Joyce, Beckett*, Los Angeles: University of California Press

Pilling, John (1976) *Samuel Beckett*, London: Routledge and Kegan Paul

Pilling, John (1994) 'Beckett's English Fiction' in John Pilling (ed.), *The Cambridge Companion to Beckett*, Cambridge: Cambridge University Press: 17–42

Pilling, John (1997) *Beckett before Godot*, Cambridge: Cambridge University Press

Sage, V. R. L. (1971) *Structure and Meaning in the Novels of Samuel Beckett*, Unpublished PhD thesis, Norwich: University of East Anglia

Sage, Victor (1977) 'Dickens and Beckett: Two Uses of Materialism', *Journal of Beckett Studies* 2: 15–39

Vonnegut, Kurt (1974) *Breakfast of Champions*, London: Cape

Winston, Mathew (1977) '*Watt*'s First Footnote', *Journal of Modern Literature* 6 (1–2): 71–80

Wood, Rupert (1993) '*Murphy*, Beckett, Guelincx, God', *Journal of Beckett Studies* 2 (2): 27–51

---

14   The gentle compositor of this book, no doubt harried and put upon, had the verso running head for this chapter as 'Rebuilding the graphic surface' throughout. I have preserved it on page 82 as a reminder that the book is not just the work of the author while hoping no other errors escape the proofing stage.

CHAPTER 6

'The technological fact of the book':
B. S. Johnson

– A page is an area on which I may place any signs I consider to communicate most nearly what I have to convey: therefore I employ, within the pocket of my publisher and the patience of my printer, typographical techniques beyond the arbitrary and constricting limits of the conventional novel. To dismiss such techniques as gimmicks, or to refuse to take them seriously, is crassly to miss the point (Johnson 1964: 176)

This quotation from B. S. Johnson's second novel, *Albert Angelo* (1964, hereafter *AA*), indicates three reasons why this work will be of considerable interest to us. This passage acknowledges, firstly, that the page is a graphic unit controlled by the author intended to communicate to an (implied) audience of readers, and, secondly, that these pages are mediated through the physical book which comes into being through the involvement of agencies other than the author himself, i.e. printers and publishers. Thirdly, the quotation is an authorial reply to criticisms received after the experiments with form in his first novel, *Travelling People* (1963, hereafter *TP*), and a pre-emptive strike against criticisms the author anticipates, since in *Albert Angelo*, in defiance of such criticism, more typographical techniques have been introduced. All Johnson's subsequent novels demonstrate this continuing determination to exploit 'the technological fact of the book' (1973b: 12).

B. S. Johnson produced seven novels in all, two volumes of poetry and a collection of short stories, as well as several plays, screenplays and television scripts, and miscellaneous joint projects. He received awards for *Travelling People*, *Trawl* and the short film *You're Human like the Rest of Them*. Despite these endeavours, by the late 1980s all that remained in bookshops for the potential reader of Johnson's work to find were two pieces both originally published in his collection of short prose, *Aren't You Rather Young to be Writing Your Memoirs?* (1973b), anthologised in separate books by the same editor, Malcolm Bradbury.[1] These selections indicate that Johnson had become emblematic of a period representative of the spirit of protest against the status quo in British fiction in the 1960s and early 1970s. As Andrew Hassam says: 'Johnson was part of a group of young British Writers working in London who looked toward Joyce and Beckett for a form of the novel which matched modern reality rather than what they saw as an ossified nineteenth-

---

1 See 'A Few Selected Sentences' in Bradbury 1987: 282–5 and 'Introduction' in Bradbury 1990: 165–83.

century realism' (1993: 4). But, far from being spokesman for any group of like-minded writers, Johnson reacted against conservative conceptions of mimesis in a very personal way. He studiously avoided the term 'realism', by then associated with convention, and set himself a new standard of mimesis, naming it, in *Albert Angelo*, 'my truth to reality' (*AA* 167). Critically, his attack on conventional realism has often been taken as an attack on mimesis itself, leading to an assumption that therefore his work must be intended to be self-reflexive rather than mimetic. But when Johnson's work clearly attempts to achieve mimesis he is seen to be caught in a double-bind and, typically, his graphic devices were understood, or rather misunderstood, in this context.

In person Johnson was often perceived as difficult and argumentative, which seems to have produced a response that implies that his work is also 'difficult' (perhaps a synonym for not conventionally realistic), but this is not the case. In her thesis *Self-Conscious Fiction and Literary Theory* Wenche Ommundsen argues:

> In spite of moments of postmodern uncertainty, he [Johnson] never seems to cast serious doubt on the existence of reality, the nature of language, or the possibility of meaning. His experimentation with the novel form may be perceived as surface disturbances which do not seriously interfere with the representational aspects of his texts. B. S. Johnson's novels are not 'difficult' in the sense that they cannot be understood unless we set aside our conventional expectations altogether (1986: 210–11 (see also Waugh 1984: 57 on Johnson 1973a))

The essential point is that all Johnson's novels and the various experiments they contain are accessible. The conventional expectations that remain may be seen as a weakness by other experimental novelists (see Burns and Sugnet 1981: 83), but it is going too far to suggest, as Ommundsen does, that Johnson's devices are only 'surface disturbances' or that they are necessarily separate from 'representational aspects'. The extent of Johnson's experimentation becomes problematic for his legacy only when surveys of his work are forced to confront the lack of formal homogeneity between the novels. Many critics have little space to deal with his texts in detail and, though Johnson's novels overlap stylistically and thematically to a certain degree, it seems difficult to discuss them side-by-side by reason of the technical complexities of their various forms. Even among favourable critics there is, as C. Kanaganayakam writes, 'little agreement about which novel deserves to be called his major work' (1985: 89).

Without a clear concept of the graphic surface, critics are ill-prepared to deal with the formal diversity of Johnson's novels and tend to go little further than list their idiosyncrasies and use Johnson's own theorising to deal with the issues raised. The 'Introduction' to *Aren't You Rather Young* ... is quoted repeatedly in most of the scattered material that comprises extant criticism of Johnson's work. Originally published shortly after Johnson's death in 1973, the 'Introduction' is generally taken, whether in sympathy with its views or in order to expose their shortcomings and contradictions, to be something of a manifesto, to the extent it has almost become B. S. Johnson, in his absence. Though the piece is a both revealing and fascinating document about Johnson and his work, its belligerent and sometimes paradoxical argumentation has helped skew the general critical reaction to Johnson's work (see White 1999: 144–9 or Coe 2004: 450). The tendency to conflate Johnson's arguments for experimentation with the experiments themselves leads to a situation in which discussion of the former often serves for discussion of the latter. Posthumous criticism, obliged to accept the fact that Johnson can no longer be persuaded to change his ways, is forced to come to terms, perhaps not happily, with the works he has left behind.

The critical situation is changing, however. Philip Tew has offered a full and detailed critical account of Johnson's work, and Picador have recently republished five of the seven novels supported by the publication of Jonathan Coe's biography of Johnson, *Like a Fiery Elephant* (2004).[2] That a revived awareness of Johnson depends on a biography is ironic since if there is one thing that distracts critics from Johnson's texts more than his heavy-handed arguments in the 'Introduction' to *Aren't You Rather Young ...* it is Johnson himself. Morton P. Levitt observes: 'What rich material he provides for the psychological critic, for the biographical critic and for the critic of society' (1981: 584). Reference to Johnson's life could hardly be avoided within the biographical context of an entry in *The Dictionary of Literary Biography*, but Levitt's second piece on Johnson links life and art too directly: 'B. S. Johnson's suicide in 1973 seems in many ways the fulfilment of his life as a novelist: there are few writers for whom life and art are so inextricably bound. This is not to suggest that one should look to Johnson's novels for the facts of his life or for the causes of his death. But ... it is impossible to consider separately his art and his life' (1985: 439). I am not arguing that Johnson's life is not of interest, or denying that Johnson's life is heavily drawn upon in his work – Coe (2004) would disprove any such claims – but a major flaw in criticism of Johnson's work has been the use of Romantic concepts of artist/creator whose life and work are cut from the same cloth. Between the Scylla and Charybdis of author and authorial theory most of the various studies are drawn into psychological and intentional analyses of the author's work (usually as a whole) in order to place him in a historical scheme in relation either to European modernism, or to British and/or 'experimental' literary traditions. Difficulties are created for interpreters when they genuinely want to stand author and texts together. Judith Mackrell states at the end of her study of *Albert Angelo*: 'It is as if Johnson's stringently puritanical notions of 'truthfulness' prevent him from fully acknowledging or even comprehending his own fiction' (1985: 52). Robert Ryf suggests of the writer's work as a whole: 'Johnson's own practice frequently belies his preachments ... the contradictions are never quite reconciled' (1977: 62). More recently Patricia Waugh has argued: 'B. S. Johnson is a good example of a writer whose literal and obsessive application of the notion of fiction as lies became damaging to his work' (1984: 98).[3] Even friends of Johnson suggest that 'he seemed imprisoned in his own theory'

---

2 Two early 1980s reprints, *Christy Malry's Own Double-Entry* (King Penguin, 1984) and *House Mother Normal* (Bloodaxe, 1984), had little impact. Picador has brought out *The Unfortunates* (1999), *Christy Malry's Own Double-Entry* (2001) and a *B. S. Johnson Omnibus* (2004) containing *Trawl, Albert Angelo* and *House Mother Normal*.

3 Waugh (1984: 99) sees Johnson not as a puritan but as a thwarted Romantic and eventually he seems

(Pacey 1974: 20) and that 'he worked himself into a cul-de-sac' (Figes 1985: 71). The lack of resolution shown in so many studies suggests to me that Johnson's accessibility and the urge towards mimesis in his work combine with his ability to open paradoxes in the relationship between life, world and book to stymie pat critical overviews.[4]

Regarding Johnson as a confused and beleaguered figure tempts us to revert to psychologism and cast him as a martyr to experimental literary puritanism but an approach via the graphic surface requires that we *must* deal with the texts themselves first and foremost, and not the author or authorial theory. Lack of space does not permit us to deal with all Johnson's work in detail so attention is restricted to his first two novels and the fourth, the infamous novel-in-a-box, *The Unfortunates* (1969). We will be able to draw some useful lessons about the reader's relationship to the graphic surface through the multiplicity of forms which are used in this selection.

Travelling People (1963)

Johnson's first novel, *Travelling People*, forms an ideal introduction to his work. As Morton Levitt says, 'the inventive, variable narrative technique of this early novel can serve to predict the imaginative and multiple forms of the novels that follow it' (1985: 576), and C. Kanaganayakam calls it 'a paradigm for his [Johnson's] later development' (1985: 89). However, Johnson himself felt *Travelling People* to be flawed and (after 1967) would not allow it to be reprinted (see Johnson 1973b: 22).[5] This decision cannot have been taken lightly by an author who, after his first major publication, determined to make his living solely as a writer, and at times had great difficulty in doing so, but it should not prevent us from studying *Travelling People*. Our critical approach should not be governed by authorial statements, particularly those made some time after original publication.

Nearly all commentators on *Travelling People*, encouraged by the book's blurb, note its debt to Laurence Sterne for some of its graphic elements. Many critics make some of mention of James Joyce, particularly *Ulysses*, which the central character is reading during the novel.[6] As Tew (2001: 131–64) has argued, such source-spotting is not sufficient. In *Travelling People*'s 'Prelude' the author figure decides on differing styles for different chapters. He adopts the approach of *Ulysses*, in a Shandean setting ('a wood and wicker-work chair of eighteenth century manufacture'), but does so in the manner of the student

---

to become a character in her own critical narrative, his life and end being explicitly compared to those of Hugo in Iris Murdoch's *Under the Net* (1954). Waugh (1995: 132) essays another portrait of Johnson as 'the Tony Hancock of the literary world of the sixties'.

4 Tew (2001) pinpoints critical shortcomings effectively, but in order to encompass Johnson has to marshal comparisons with theorists and philosophers as diverse as Bataille, Bhaskar, Bourdieu, Cassirer, Habermas, Lefebvre, Merleau-Ponty, Sartre and Nietzsche.

5 This is not unique. Graham Greene suppressed his second two novels for similar reasons.

6 Connections to early Beckett are also invited by the blurb (written by Johnson), but they will be more apparent in *Albert Angelo*.

narrator of Flann O'Brien's *At Swim-Two-Birds*.[7] Through this synthesis Johnson places his novel simultaneously in both the experimental and the comic traditions but he goes on:

> Furthermore, I meditated ... Dr. Johnson's remarks about each member of an audience always being aware that he is in a theatre could with complete relevance be applied also to the novel reader, who surely always knows that he is reading a book and not, for instance, taking part in a punitive raid on the curiously-shaped inhabitants of another planet. From this I concluded that it was not only permissible to expose the mechanism of a novel, but by so doing I should come nearer to reality and truth.

In referencing science fiction he updates the available breadth of references and new possibilities (e.g. the film script). And, in deciding not to attempt to create any 'suspension of disbelief' (essentially calling for ontological awareness as a movement towards truth), Johnson puts his own stamp on the sum of his intertexts.

Johnson also claims the graphic surface of *Travelling People* with a note on the last page that says, 'THIS BOOK WAS DESIGNED BY RFS AND THE AUTHOR'. This is not a suspect claim, like those of the narrator figures in *Murphy* and *Watt*, undermined within the text, but an announcement of hands-on involvement and acknowledgement of the book as collaboratively produced artefact. The lower half of the last page is given over to technical information about the typeface, its italic and the paper itself. Even as a first novel of its day *Travelling People* is luxuriously produced; the epigraph, dedication, and each chapter title have a full right-hand page to announce themselves, with a blank verso. This is also true for each 'interlude' and 'interruption', and every journal entry in chapter 6 begins on the right-hand page, too. These divisions nearly all mark changes of literary form, ranging from streams of consciousness to the more neutral form of a film script.

What is the reader to make of this profusion of different forms? One effect is the distancing of the reader from the central character which occurs through the use of a variety of modes instead of a single uniform style (see Tredell 2000: 42). The name of the central character, Henry Henry (product of 'his parents' Shandean fixation with economy in nomenclature' (*TP* 23)), reinforces this distancing even as it makes it difficult to establish at what level of formality other characters address him. The overall suggestion is that the reader should remain aware of his fictional status and therefore not take Henry, and particularly his writing in the letter and journal chapters, quite at face value. For example, Henry makes an observation about the Stromboli Club owner, Maurie: 'Last night I noticed that he was *made up*' (*TP* 151, Johnson's italics). A game is being played here, between author and reader, at the expense of the characters.

Authorial powers, not substantively different from those of an omniscient author in a more conventional novel, are explicitly flaunted in *Travelling People* in a number of ways that to demonstrate what the convention involves. In the section entitled 'Another Interruption' within chapter 6, the author figure takes over from Henry's journal, emphasising

---

7 Compare Johnson 1963: 11 with O'Brien 1967 [1939]: 9. See also Tredell 2000: 49.

his superior literary capability: 'Henry was unable to find words to describe the events of Saturday, August 24th; I am under no such difficulty, however, and feel it no less than a duty to record what happened' (*TP* 171). The author can fill in the gaps which the 'writing' characters can't write. Similarly he boasts his omniscience by offering the reader information from beyond the temporal scope of the novel. We are told that Kim 'was not to cry again for fifteen months, when a kettle scalded her; but only I know that, and you, too, now' (*TP* 245). His complete access to his characters' thoughts is also made clear. After their first sexual bout on the Roman hill fort Henry and Kim relax: 'Soon, Kim went to sleep, and Henry went into the back of his mind, a private world where no one could ever penetrate; always excepting myself, of course' (*TP* 255).

The author describes his characters as 'puppets' (*TP* 155) exactly as *Murphy* does, though since they are 'other puppets' the central character is included in this class, too. *Murphy* and O'Brien's *At Swim-Two-Birds* are behind the author's first 'Interruption' when he feels it incumbent upon him to give Henry some background against the fact that 'Henry is born at twenty-six years old, completely bespoken as regards prejudices, predilections, proclivities, and so on; which the reader probably considers not entirely natural, or even as smacking a little of the cantrips of mediaeval necromancers' (*TP* 155).[8] The status of characters as fiction, and the way that we, the readers, may invest them with a life outside the boundaries of the text, is made very apparent. Another example occurs when we read that Henry has discovered that 'Kim was unique, as individual as any woman in Henry's experience; about which experience the reader is probably pruriently curious, but must contain himself because I have already provided Henry with as much of a past as is necessary for an understanding of his actions' (*TP* 273-4). Here the reader's curiosity about character's 'lives' becomes suspect, and mention of it is craftily placed before the main sex scene in the text to give the reader extra pause to examine his or her interest in it. The author goes on to inveigle the reader into some more of the necromancy of the authorial role when he closes a section of chapter 8 with: 'And there I think I shall draw a veil of asterisks over the scene' (*TP* 272). This reanimates the cliché in a bizarre way. The dead metaphor of drawing a veil over a scene, originating in (or at least suggesting) the theatre, regains a physical veil: the asterisks and the blank space that surrounds them. The author lays claim to the dividing device between the sections of this chapter with the suggestion that the opacity of the page may actually be used to conceal things. This idea is further developed, as we shall see, in *Albert Angelo*, but here it serves to note the control the author exerts over the 'staging' of the narrative.

Similarly, when the author interrupts Henry's journal a third time: 'I should here issue a caveat that the rocks and rapids of polemics lie ahead, and that any reader desirous of avoiding them should shoulder the vessel of his prejudices and bear it overland to page 193' (*TP* 187). On such occasions the author presents himself as a figure outside the text, a someone for whom the book itself is a *fait accompli* in the same way that it is for the reader (see also *TP* 248, 250). The difference is, of course, that the author figure, although

---

8 According to the *OED* a 'cantrip' can variously mean a horoscope, a spell or a mischievous trick.

he can seemingly refer backwards and forwards within the book as though he has some kind of external overview, exists only as an extrapolation from the text, a phantom. This is not the actual writer but what Foucault calls the 'author function' and 'the principle of thrift in the proliferation of meaning' (1979: 159). It is this phantasmal figure on to whom we project everything we surmise through the central and other characters about the author of the text. At odds with the decreasing narratorial competence seen in Beckett's work (actually a position of strength) Johnson's authorial narrator is conscious of the frailty of his power and lack of control over his reader's hypothesising. I believe the strategies used in *Travelling People* are Johnson's first attempt (without the benefit of Foucault) to expose to the reader what he identifies as the characteristics of this multifarious function and the peculiar ways in which it operates.

Johnson's exposure of authorial powers in *Travelling People* is only partial, however, since, though brought out into the open, the premises and conventions of the narrative remain in place throughout the text. Far more interesting and radical things occur in chapters where the garrulous author figure is not visible (though he is as ever behind the scenes), and they take place at the level of the graphic surface of the text.

The major graphic elements of *Travelling People* appear within the chapters composed of interior monologues. Chapter 4 of *Travelling People* presents the reader with a graphic rearrangement of the page layout in the course of a stream of consciousness sequence. Within this chapter we travel with Henry on the underground from Bank to King's Cross and from there, on foot, to Euston Station (*TP* 35-43). His internal monologue is separated into line-spaced paragraphs which are wholly indented except for their first lines. Many of these thought paragraphs begin with Henry's reading of signs or advertisements as he travels through what Mackrell calls 'the onslaught of external stimuli' (1985: 46). The influence of advertising is a constant in the early chapters of this novel, from italicised imagined ads, to a booksellers' catalogue entry for the supposed dictionary of graffiti, to the memory of a recruitment session that explains Henry's loathing of the business, but what makes this usage fresh is the graphic element. After the single word cue 'Escalator' the page layout alters. Representing the advertisements alongside underground escalators the text of fictional adverts is set in narrow italicised paragraphs spaced diagonally across the page, left to right going down and right to left coming up:

I Married the Virgin
Mary. The Passionate
Story of Joseph, the
Earthly Step-Father of
Our Lord. Starring …

      Fineform Foundation
      Fillets for Successful
      Stately Sylphs who …

           Guinness is Good for …

Henry, yes, very.

Fineform Foundation
Fillets for ...
  Security and 4 ½%! The
  only Building Society
  which offers you
  assets ...

Fineform Foundation ...

The appearance of Henry's thoughts in roman face bring the movement back to the left-hand margin. The mimesis attempted does not attempt to produce the advertisements in facsimile but is, instead, iconic in that the words of the ads are broken to fit the representational form, i.e. oblong posters appearing in diagonal relation to each other. The mimetic impulse of the sequence is concentrated on providing a representation of the action of Henry's mind. We see this in the way that as some adverts are repeated he reads less and less them each time: '*Fineform Foundation Fillets for Successful Stately Sylphs who ...*' becomes gradually '*Finef ...*'. Henry needs to read less to recognise the repeated ad, as does the reader. The link between character and reader has become extremely close here: they both take part in the apprehension of external stimuli of a textual kind, and because those external stimuli are textually identical Henry and the reader are going through almost exactly the same process. Tew (2001: 133) calls this passage process mimesis (see also 83). The parallel between internal and external reality is as close as printed text can bring it. We might argue that the textual representation of the posters misses the typographic, graphic and colour elements of 'real' Underground posters but they are as real as anything in Henry's textual world. Furthermore we are not looking through Henry's eyes: that is not what stream of consciousness attempts to represent at all. We are, literally, reading Henry's mind.

Mackrell argues that 'in all of Johnson's early works, the direct representation of consciousness tends to be an uneasy tension between literariness and literalness that is never fully resolved', but this is to step back from her earlier recognition that Johnson's devices 'function less as alienating disruptions of the fiction than as extensions of the novel's mimetic range' (1985: 50, 48, referring to *AA*). The literalness added to the conventional literariness of fictional prose may seem unresolved, but conventional printed prose does not even recognise that its representational capacities with regard to character consciousness are engaged in a contradiction. No one really thinks in print but print is the best medium for the depiction of consciousness we have. Johnson's experiments in *Travelling People* ask, how can we improve the representation of consciousness and its interaction with the world? Setting aside 'process mimesis', I would like to call approaches to literary representation through the graphic surface *graphic mimesis*.

Travelling People's seventh chapter contains a second example in the stream of consciousness of club proprietor Maurie Bunde who, as his name suggests, is close to death. We are presented with a complete record of Maurie's mental life over the last day of his life. The chapter begins with the reader introduced into his mind during a dream, which is given equal textual weight to his waking consciousness. Speech is indicated by italicisation, but the reader reads only Maurie's speech: the words of those he is speaking with must be inferred into the line spaces left to them. These gaps and those representing benign unconsciousness or dreamless sleep form the only white spaces in the text. When Maurie has a heart attack, while attempting to learn the racing crawl in his pool, this is represented by sections of the pages being printed 'grey': as Maurie races Dunne he lapses into a page and a half of speckles, followed by a brief return to consciousness and thereafter a relapse into a half-page of wavy lines reminiscent of a Bridget Riley op-art painting. Later, after a partial recovery and a refusal to accept his condition, Maurie suffers a fatal heart attack while demanding manual satisfaction from his mistress Kim. This is followed by two and a half entirely black pages. Contemporary critics were quick to spot the reference to Sterne's black page in *Tristram Shandy* (1985: 61–2). Unfortunately most seem to have contented themselves with this without examining how Johnson's use of the device differs from that of Sterne. Bernard Bergonzi says, approvingly: '*Travelling People* is an extremely entertaining novel with an obvious debt to Sterne in its typographical eccentricities: as, for instance, when one character has a heart attack and Johnson illustrates its effect with a blank page printed entirely in black' (1970: 205). We need to look a little closer at what is involved here. Certainly the bottom half of page 224 is printed entirely in black, but 225–6 is actually a black sheet of paper pasted into the fold of the pages (and consequently less free to turn over). This is certainly not a *blank* page. Quite the opposite in fact since, although there is nothing to read, nothing may be written here either, unlike the gaps in the text representing sleep and dialogue.

The employment of these devices within a sequence of stream of consciousness greatly affects their implications. It is important to note that all of the breaks in Maurie's verbal consciousness occupy the entire page width, implicating the whole field of the page in the representation of his consciousness. The margins of these pages, even page numbers, are all subsumed to this representation. They are technical and aesthetic conventions which, should the author demand it, can be put aside. In this exceptional instance they are, for the objectives of the writer are not simply a knowing reference to previous graphic devices but an attempt to convey, as completely as possible, the mimetic representation of a character's thoughts through the medium of the book. Unlike Sterne's black page, which forms a memorial tribute to Yorick, this black page represents, in graphic mimesis, the state of death itself. For all the novel's satire of Maurie's upper-class views and bisexuality the black page here is a bleak moment that we bypass guiltily, with relief.

The success of these graphic devices should not be underestimated. Johnson's eventual rejection of the novel has other causes: 'Since *Travelling People* is part truth and part fiction it now embarrasses me and I will not allow it to be reprinted; though I am still pleased that its devices work' (1973b: 22). The embarrassment of *Travelling People* does relate to the presence of the author in the text, but not to his status of author as controller, his treatment of characters as puppets or his manipulation of structure and plot. Instead it relates to an avenue of interpretation that he has not taken charge of, has overlooked, an aspect of narrative which is so conventional as to seldom be explicitly commented upon. Although Johnson, unlike Beckett in *Murphy*, consigns his central character to the status of puppet this does not prevent the reader 'reading in' the idea that within the main character there is likely to be a part or an indication of a part of the character of the author himself or herself. This is another aspect of the author function and, although Foucault (1979: 112) argues that it would be 'wrong to equate the real writer with the author', the reader is left to construe what he or she will about the author outside the text. In this text the reader is quite likely, I think, to imagine that there is some kind of objective correlative between Henry and Johnson. Johnson was not able to escape this 'English disease', as he later called it (1973b: 22), until his second novel and there is considerable evidence that *Travelling People* is riddled with it.

In the concluding chapter of *Travelling People* we read that an older and wiser Henry 'preferred himself as he was now, perhaps fortunately, though he still retained a slightly ashamed admiration for his former selves' (*TP* 297). In the picaresque adventures of this character, a mature student just out of university, it is easy to see the shade(s) of a young Bryan Johnson described, with 'slightly ashamed admiration', by a somewhat older author. I believe this is where the 'embarrassment' the author later attributed to this book originates. Henry beats all comers in battles of words, wits and fisticuffs in the course of the novel. He lectures Kim on life and love, earns her admiration and respect and finally, assuming the mantle of Lancelot, treats her to a night of Olympian sexual endeavour. The problem Johnson found in looking back at *Travelling People* is that it is virtually impossible for a reader to tell what might relate to the life of the author and what might be completely fiction as long as the narrative remains within the bounds of conventional realism. By the time of 'Disintegration' in *Albert Angelo,* the author wants nothing to do with the untruths and half-truths involved in such attempts to disguise the umbilical cord of the objective correlative. By the end of that novel Johnson's view is to reject character altogether and seek a more direct mediation between writer and reader. Once he had done so he could no longer look favourably upon *Travelling People* as a whole again, but the success of its graphic devices would continue to inspire him, as we shall see.

Albert Angelo (1964)

Albert Angelo is divided into five parts: 'Prologue', 'Exposition', 'Development', 'Disintegration', and 'Coda', with the second and third comprising the bulk of the text. Within these five parts are a total of twenty-seven sections (separated within parts by a line of five asterisks) and these sections offer a sum of around twenty differing styles or narrative methods. Many of these sections introduce graphic devices, or rearrange the graphic surface to convey information in different ways.

Through this plethora of strategies *Albert Angelo* tells, or perhaps it would be better to say begins to tell, the story of a supply teacher and would-be architect in north and east London. My reservation here arises because in the fourth part of the novel an authorial presence violently interrupts the narrative (Johnson 1964 (subsequently *AA*): 167). Contemporary critics, predictably more satisfied with the most conventional parts of the novel, were disappointed that the story of Albert Albert was not taken to a conventional conclusion. The majority of studies of the novel tend to treat 'Disintegration' *as* the novel, or work backwards from this point,[9] but I would like to approach it as the reader does, through the rest of the narrative, to see how it is hinted at, predicted and justified. In this way we will be able to see that within the narrative that precedes it, and in 'Disintegration' itself, the graphic surface provides important pointers towards a more productive interpretation of the book as a whole.

The first part of *Albert Angelo*, 'Prologue', is composed of two short sections. The first is a three-way dialogue, presented with each speaker formally attributed before the speech in italics. As such this section resembles, but is not, dramatic form. The layout of the dialogue in this section uses the graphic surface for the specific needs of the narrative and in so doing it discards the conventional, speech-marked form for dialogue. The same form of presentation returns for Albert's second dialogue with Joseph on pages 142–6. But throughout *Albert Angelo* the presentation of dialogue varies in form according to the needs of the section. For example, while the conventional form (inverted commas) appears in the first three sections of Exposition, Development's second section uses single and double dashes for first- and third-person speech, and the internal monologue of the fourth section of 'Development' presents speech in capitals. The significance of these changes may be limited to their respective contributions to the clarity of the particular sections, but the overall effect of such a variety is to establish the epistemological individuality of the sections, each of which sets a distinctive problem for the reader.

This can be further shown by the way that in the second part of *Albert Angelo*, 'Exposition', the narrative pronoun migrates from 'I' to 'they', visiting all stations in between. After the 'I' section, describing a visit to his parents, Albert narrates a day in his life as a supply teacher in the second person. This is followed by a third-person narration with Albert as 'he' which deals with the beginnings of his failed romance with Jenny. Then Albert narrates again in the first-person plural, for himself and his similarly unlucky-in-love mate, Terry. In the second-person plural address he cynically lectures his class on God.[10] Finally we have Albert and his ex-girlfriend, Jenny, narrated as 'they' on a joint trip to Ireland. 'Exposition' forces the reader to adjust perspective each time, and in so doing generates some awareness of how each section is focalised, and the effect the narrative pronoun has on the reader.

The most striking and original elements in *Albert Angelo* all exhibit this fascination with the reader's hypothesising during the reading of a text. For example, the third-person sections of 'Exposition' are both narrated in the past tense, full of the awareness that, though they depict the beginnings and high point of the romance between Albert and Jenny, those times are definitely gone. Yet to understand this it is necessary for the reader to 'read in' the identities of the protagonists through context and detail. It is not

---

9 See Kennedy 1974: 158–61; Tredell 1985: 64–70; Thielemans 1985: 83; Ryf 1977: 60; Levitt 1981: 577.
10 This exercise brings to mind James Kelman's *A Disaffection* (1989).

immediately clear who the 'he', 'she' and 'they' referred to are. In the first of these two sections a journey depicted as a sequence of architecture is characteristic of the discourse associated with Albert, and eventually things are clarified by the attributed dialogue in the last two lines: 'There will be other times,' she said, Jenny. / 'All the other times in the world,' he said, Albert' (50). The device of attribution of speech is exposed here as a device to answer an epistemological problem of reading which is a familiar (if often unconscious) refrain for the hypothesising reader: 'Who is speaking?'[11] In the third-person plural no clues are given as to the protagonists' identities but 'they' are, I would suggest, routinely attached to the previous Albert and Jenny sequence by the attentive reader. Even if not, these intimate moments will be 'remembered' in Albert's internal monologue in the second section of 'Development'.

Overall the result of the movement of the narrative in and out of Albert's consciousness in 'Exposition' challenges the reader's interpretative abilities. The adaptations of the text to its varying tasks demand that the reader adapt, in turn, to them. The reader of *Albert Angelo* has to think on his or her feet in order to negotiate its devices, particularly the graphic-based ones, which appear during the course of the novel with little fanfare.

Initially the use of the graphic surface in *Albert Angelo* does seem to be designed to attract the attention of the reader to the conventions of mimetic representation. One example is the 'specially-designed type-characters' (e.g. 31, 42) that frame physical descriptions of Albert's pupils. The intent behind the use of these characters seems to be to highlight an aspect of the text that may often be elided by readers, and in so doing draw attention to the fact that elisions do take place when we read. We might compare the following 'authorial' statement in *Christy Malry's Own Double-Entry*: 'Many readers, I should not be surprised to learn if appropriate evidence were capable of being researched, do not read such descriptions at all, but skip to the next dialogue or more readily assimilable section' (Johnson 1973a: 51). The symbol used in *Albert Angelo* to frame description may thus be taken as a licence to skip these brief descriptions. Nicholas Tredell points out: 'In a way, the precise details of the physical descriptions do not matter; this is why ... readers often glide over them. It is simply the fact that a person or object has specifiable characteristics that counts' (1985: 66 and 2000: 58–60). Though it is a graphic device the description marks function much like the phrase 'so it goes' that occurs repeatedly in Kurt Vonnegut's *Slaughterhouse Five* (1970) whenever anything, irrespective of whether it is human or not, is said to have died. Johnson's typographic squiggle works as a sign of repetition for the reader: 'description of physical characteristics here'.

Between the unique symbols we find a few sharp observations of visual impressions, for example: 'Blue eyes, staring, postbox mouth, ears like open cardoors' (*AA* 45). At one level this is a move back to the mimetic convention – a character being pictured as a set of visual attributes rather than a column of statistics – but, as we have noted earlier, the framing of the description exposes the convention and makes it very clear that a majority of

---

11 This question is one of some interest in literary theory and an explicit element of Brooke-Rose's *Thru*, discussed in Chapter 7 .

what we get as description is typically superfluous. This is an important aspect of the device here because, significantly, the vast majority of the children so described will play no further part in the novel; their descriptions are indeed merely ciphers, symbols of what constitutes a 'character' in a novel. Shlomith Rimmon-Kenan puts it: 'in the story character is a construct, put together by the reader from various indications dispersed throughout the text' (1983: 36). Yet while these framed descriptions are simply single visual indications, never-to-be-developed fragments of potential characters, a brief impression is all that most pupils will mean to the supply teacher, whether that impression is a visual, aural or written trace. So, ultimately, the framing device performs a mimetic function.

In addition to the suggestion of character by brief description, *Albert Angelo* also generates 'characters' by the use of proper names. In Barthes's words: 'The proper name acts as a magnetic field for the semes' (1975: 67). Following Barthes, and furthering her discussion of character in *Narrative Fiction*, Rimmon-Kenan adds that a 'fundamental cohesive factor is the proper name' (1983: 39). Our readerly expectations are raised by the use of the name and our conditioned reaction to the textual signal of a proper name is to look for a plot rationale for its inclusion.

This is pushed to its limits in the second section of 'Exposition': the second-person singular narration leads us into a complete calling of the register for 3B, which proceeds as reported dialogue over four pages. Of course, we realise that there is no 3B, just a list of names, but even this list of names, as information pertinent to the rest of the novel, is superfluous. 3B is not the class with whom Albert is in conflict in 'Development'. This is apparent not only because that class seems older and more disruptive but because none of their names corresponds with those of 3B. What the calling of this register provides, beyond an excess of verisimilitude, is a mini, and minimal, narrative. It is introduced with: 'You open the register, and glance down the names. Several Greek-looking ones, a Mustapha, and half a dozen Irish. Not a West Indian district, apparently. You look for special notes: there is only one, Linda Taylor, mild epileptic, besides three with "S" against their names for spectacles' (*AA* 32). Thus primed the reader has several points to look out for; the Greek names, the Irish ones and the epileptic girl. This is, at its most basic, a demonstration of an aspect of the process of reading, gathering information about characters, the core of whose construction is usually the proper name. But this narrative is not without a representational aspect: it can be seen as sociological, illustrating the multi-ethnic state of London over which certain cultural and racial groups are distributed. The mimesis here is more than technique; it gives, and depends on, information.

In addition to raising points about the significance of naming within narrative, the reading of the register for 3B involves an alteration to the layout of the page that reorganises its representational capabilities. Naturally, i.e. according to the conventional indented rendering of speech, this sequence of name and response occupies mostly only the left-hand portion of the page. Such an extended sequence as this would already appear unusual and attract attention to itself, but the conventions of reported dialogue are broken graphically where a column appears on the right-hand side. Here (*AA* 35–6) Albert is allowed some comment in italics, sometimes via the second-person singular narration yet at others more directly:

'Now the boys. Christopher Arbor.'
'Yerp!'

> *You look hard at him. You decide to let*
> *him get away with it this time.*

'David Bufton.'
'Yerp. Sir.'
'Alan Burdick.'
'Yer-r-r-r-r-p!'
'Look, the next boy who tries to be funny while I'm calling the register is
going to regret it. Georgiou Constantenou.'
'Yes, sir.'
'James Day. James Day?'

> *You will risk a joke.*

'James Day seems away.'

> *Good, they laughed a little.*

'Owen Evans.'
'Here, sir.'

This device has significant implications. The disruption of the graphic surface draws
attention to the device as a device, but, like the descriptions framed by special characters,
the graphic separation of thought and dialogue operates mimetically, making a distinction
between Albert's 'external' dialogue with the class and his 'internal', private thoughts.
The initially defamiliarising change to the graphic surface is rapidly normalised by the
reader and understood as an alternative mimesis. This double-impression in its turn
exposes those more conventional devices as mimetic devices, and not a direct transcription of external reality. As Nicholas Tredell states: 'All the devices of *Albert Angelo*,
conventional and experimental, come, in the reading process, into a state of dynamic
activity, playing against and de-automatizing each other, disrupting the 'organic unity',
impeding and displacing the narrative flow' (1985: 64–5). Certainly we can identify the
defamiliarisation of conventional mimesis, but these graphic devices go further than that,
seeking to explore a new, more ambitious level of mimesis.

The use of the divided page is expanded upon in the largest section within
'Development', in which Albert is, literally, up against an older and more disruptive class.
There the interior (thought) and exterior (speech) are rigidly split into two columns (see
Figure 6.1). Albert's consciousness is present, in one column or the other, throughout,
whether he is reading privately about architecture, teaching geology or drifting into a
sequence of sexually stimulating memories of his time with Jenny. In this arrangement,
however, his thought may appear simultaneously with the speech of others, introduced by
a long dash, or his own, simply indented.

As we have seen in our discussion of Brian McHale's work on the division of text into
columns within narrative in Chapter 1, the reader is required to improvise an order of reading.
This does not happen in the first divided section quoted: everything in that could be – and

——Ma famly? You bin
sayin' fings about ma famly?
—— I'll get you, just you
wait!
—— Watch it, cocker, or
you'll be 'avin' a visit from
the Corps.
—— I'm terrified.
—— Read it out to 'er.
—— No, shush, Albert'll see
it.
—— I don't care. 'E wouldn't
get it off me anyway.
—— The Corps...
——Go on, read it, ent it
funny...

**What the hell d'you
mean by making so much
noise! Silence!**

*Ah, Jenny, oh god, god,
god! My love, that's it, my
love, you can never go back,
that high, yet how I miss it!
The love! Singular, only,
only one, the love, the love.
Not so much her, Jenny, but
the love, for there were —
were there? — bad things —
weren't there? — about her I
don't miss. But do I, were
they part of the love? They
must have been, yes, all part
of the love, part of the pain
and the pleasure and the
joy, the joyous in the rain
and the suffering...
Bloody noise!*

Figure 6.1: Parallel columns from *Albert Angelo* (1964: 88)

was designed to be - read in sequence from left to right. In this instance, however, stream of consciousness is set against direct external speech. As Philip Tew says: 'the reader feels located and dislocated simultaneously' (2001: 168). For the reader this is internal monologue *plus*; the text gives access to the external world of the character too, structuring two other aspects of representation as well (what he hears, and what he actually says). The reader has to relate clips of dialogue from a number of speakers to the continuous stream of Albert's thoughts which, chronologically, must be simultaneous. This simultaneity works by the specific graphic device of parallel lineation in which space *equals* time.[12] Through this device we can read a fairly straightforward mimetic narrative which shows that while Albert is occupied internally the class becomes disruptive; this is the product of non-interaction with them and Albert's attempt to live in two worlds. Like some chapters of *Travelling People* this section attempts to convey, as completely as possible, a mimetic representation of a character's thoughts through the medium of the book (not simply prose).

12 Johnson takes this much further in *House Mother Normal* (1971), which is composed of nine internal monologues, each of twenty-one pages, covering the same period of time; the duration of a geriatric social evening. In this way the same events can be seen through different character consciousnesses and compared in the codex form of the book.

McHale's (1987) reaction to disruption of the graphic surface totally bypasses this mimesis and the important opposition which this particular device sets up. The ontological awareness into which McHale retreats is a side-effect, and his reaction merely an acknowledgement that the layout is unconventional, therefore to some extent defamiliarising. The two columns are at odds with each other in a number of ways: teacher/class; individual/group; internal/external; order/chaos; all of which are represented and paralleled textually by the challenge set for the reader by the dual columns. It is literally impossible to read both columns at the same time, our reading, therefore, has to be on one side or the other at any particular point in time. The conceptual allegory of conflict between teacher and class formed by the textual device is highly significant, as we shall see, while the graphic presentation of the conflict also clearly serves mimetic ends.

Another example of graphic mimesis in *Albert Angelo* cuts out narratorial mediation entirely. Suddenly the reader comes upon the unheralded reproduction of a spiritualist reader's advertising card, front and rear '(BE SURE TO READ OTHER SIDE)' over two pages (*AA* 120–1).

This device is, I believe, a development based on the Suk's astrological 'Thema Coeli' in *Murphy*. Johnson's spiritualist's card is quite different. It is laid out in a variety of typefaces in several different sizes, with an illustration of its own, all on toned blocks. Although Madame Mae clearly operates in the Angel, neither the content nor the spiritualist is referred to elsewhere in the text. In fact, these two pages have every appearance of being a copy of an existing document, from outside the text, not authored by the same author. What are we to make of this?

Nicholas Tredell tells us that 'This [device] transfers to the novel a technique with which we are acquainted in twentieth century visual art: in collage, in the *objet trouvé*: in pop art, an artefact (often bearing a printed legend) is removed from its mundane context and placed against disparate artefacts in a context traditionally associated with art, and it is thus defamiliarized, seen afresh' (1985: 66. See also 2001: 60–1). Though I would agree that visual art is this device's source of inspiration, I think it is necessary to point out that we are only actually presented with two-dimensional monochrome copies of the Madame Mae card, not a card itself (although this would have been possible). One can easily imagine, for example, the actual card being printed in blue ink on magenta card, but those aspects of it, its colour, its separateness, its full reality, aren't available to us.[13] Tredell is right, however, when he suggests that this piece of printed ephemera is defamiliarised and seen afresh in its reproduced state. Whereas such a piece of paper would be unlikely to detain us a moment when encountered outside the book, we are, I think, obliged to study it and ask ourselves why it has been included. Perhaps the main point about Madame Mae is 'She enjoys the enviable reputation of telling the truth!' which is something central to Johnson's writing throughout his career.

---

13 The full reality of the card would only be another set of signs like the textual version, but a certain constriction of these signs has taken place in the representation of the card as part of a monochrome codex form.

Regarding the question of telling the truth there are, on the second 'side' of Madame Mae's card, a series of questions, several of which have some relevance to Albert's situation in the plot of the book so far. In fact they are so general as to be questions any reader could step back from most novels and ask in reference to the characters with the proviso '*DO – YOU – WISH – TO – KNOW?*' An important clue to the significance of the reproduced card comes over the page when three segments from children's compositions seem to answer questions like 'When and whom will you marry?' 'How long will you live?' and 'If you have enemies and who?' for Mr Albert or 'Alburt'. Instead of this advertisement being remembered and quoted by the characters in the novel, as the Suk's predictions are in *Murphy*, here it is left to the reader to relate this text to the text at large, and its questions to the characters. It is the reader, not the characters, who really needs to know how things will turn out. And this teleological need is ironically associated here with spiritualism, itself often associated with fraudulent charlatanism and an activity that seeks information from or about those who are dead or otherwise missing.

The wish to know is central to the operation of the most remarked-upon graphic device within *Albert Angelo* where holes are cut in some of the pages. In the original and American editions this device operates as follows: a short section on pages 147–9 has Albert with Terry in Georgiou's café, explaining his idea of letting his class express their feelings about him, but the last five lines of page 148 are blank, with the section continuing at the top of page 149. Under the line of asterisks, indicating the start of a new section, a text-width hole is cut in pages 149–52 revealing the penultimate three lines of page 153.[14] The words seen through the gap are 'struggled to take back his knife, and inflicted on him a mortal wound above his right eye (the blade penetrating to a depth of two inches) from which he died instantly'. The device allows the reader to see violence ahead. The blank space at the bottom of page 148 means that there can be no 'backward' glances through the hole (at least in copies I have seen). On pages 150 and 152 we find the narrative reaching right down to the hole but continuing on pages 151 and 153 uninterrupted (see also Tew 2002: 15).

The section beginning on page 150, after the asterisks above the hole on 149, is a clipped first-person account of an eventful night out with Terry with a pseudo-Berlin title, *Cablestrasse*, and without paragraph indents.[15] Alarmingly, our first glance (for the novelty of the device cannot fail to engage our attention) of 151 imposed on 153 reads 'Terry / struggled to take back his knife ...'. A conventional linear reading will, however, show us that Albert's bullish behaviour does not lead to a knife-fight at this point. Instead, over the page, Terry and Albert have high jinks in a bombed industrial area and get a talking-to from a policeman. The sequence ends, half-way down page 153, like this:

---

14 Coe (2004: 18) rather awkwardly indicates this by stating there is 'a rectangular hole cut through two of the recto pages.'

15 Cable Street was the scene of famous riots between British fascist and anti-fascist groups during the 1930s.

> Very reasonable copper. Not narked. Just said not the time to appreciate architecture, as this was Stepney and any minute a drunken man might rush out of a house with a knife in his hand and stick it into the first person he saw; who might well be me.

This manages to preserve the suspicion that the violent end anticipated since page 149 may still come to Albert in the next section, but ultimately the text seen through the hole turns out to be an account of a factual death some four hundred years ago. The last line of the page (and the section) and therefore not visible through the hole/window simply states 'Christopher Marlowe, Poet, February 1564 to May 1593'.[16] The dramatist is mentioned neither previously nor subsequently and does not appear even among the longest list of books noted on Albert's shelf. All we have is a seedy, slightly mysterious, killing in Deptford, unless we conflate this episode with one towards the end of *Travelling People*. After Maurie Bunde's death Henry and Kim set out to shirk the responsibilities laid upon them by Maurie's successor Trevor and his moll Mira. This consists of driving into Pwllheli and having a working-class night out:

> They ... drove several times around the town looking for a place to have a drink. Finally, again almost simultaneously, they chose a little workingclass beerhouse a few doors from the fish and chip saloon they had left only a little earlier.
>
> Henry went through the door of the single bar like Christopher Marlowe into Eleanor Bull's tavern at Deptford Strand on 30th May, 1593.
>
> 'Ho, Landlord,' he cried, stuffed with hubris to the eyeballs, 'Come! A rehoboam of Rhenish for my company and I!' (*TP* 261)

Henry buys a round, contributes a music-hall song to the evening's singing and is roundly well received into the community, working-class roots being stronger than national loyalties. This adds up to a feeling of belonging and identity not available at the upper-class Stromboli Club. This identity is personified in Marlowe:

> On Henry, this cheap, weak beer had the same exorcising, re-cleansing effect as the fish and chips. He bought himself another, a pint this time.
>
> 'I was weaned on this stuff,' he said, loudly, Christopher Marlowe sweeping back into him.
>
> 'That explains a lot of things,' laughed Kim, and Kit returned to the shades (*TP* 262)

The identification of Henry with Marlowe suggests, more clearly than anything in *Albert Angelo* does, a link between Albert and Marlowe. Whereas Henry's relation to Marlowe is fairly direct – a persona he can assume – Albert's relation is less obvious. While both Henry and Albert are to some degree objective correlatives for Johnson, the Marlowe figure is an objective correlative of an objective correlative. His demise prefigures that of Albert himself, both as a character (Albert's demise in Coda) and as a device (where the objective correlative is dropped in Disintegration).

---

16 Disappointingly, the Marlowe reference is often visible in copies of the 2004 *Omnibus*.

In the short term, the present of a first reading, Marlowe's fate, which we initially feared would befall Albert, must keep the possibility of a stabbing current, especially as, when we turn over, we begin to read the series of verdicts on Albert by his pupils indicating the depth of their hostility. In view of Albert's physical violence towards the class we must take the anecdote as a warning. It would be possible to reach this conclusion without the hole in the pages, and we must go a little further to uncover how this physical change to the pages of the book affects the reading process.

What the device of the hole does is to disrupt temporarily the linear flow of the narrative, and to a certain extent throw out the normal process of reading. As Shlomith Rimmon-Kenan says:

> the process of reading is largely an attempt to integrate the various data, to establish maximum relevance between the diverse details, to form hypotheses as to what happened, what is happening and what is going to happen in the narrative ... The reader does not wait until the end of the narrative, but starts forming connections and constructing hypotheses at an early stage (1977: 9)

This process usually consists of simply assimilating the details and implications of what has been read, but this forward-seeing device conspires to offer information from a point beyond the site of reading. The reader's hypotheses must then take that into account; and the reading of the text, between the point at which the hole becomes visible and the exact point which it spies ahead to, becomes peculiarly fraught. Patricia Waugh reads the holes in the pages in the following way: 'The reader is forced to reflect upon the conventions not only of narrative suspense (which works essentially by deliberately impeding the completion of the action or the explanation of a story, while gradually filling in "blanks" in the text) but also of the contextual basis of "meaning" both inside and outside fictional texts' (1984: 96). But the device is, I believe, actually more specific than this, more loaded. I would venture that one hypothesis that presents itself to many readers will be 'What if it is Albert that is killed?' which inevitably leads to 'If Albert dies what's in the rest of the book?' This device, and the Madame Mae section, do not ultimately make the reader aware of the physical nature of the book so much as they expose the mechanisms of the reader's ongoing hypothesising from the text and, through this, the relationship between the reader's hypothesising and the technical operation of the book itself as a vehicle for text. In the normal linear progression of narrative the crisis point of hypothesising is closely related to the end of the book which is materially apparent in the physical number of pages we will have to turn to reach it. Here the section between the sighting and passing of the hole almost constitutes a mini-narrative, a teleological drama, in which we are shown the last pages but must read those which intervene to understand their significance. We may argue that Johnson did not intend to make this point when he used this (possibly unique) graphic device, but that would not mean the device did not operate in this way.

'Disintegration' suggests that 'the future-seeing holes ... [are used] as much to draw attention to the possibilities as to make my point about death and poetry' (175–6). Mackrell (1985: 51) is right to ask, 'What point?' The last clause of the statement suggests we take account of the exchange between Albert and his flatmates in the first section of 'Prologue' where Joseph suggests that Albert's buildings will be built after his death: '*Luke said:* Like poets, after they're dead. / *Albert said:* Like poets, just. / *Luke said:* Fucking lot of good that is, mate. I mean, when you're dead you're fucking dead, aren't you? / *Albert said:* No' (*AA* 13). Like Marlowe, the 'poet' may leave something behind: it may only be his death, but it may be solid printed evidence of his existence, too.

The fact that the hole allows us to see something that can be linked only tangentially to Albert Albert, the central character of the text, certainly does fall within Johnson's intentions for the device. The deflation of the reader's hypotheses is built up to on page 152, where Albert records:

> Suddenly had an epiphany on sight of the roofline (*it hit me, it hit me: some one, some people, humankind, had thought about that roofline, had conceived it; it wasn't brilliant, or graceful, it was just of humankind, man's, sweated from his conscious*) and stopped to write it down (*AA* 152)

Consider this, disregarding the architectural reference to roofline (something we will have some justification for doing once we reach 'Disintegration'); it could be taken as praise for the mechanism of the book, for the thought and organisation that has goes into it (after all 'roofline' is only one word within the edifice of the book) and particularly for the considerable efforts that have gone into the constructing of this particular graphic device. The bathetic outcome to the artifice here tends to devalue or ironise the above quotation, though I would suggest that the fact that the policeman demands to see what he has written and Albert obliges with the words 'Showed him piece of paper – much good it would do him' prefigures this result.

The reversal of expectations around the holed pages shows the text continuing to ironise the teleological needs of the reader while making demands of his or her hypothesising activity.[17] Tredell argues, 'When we consider, in retrospect, the supposedly proleptic holes, we see that these point up a device which we might call false prolepsis: an arousing in a narrative, by selective or distorted anticipation, of reader expectations that are subsequently, to a greater or lesser extent, disconfirmed' (1985: 67).

The effect itself, the defeat of expectations, also has a larger relevance within *Albert Angelo*, for we see false prolepsis at play on a grand scale when, at the end of 'Development' more architectural description focalised through Albert is broken off with ' – OH, FUCK ALL THIS LYING!' (163). 'Disintegration' follows. We shall see how the reader might negotiate this change, and renegotiate his reading in light of it, in the following section.

'Disintegration': shifting the goalposts

'Disintegration', the fourth part of *Albert Angelo*, seems to be largely a hectoring first person rant. Albert is summarily abandoned, exposed as a character in a fiction, and ridiculed as

---

17 Teleological need (rather than teleology) is subject to irony because it has the desire for an end result. Hypothesising, though it involves consideration of end results, is not so easy to disconcert because it is provisional and ongoing.

a disguise for actual facts. On page 167 the new voice expresses three basic things that he feels the narrative thus far has falsified and which must now be brought into the open:

(1) The author has something better to offer than just a story to tell: 'Im trying to say something not tell a story telling stories is telling lies and I want to tell the truth about me about my experience about my truth about my truth to reality'.

(2) The author is no longer satisfied with using an objective correlative for himself: 'im my hero though what a useless appellation my first character then im trying to say something about me through him albert an architect when whats the point in covering up covering up covering over pretending pretending i can say anything through him that is anything that I would be interested in saying'.

(3) The subject is writing, not architecture: 'what im really trying to write about is writing not all this stuff about architecture trying to say something about writing about my writing'.

The essential problem for the reader of *Albert Angelo* on reaching 'Disintegration' is the realisation that a considerable number of his or her hypotheses constructed during their reading of the narrative are rendered invalid. Disintegrated. Judith Mackrell claims the effect is to:

> irritatingly belittle Johnson's achievements within the main body of the narrative (not simply the creation of a vivid and detailed fictional world, but also the exploration of the ways in which different styles and forms shape and illuminate their material precisely by virtue of their different methods of selection and structuring) (1985: 52)

I would disagree, at least with the belittling part of this quotation. What 'Disintegration' does do is make us reconsider what we have read and focuses the reader's attention upon his or her own hypotheses, and, since we do not wish to discard them having come this far, how they might be changed, adapted and readjusted to the new situation. All that 'Disintegration' does (as prefigured by the device of the holed pages) is exaggerate, and so call attention to, the working of this process.

The sudden rejection of what has gone before in 'Disintegration' does not erase it. Though we see, in *Albert Angelo*, an author attempting to enter and occupy his text to the degree that the difference between him and his narrating voice is shaved as thin as possible, we will still end up at odds with the text if we concentrate on Johnson. When we encounter the author figure in 'Disintegration' we are not suddenly transported into a literary manifesto (although some paragraphs of this part do have that tone) or a psychological study; we, the readers, remain within the novel *Albert Angelo*: all we have done is physically turned a couple of pages. The author is no more nor less the author than he was during the narrative. In fact, his qualification for that title, in its formal sense, depends on what has gone before. All that has happened is that he has dropped all the narrative devices that shielded him from view during the previous parts of the text.

Thus, the first problem that the reader has to contend with in 'Disintegration' is what status to assign the new voice. In view of the first-person sections that have gone before, Morton P. Levitt describes the interruption by this new voice thus: 'Albert breaks down (or is it Johnson?), admits that he has been writing a novel and explains his strategies' (1981: 577). This is, I think, an unwarranted interpretation. There is little evidence within the text for believing Albert to be his own author in the way that Tristram Shandy is presented as the author of *The Life and Opinions of Tristram Shandy*. Nor will the concept of the implied author be very helpful here. Bernard Bergonzi explains:

> Although it would be possible to assimilate this effect to modes of fiction by saying that the author's 'second self' has undergone a rapid and violent change of persona, this is surely to soften its impact excessively (in private conversation B. S. Johnson has violently protested against any such interpretation) (1970: 206)

It would be easy to dismiss Johnson's opinions if they were only that, as in the controversial 'Introduction' to *Aren't You Rather Young* ..., or only reported by a critic, as in the Bergonzi quote. Here, however, they are expressed as part of the novel itself, and the identity of the literary interloper of 'Disintegration' can only be that of some author figure. If *the* author does not (cannot) manage to enter the text personally it is not for the want of trying.

In fact from the perspective of having read *Albert Angelo* up to the point of 'Disintegration' I do not think we can have failed to suspect that this 'author', or one very like him, existed as a metatext of the narrative. This is an aspect of the 'complex operation which constructs a certain rational being we call "author"' (Foucault 1979: 150). I suggest the reader routinely suspects the major or first character of being in some respects an 'objective correlative' of the author outside the text. As a result it would be surprising to learn at this point that Johnson had never been a supply teacher at all.[18] And if we look back on the text we can see several direct suggestions that Albert is a surrogate for someone.

In the following passage, his function as a supply teacher acts as a metaphor for the role the character is asked to play on behalf of the author:

> Always in supply there is this mysterious figure whom you are replacing. You try to build up your own conception of him from what others let fall in conversation, from his room, his desk, his children. Mr. MacKenzie. Whom you are replacing (*AA* 38)

Furthermore, in the first person Albert tells us of how the stagy and unlikely portico to his parents' house affects his behaviour:

> I would make exits and entrances and imagine a vast audience watching every movement I made. This behaving as though an audience were watching has become part of me, is my character, is me, and on one level I am always thinking and acting in a film for such a film audience (*AA* 22)

This statement actually operates on as many levels as Albert does. It is mimetic, allegorical and metatextual. Firstly, there is a mimetic admission of a certain psychological outlook from the character Albert, consistent with his interest in architecture throughout the text. Secondly, the architecture-as-stage-set metaphor operates in a conventional symbolic or allegorical way for the reader aware (as 'Disintegration' makes explicit) that architecture

---

18 Albert's teaching activities are not denied, only his architectural ones. See Ghose 1985: 29.

stands for writing in this text. The combination of these two ideas, that architecture provides scenery, in the sense of surroundings for the characters, and at the same time, like theatrical scenery, represents something other than itself, feeds a third idea at a metatextual level; that Albert *is* a fictional character who is acting, not in a film but in a fiction, for an implied director/author and a reading audience. 'Disintegration' brings the whole set crashing down, doing away with the theatrical illusion of conventional representation.

In *Albert Angelo*'s epigraph, taken from Beckett's *The Unnamable* – 'when I think of the time I've wasted with these bran-dips, beginning with Murphy, who wasn't even the first, when I had me, on the premises, within easy reach' – we may see some justification for 'Disintegration''s rending of the fictional curtain between reader and writer but not, as both Mackrell and Bergonzi both point out, licence to offer autobiography instead of fiction.[19]

The Unnamable appears to be making similar moves to those made in Disintegration; for example, everything in previous works by the author is described as 'all lies' (1958: 20). But for Johnson lies disguise the truth, while in Beckett everything, including truth, has to be invented, so that in *The Unnamable* the extent of the lies is virtually total: 'Ah yes, all lies, God and man, nature and the light of day, the heart's outpourings and the means of understanding, all invented, basely, by me alone' (ibid.).

Again, there *appears to be* a similarity between *Albert Angelo* and *The Unnamable* in the rejection of substitute characters, but in Beckett this has a different motivation: 'All these Murphys, Molloys and Malones do not fool me. They have made me waste my time, suffer for nothing, speak of them, when, in order to stop speaking, I should have spoken of me and of me alone' (ibid.: 19). The intention is to *stop* speaking rather than to speak more truthfully. The narrating voice of *The Unnamable* which rejects its forerunners is not Beckett's voice and is not meant to be understood as such, describing itself in the following way: 'I'm a big talking ball, talking about things that do not exist' (ibid.: 21). Johnson, on the other hand, is committed both to mimesis and to admitting his own human presence. As Philip Tew writes: 'For Johnson *everything is embedded* and *material*, even his own act of writing' (1998: 182 and see 2001: 143).

We might like to remember Pope's satirical take on aposiopesis in *Peri Bathous ... The Art of Sinking in Poetry*: 'An excellent Figure for the ignorant as, *What shall I say?* when one has nothing to say; or *I can no more*, when one really can no more: Expressions which the gentle Reader is so good, as never to take in earnest' (1968: 46). Of course, *The Unnamable* voice that wishes to stop speaking has another hundred pages to go at this point, and will invent Mahood and Worm, and state, in the famous last line, 'you must go on, I can't go on, I'll go on'. Johnson, similarly, although he calls Disintegration 'an almighty aposiopesis' does not dry up, he simply cannot go on as before.

The dramatic interruption near the end of *Albert Angelo* is an attempt to enact teleology; the discovery of final causes. In the conventional objective-correlative-using text

---

19 There is, however, some Beckettian precedent for the *manner* of Johnson's break with description in *Malone Dies*: 'A stream at long intervals bestrid – but to hell with all this fucking scenery' (1962 [1958]: 131).

such final causes are not to be discovered; they remain cloaked in fiction. In *Albert Angelo*, however, the ironisation of readers' teleological needs implicit in earlier devices – the reading of the register, Madame Mae's card, the proleptic holes – is shown to have been applied to 'false' narrative situations of the kind that the aposiopesis of 'Disintegration' explodes. What now emerges is a serious attempt to replace fiction with 'truth'.

In the event, this proves not a little tricky. When we are offered 'A few instances of the lies', which we might perhaps read as 'factual bases', the problem arises that we have to take these on trust just as we initially did those in the narrative. Johnson tells us much about himself through objective correlative in *Travelling People* and *Albert Angelo*, and even more directly in his subsequent novels *Trawl* and *The Unfortunates*. In his studies of Johnson's third novel, *Trawl*, which is presented as a novel though it largely consists of autobiographical material, Andrew Hassam is 'haunted by the spectre of an unsubstantiated biographical raw material to which the works appear to refer' (1986: 63, see also 1988). There is nothing to check Johnson's truths against.[20] While Hassam finds *Trawl* an indeterminate form, we must reflect on the indeterminacy caused within *Albert Angelo* by the fact that it contains two 'truths'; one occupying the first three parts and the bulk of the text, the other following. What 'Disintegration' does is simply exemplify a few name changes, shifts, relocations and exaggerations, and emphasise their triviality. The problem for the reader is: how can we recognise that any of these details, offered us as truth, are any more valid than those offered us within the 'lies' of Albert's narrative? This problem is spotted by the character Malone in *Malone Dies* where he says of his creation, Sapo: 'And yet I write about myself with the same pencil and in the same exercise book as I write about him' (1962: 41–2).[21] Johnson, in attempting to impose himself on the narrative at a plane somewhat higher than Malone, has raised the stakes but the gamble still carries the same risk. As readers we are at liberty to realise that the new 'truth' is not actually offered us on any new authority, but only the same authority as before in a different mode, or mood. Certainly one truth seems meant to supersede the other when the author figure claims superiority to Albert Albert, but what if another author figure steps from the wings, and so on, to infinite regress? This is the lesson of Beckett's trilogy which culminates in *The Unnamable*. It seems to me, however, that Johnson thrusts himself so aggressively into the text here in order to do his best to disallow this possibility. Despite the Beckett epigraph the impulse behind 'Disintegration' is to travel in exactly the opposite direction.

What we are left with though is a sequence of details, a mere sketch of a narrative, as in the mini-narrative of Albert's reading of the register, parasitising on a greater one. Indeed, it is only through reference to Albert's narrative that these details have any relevance for us at all (compare Beckett's 'Addenda' to *Watt* discussed in Chapter 5). Johnson admits that pointing out every 'lie' would be 'so tedious'; so the majority of these small lies are there-

---

20 Alan Burns had two chapters of a biography printed (1997) and Jonathan Coe has given us a complete biography (2004).

21 Essentially this is a realisation that the text on the page recognises no levels. Which is not to say that the reader can't recognise the hierarchical relationship between Malone and Sapo.

fore allowed to stand. Yet if we were to replace the exemplified lies with the supposed truths a rereading would not change our understanding substantially. Parrinder pertinently asks: 'What relevance, after all, do such unverifiable assertions have for the reader?' (1977: 48). Any more of them would be tedious and pointless, as Johnson tacitly acknowledges by stopping. These details really have a relevance only to Johnson's *own* reading; '*my* truth to reality'. Only the man who knows the reality represented in the text intimately could be dissatisfied with the equivalent details that have replaced the actual ones. This is perhaps what lies behind the following admission: 'I have to write, I have to tell the truth, it's compulsive, yet at the same time agonising' (*AA* 168).[22] The reader may, however, be irritated by these trivial details exactly because they do not add anything to his or her reading. It is as if Johnson wished to go back and change the physical descriptions framed between his specially-designed marks. Nothing outside those marks would be altered.

The 'corrections' to the narrative may be of more interest for the reader only when they address its larger elements. We do learn additional details when the abortive romance is discussed; and we also learn of the cathartic effects of writing this sequence out (although these events will feature again in *Trawl* and, more tangentially, in *The Unfortunates*). Here, at least, the exposure of 'lies' becomes productive and gives this sequence a painfully self-conscious confessional feel. This is short-lived, however, and soon closed off embarrassedly with 'enough of this emotional sewerage'.

The whole purpose of correcting the 'lies' attendant on fictionalisation is not really a personal confession but a literary one. The thrust of the 'Prelude' to *Travelling People*, an 'authorial' preface already discussed, offers some support to the idea that deceit between writer and reader is to be avoided, and that earlier novel goes some way to exposing authorial presence and power, but, as we have seen, other conventional mechanisms, particularly the objective correlative, remain in place. By the standards of *Albert Angelo*, *Travelling People* has failed. The objective is no longer to draw nearer to reality and truth, but to achieve them. Disintegration is an act of narrative violence towards these ends.

What Johnson is doing as he exposes the convention of the objective correlative is to set himself a new goal. Johan Thielemans puts it: 'What has been radically rejected is here reintroduced as an ideal to be reached. By destroying the "illusion' ... Johnson tries to save that very illusion and turn it into a valid attempt to speak the truth. The rejection is also a recuperation' (1985: 84).

The 'Last Interruption' to *Travelling People* also offers some hint to the motivation behind 'Disintegration' and the bolder questions asked of the form in *Albert Angelo*. Here the author tells us of Henry's desire for 'society to be as it says it is, not how it actually is' (*TP* 192).[23] I believe this quality, translated into literary terms, may also be attributed to the author figure of *Albert Angelo*. He wants mimetic novels, texts which represent life, not

---

22 This quotation might be seen as a personalised version of 'I have no voice and must speak, that is all I know' (Beckett 1958: 23).

23 See also Johnson 1973a: 116: 'What it [society] does in practice is not what it says it does. It does not care for human life ... but you know the ways in which we are all diminished: I should not need to rehearse them further.'

supposedly realistic novels that mimic the conventions of other novels. But this argument does not remain purely one of literary technique; it turns out to be the problems of representing different aspects of society that provide the voice for the alternative view of mimesis, and this voice has its own graphic characteristics.

Reintegration: order and chaos

As we have seen, the graphic devices of *Albert Angelo* offer a series of striking challenges to the reader through which mimetic information may be imparted. The re-integration of the text requires us to assimilate the lessons of these devices, to understand the conflicts within the narrative which they develop and their part in creating the context in which 'Disintegration' happens.

In terms of plot, the major conflict in *Albert Angelo* is between Albert and his class. Within the long double-columned section of 'Development' Albert's discourse, internal and external, expounds accepted knowledge about architecture and geology and includes words he reads from a printed book. He is also personally responsible for order in the class, and attempts to impose it. The pupils' speech, however, opposes and resists Albert's discourse (see Tredell 2000: 66–7, 72–3). Though Albert's discourse dominates the speech column for long periods the class manages to get its language into his consciousness when he reads the note with its ribald poem they have been passing around. The class also manage 'physical' effects: stealing Albert's pen, defacing his architecture book and temporarily abducting the sample of gneiss which is his souvenir of his holiday with Jenny. The memories Albert starts to recall as a result of handling this item lead him mentally away from the classroom, and while Albert moons over Jenny internally he allows the class their most expansive penetration of the speech column. The class, whose interior thoughts are unvoiced, remain aware of the external world noting ''E's got that dozy look', and, when Albert is roused from his reverie, a class member is quick to observe its effect: 'Oh, Albie's got lead in 'is pencil' (*AA* 89). It is as though the left-hand column knows what the right-hand is doing, and there is a compelling reason for this: outside class Albert's escapades with Terry are conspicuously those of teenagers; hanging around in cafés, kicking beer cans, throwing milk bottles. Another link can be seen when we realise that Albert's near-fracas with the West Indians (*AA* 150–1) shows marked similarities to adventures recounted (or made up) by members of his class in the composition '*What a scrap*' (64–5) in which there is a gang fight (leading to camaraderie) with a group containing some West Indians.

Overall the novel shows that Albert has a good deal of sympathy for his charges, notably in terms of social class, but he is compromised by his role as teacher. There are parallels here with the situation of teacher Patrick Doyle in James Kelman's *A Disaffection*. In *Albert Angelo*, however, instead of the problem being repeatedly rehearsed in the protagonist's head, as it is in Kelman's novel, the division and the tension between being one of 'us' and one of 'them' is demonstrated graphically on the pages. The two-columned section shows the interplay of opposed discourses, official and unofficial, in the class, while on a larger scale the two discourses occupy different sections within 'Development', offering pro- and anti-Albert sympathies to the reader.

Throughout 'Development' we see Albert's narrative – as centred on him, the sort of narrative that filled 'Exposition' – lose ground to other types. This part begins with four short narratives presented as classroom compositions drawn from the children's lives. Midway through the section there are three short segments of similar narrative which include Mr Albert, and, finally, towards the end there are nineteen short, but largely hostile, compositions on the subject of Mr Albert set by him in a vain hope of alleviating some of the classroom tension. The power struggle between Albert and this class is represented graphically throughout. The sum of these sections is to provide an alternative viewpoint, or a number of alternative viewpoints, upon the central character, and simultaneously to provide an alternative language to that of Albert and his narrator. All the class work is presented with 'uncorrected' idiosyncratic spelling and grammar. This does not, however, prevent shrewd judgements:

> i think he trise his hardest But i think he has a bit more go in him but he dont want to yuse it on us he is quite tall and on the plup side But i cant tallk somtimes when we all sit down to work he sets us the Boy's including me just fuk about in class and take the mike out of him we also somtimes just take no notis and just carey on withe what we are dowing somtimes i think he must fell like just droping avver thing and give up but he just perseyveres (*AA* 158)

These 'compositions' constitute the prose voices of the class whose taming is Albert's job, and one he is uncomfortable with. Firstly, he realises that 'the school *is* a microcosm of society as a whole' (*AA* 133). And secondly that he is an enforcer for that society. His encounters with the class and his access to their writings, which (in a sense) form a dialogue, bring about a realisation of how 'unnatural' what he attempts to make them conform to is:

> Unless you came to this school you just wouldn't believe half the things that go on. You'd hardly see it as a school at all as you know schools: there's no set of rules, or even habits, to which the kids will conform or that they will even acknowledge. I've never been anywhere before, for instance, where they do not even accept that they must not talk in class: when I shut them up they resent it as though I am curtailing an inalienable freedom. And I see their point, in a way, too. (*AA* 132)

Once again, we see Albert expressing a guilty sympathy for his class and an acknowledgement of the way that his voice excludes theirs.[24]

The autonomy and difference of the voices of Albert's class is signalled by the textual vitality of 'their' pieces: some have titles, some don't; some have underlined words; some are partly or entirely capitalised; length varies from a page to a few lines, with some laid out in letter form; one piece is even laid out like a poem. This lack of uniformity attempts to reflect the idiosyncrasies of the children while the conventions of the printed book deny calligraphic reproduction of the numerous hands these pieces purport to be from. The

---

24 Tew has consistently argued that class conflict is a vital factor in Johnson's writing.

brief sections of children's prose are typographic representations which stand in for an accurate or facsimile representation of their writings. They constitute a mode of graphic mimesis which moves closer to what the novel intends to represent but the goal is ultimately unattainable. These devices show the *reductio ad absurdum* of literary mimesis by the means of their own shortcomings. Every move towards the goal of representation in text discovers its objective to be a mirage. For all their diversity the class texts are all 'brought into line' by the printed book.

In 'Disintegration' Albert's sympathy for the language of his pupils has been exchanged for the author figure's appropriation of their graphic voice. The author selects this particular voice from those used previously because of its opposition to order, the conventional order, whose representative was Albert. Just as the character is overthrown so is the architectural discourse associated with him, and the grammatical voice of conventional mimesis with it. This point hasn't penetrated many critical readings because of misunderstandings surrounding the use of the graphic surface. Bernard Bergonzi, having quoted part of 'Disintegration', comments that 'Johnson nevertheless remains imprisoned in his typographical dimension [as] is evident from the obtrusiveness of his lack of punctuation' (1968: 199). For Johnson the voice of disorder is the voice of truth and he argues that 'there is a great temptation for a writer to impose his own pattern, an arbitrary pattern which must falsify, cannot do anything other than falsify' (*AA* 170). Adopting the style of the unedited vitriol against the character within the fiction, the voice of 'Disintegration' vents, from a superior position, similar criticism of the inadequacy of Albert.

The variety of styles and devices used in the text form both the tools and the solution of the quest for literary rejection and recuperation. We have seen enough changes of style, and original graphic effects, to suggest that *Albert Angelo* consists of a literary collage: a selection of patterns. This approach works in two ways: firstly, as a disconcerting disunity of style designed to expose the assumptions and shortcomings of the conventional novel; and secondly, as an attempt to recreate for the reader the different situations of everyday life, i.e. as a sequence of mimetic devices. The author ultimately claims that *Albert Angelo* 'attempts to *reproduce* the moment-to-moment fragmentariness of life, my life, and to echo it in technique, the fragmentariness, a collage made up of the fragments of my own life' (169, my emphasis). The novel is a motivated collage of graphic mimesis, yet the fact that its efforts remain only 'attempts' indicates the difficulty of the author's objective.

In 'Disintegration' Johnson lists just some of the problems of providing this 'truth to reality'. There are problems of memory – 'I don't remember anything like everything, or even enough, so in writing about it I'm at a disadvantage straight away, really, trying to put down what is true' (*AA* 171). Then there is the temporal dimension to be considered:

> – So that's another shifting of reality, in the course of the book I've come to see differently events I believed to be fixed, changed my mind about Muriel, I have this other girl, Virginia now, at the time of writing, very happy too, but who knows what else will have shifted by galleyproof stage, or pageproof stage, or by publication day, or by the time you are reading this? (*AA* 172)

The quotation above indicates the fact that writing and publication are by no means direct and the transcription of a novel to a physical book is a cumbersome process which takes time but, ultimately, fixes the text but is unable to pin down life/truth. Having heard of the death of an incidental character's unmentioned wife, the author concedes: 'you just can't keep up with it, life' (*AA* 173). There is a demonstration of this in the Bloomian jaunt Albert takes in 'Development' during which he achieves no furthering of his architectural pretensions. 'Three lines …' Albert laments at the end of it, in terms that easily translate from architecture to literature. However, the day in which only 'three lines' have been produced takes twenty pages of stream of consciousness prose to tell. Here is an implicit Shandean admission that, though he is attempting a far less comprehensive record than Tristram, the writer of the text is at once fed by reality and forestalled by it. In this manner the printed book offers less of a truthful representation of life than a contrast to it. There is, however, no alternative. Since the uncertainty and fluidity of the present cannot be captured in the laborious medium of the book all the author can do, with his incomplete memory, is record what *has been* experienced as fully and accurately as possible and hope to arrange it such a way as to reconstitute it in the mind of the reader.

The elimination of the imperfections of his chosen communicative device was Johnson's aim: 'I want my ideas to be expressed so precisely that the very minimum room for interpretation is left. Indeed I would go further and say that to the extent that a reader can impose his own imagination on my words, then that piece of writing is a failure' (1973b: 28). It thus becomes clear that the author is placing considerable weight on his graphic experiments as the means of expressing his ideas precisely. His carefully prepared graphic devices are designed to offer his vision of 'truth', a message without the usual literary 'noise', and the technical standard he sets in his development of them is extremely high. To a certain extent Parrinder is right to say that Johnson has set himself 'an impossible technical standard' (1977: 49). Yet the quotation above is from Johnson at his most doctrinaire; his deliberately controversial statement is not necessarily to be taken at face value. In the same piece Johnson admits he cannot control the fluidity of language; 'I can only use words to mean something to me, and there is simply the hope (not even the expectation) that they will mean the same thing to anyone else' (1973b: 28). And the same argument and caveat are present, without being pursued, in *Albert Angelo*: ' – Further, since each reader brings to each word his own however slightly different idiosyncratic meaning, how can I be expected to make my own – but you must be tired' (170). We might also compare the ironically indignant narrator of *Christy Malry's Own Double-Entry*:

> I have often read and heard said, many readers apparently prefer to imagine the characters for themselves. That is what draws them to the novel, that it stimulates their imagination! Imagining my characters, indeed! Investing them with characteristics quite unknown to me, or even at variance with such description as I have given! … What writer can compete with the reader's imagination! (1973a: 51)

This quotation seems to me to acknowledge the imperfections *and* the advantages of writing as a means for attempted communication between author and reader. The comic indignation comes from an author character who is a creature of ink on paper himself.

Johnson is ultimately conscious that all must be subjugated to the discipline of print. Even if the author's technical involvement is not stated in *Albert Angelo* as it was in *Travelling People*, it is clear from the devices he uses, and the way he discusses them in the 'Introduction' to *Aren't You Rather Young* … , that Johnson sees himself working with words as print, constituted of ink and paper, as much as he does with words as language. It is crucial to our understanding all of his graphic manoeuvring that Johnson does not recognise the artifice of the book as a pattern or a falsification; the technological fact of the book is a given.

Another pointer to this attitude is the fact that the author remains unnamed (unnameable?) within the text, even in 'Disintegration'. This holds true for most of Johnson's other novels too, including the largely autobiographical *Trawl*.[25] This follows the convention which has applied throughout most of the history of the novel: that the author is unnamed within the text.[26] Withholding a name seems to be a position of power, or perhaps the one of least vulnerability, of most resistance to the danger of becoming a 'character'. To take *Lolita* as a comparison; though there is the internal claim that this text is presented as a case study by a practising psychiatrist, the name on the title page is that of Vladimir Nabokov, and this is one convention Johnson still relies upon.

Patricia Waugh asks, in *Metafiction*, 'What is the "frame" that separates reality from "fiction"? Is it more than the front and back covers of a book, the rising and lowering of a curtain, the title and the end?' (1984: 28). The physical object of the book does offer a border or threshold, at least between text and world, and this is where Johnson places his name. He seems to regard the title page and the spine of the book as offering a kind of truth untainted by the possibility of 'lies' within. But the following of this convention is in no way apologetic.

The book is an intermediary device, a vehicle for text, whose operation Johnson tampered with throughout his career in order to improve it. In his subsequent works the numerous graphic and typographic skills developed in his first two novels are no longer put into service for an objective correlative but always within texts that are pointedly conscious that there is an orchestrating author from their beginning, always seeking new forms of graphic mimesis to bring them closer to what they wish to represent. These works are self-reflexive *and* mimetic, conscious that the text relates to the real only through the reader, and that it is up to that reader, as user, to 'mind the gap' between the two.

Albert Angelo's short 'Coda' seems to offer the chance to close off loose ends from the old schema where the character Albert Albert was central, but his brief, elliptic disposal by

---

25 The exception might be *The Unfortunates* (1969/1999) since its packaging includes a reproduction of the newspaper football report that brought about the visit to Nottingham which is recounted, in fragments, in that novel. The byline is included.

26 Before titles were a convention the first name in the text was often used as a title. In later periods titles allowed authorial anonymity to become a convention. See Genette (1997) for a discussion of anonymity, pseudonymity and onymity.

his students merely confirms the suspicion that he can no longer be taken seriously. The final section of 'Coda', which closes the novel, is, appropriately enough, a schoolroom composition on the subject of death, but not Albert's. What we get is a girlish report of the funeral of her big sister's friend's mother as told by her own mother which offers a cynical view of the whole process: 'it was Just a gerate wast of time and all that work fore relly nothing Just a shocking display of funeralization on behaf of the furm that was calld in' (*AA* 180). Yet this childish view, which does not mention the real Albert at all, can be seen, in its tone and language, to offer a challenge to those, critics and readers alike, who would dismiss *Albert Angelo* as a 'gerate wast of time'. Our correspondent does not get to grips with the death of Albert (the objective correlative for Johnson himself) at all, although, as part of the class (we might hypothesise), she is linked to those responsible for the bundling of Albert into the canal. *Albert Angelo* thus closes with a prophetic parable. Quite simply, in a cunning switch applicable to his entire career, Johnson predicts his own critical mugging by those he has done his best to educate.

The Unfortunates (1969)

After *Albert Angelo* Johnson wrote *Trawl* (1966), an account of the experience of being on a commercial fishing voyage to the Barents sea, largely composed of personal intro-spection. With its tall page format (shorter line length), dots to indicate gaps rather than conventional paragraphing, and uniform style, the standardisation of *Trawl*'s graphic surface is somewhat anomalous within Johnson's work. As Andrew Gibson says:

> the typographical variations which are so marked a feature of Johnson's texts are not merely superficial or playful. Johnson was obsessed with the idea that the experience of books is, in the first instance, material, and that the material experience of the thing determines the experience that follows it, that the material conventions of the book sketch in the background for other, more complex cognitive and perceptual grids involved in reading and interpretation. In fact, Johnson's typographical experiments are the most concrete embodiments possible of a principle of multiplicity evident everywhere in his work, and bring his novels as close as printed text can come to that principle in its sheer materiality ... (1999: 94)

After *Trawl* Johnson returned to multiplicity with a vengeance in his infamous novel-in-a-box, *The Unfortunates*: twenty-seven unbound sections of varying lengths to be read in any order except for 'First' and 'Last'. Though often critically paired with *Trawl* because of their shared confessional elements *The Unfortunates* offers Johnson's most extreme experiment in the materiality of the text. The format of *The Unfortunates* is memorable and marketable too: 'an excellent way of attracting publicity' (Coe 1999: x).[27] As Coe

---

27 The proffered randomisation is not wholly unique: French writer Mark Saporta's *Composition No.1* (1962) was originally loose leaf. Coe (2004: 230–1) makes clear that Johnson knew of it. The British Library has a copy which, unfortunately, has been bound.

suggests, there is the prospect of '*fun*' with this form but the subject – a memorial of a friend dying of cancer – doesn't take up this option. There are now two editions; the original and the 1999 reissue, which differ in a number of ways; the latter having a different cover, an introduction by Jonathan Coe and restored text.[28]

It is not straightforward to reference *The Unfortunates*; each section has its own numbering starting at 1. The sections are distinguishable to the reader by lines of printer's ornament at the head of each first page but such devices are not available for the critic to reproduce. References therefore need to be keyed to the first words of the individual sections. Furthermore, since every reading will be randomised across the untitled sections (at least), it makes it fruitless for commentators to discuss their individual orders of reading since no one else will share them. In this sense randomness as an experience for the reader immediately gives way to specificity. In his reading Gibson mentions the physical characteristics of the worn and yellowing British Library edition which at least will have been the text read by several others. But this doesn't begin to ask whether Gibson's experience of the text is the same as his predecessor's (did either shuffle the sections as the text instructs?).

As Tredell (2000: 100) points out, *The Unfortunates* involves the reader in constructing the novel's '*syuzhet*', or structuring of content, but there is more than one '*fabula*', or story, in the novel. The first is the day-long story of reporting on a football match and the memories it conjures up. The second is the much longer relationship between the author figure and Tony, the academic friend who dies of cancer, from its beginning to the funeral. The two *fabulae* overlap in the sections in which locations prompt memories but there are several sections which contribute to one *fabula* only, and make no contribution to the other. A particular area of ambiguity is that, while we can retrieve chronology of the day and of the relationship, the order of the memories when not tied to locations in the first *fabula* isn't possible to reconstruct. That we can reconstruct these *fabulae* at all argues against genuine randomness in content, and friends and critics have found this a problem: Ghose (1985: 33) recounts arguing with Johnson about it, Parrinder (1977: 45) dismisses the randomness as 'superfluous' and Judith Mackrell argues that 'Reading *The Unfortunates* is in certain respects … not unlike reading a conventionally structured novel which makes use of flashbacks within a linear chronology' (1985: 55).

Johnson later described this novel's form as a 'physical tangible metaphor for randomness and the nature of cancer' (1973b: 25) and Tredell rightly adds 'the workings of the mind' and 'existence' (2000: 99) but the detractors are right to object to 'randomness'. A page from another text entirely, found documents such as the Madame Mae card of *Albert Angelo,* even the football report (butchered by the subs as predicted) from the box, might have been included to indicate a more random selection of content. Johnson's metaphor only fully relates to the *experience* of the text in a random order. The random ordering of the sections disorders any temporal logic that might subsequently be reconstructed and, through material in individual sections that appears to be out of

---

28 And, at least in my copy, one incorrectly bound section.

sequence (problematising 'the interpretative relations between its different parts' (Mackrell 1985: 55)), the experience of reading *The Unfortunates* does contain ample evidence of randomisation. That is, the possible retrieval of temporal order foregrounds the actual disorder. Thus the 'flaw' noted by critics allows us to see the full effect of the randomising of the sections: even if everything is not necessarily in its best order, the text *will* be different for each individual reader. As a result Gibson is able to argue that: 'for any given reader, Tony's decline and death are secreted at an unpredictable place in the text. They appear according to no logic, temporal or other, and have the force of unpredictable events, an irreducible singularity' (1999: 96). In this way Johnson has achieved an effect (albeit more finite) of variation of individual texts of the type pioneered by Sterne's marbled page (see Chapter 2). Though the format is finally explicable, this is appropriate because neither cancer or psychology is utterly random. And, ultimately, there is more to gain from the format than the partial experience of randomness.

Tredell argues that 'more than any other of Johnson's variations of format this one presses against the limits of, and thus highlights, the book as physical artefact' (2000: 99). But even this favourable statement underplays Johnson's achievement: the limits of the bound book are exceeded by this novel and, while we might reflect on the book as artefact when we next read one, *The Unfortunates* is something different. As Philip Tew remarks: 'This is an opening out not just of the form but of the literal experience (from the moment of opening the box …)' (2001: 84).

Parrinder's (1977: 45) statement: 'It was uncomfortably typical of Johnson that the "random order" effect in *The Unfortunates* should seem superfluous' misses the point. Breaking the back of the book, de-inventing the wheel rather than re-inventing it, defamiliarises the experience of reading and foregrounds the sections, the units beyond which Johnson couldn't randomise. The effect of reading these sections is very different in physical terms from reading a novel, though the experience of *completing* a book seems to me to be conjured up by every section. In working through our individual order of sections, finishing and leaving behind these fragile items, much less distinguishable from one another than any grouping of novels, we whittle the text away, have done with it, time and time again. The form itself generates poignancy, there being no better example than the shortest section which bears the following paragraph only:

> June rang on the Saturday, was it, or the Thursday before, no, quite late, we had already arranged to go, though what arrangements could we have needed to make, saying there was no need for us to come down now, on Sunday, for he had died that evening, had not recovered consciousness that morning from his sleep, but previously there had been the opposite of a relapse, three days when his mind had been virtually normal, for which she had been grateful, June, it had seemed like a miracle, though he still could not move, his mind had come back and they had talked very seriously about everything, for the first time had talked about death.

My quotation here falls very short of the effect of the original in which the reader is left holding a frail single sheet of mostly white paper. Once again, and far more appropriately than *Travelling People*'s black page, Johnson has achieved something beyond the capabilities of prose alone. Hostile criticism fails to comprehend the new form as a move towards the reinvigoration of the novel when what *The Unfortunates* really does is ask questions of role of the comfortably solid presence of the book in the novel as a medium of representation.

There is not room in this book to go into how Johnson continued to use the graphic surface in his three remaining novels, beyond indicating that it is crucial to the functioning of *House Mother Normal* and *See the Old Lady Decently* and offers a key metaphor within the black comedy of *Christy Malry's Own Double-Entry*. In each case the critical reception Johnson had experienced with *Travelling People*, and attempted to pre-empt in the passage from *Albert Angelo* quoted at the beginning of this chapter, was repeated. Despite flirtations with the literary establishment Johnson would remain at odds with his critics throughout his career and beyond it.

The result has been, until recently, a relatively unproductive dialogue between his novels and literary criticism. They have been viably seen as a kind of shock tactic against complacent reading and Johnson's continued use of the graphic surface can broadly be seen to embody a political alignment against literary convention and social conservatism. But a greater degree of specificity is required to draw full value from these works; the varied and complex devices used by Johnson in testing the representational capabilities of the graphic surface are still under-acknowledged. For example, conventional criticism has never been able to integrate the 'Disintegration' of *Albert Angelo* into the novel as a whole, and one of the sticking points has clearly been the graphic surface of these pages. The solution to the problem set the reader by 'Disintegration' requires a view of the text as not divorced from the world.[29] Close analysis of the use of the graphic surface allows us to see Johnson's faith in a representational connection as mediated by 'the technological fact of the book' and how his work as a whole ultimately strikes against the homogenisation of representation and any critically sanctioned surrender to the economy of perception which assimilates texts only to other texts, not texts to life.

References

Barthes, Roland (1975) *S/Z*, London: Cape (translated by Richard Miller)
Beckett, Samuel (1958) *The Unnamable*, London: Calder and Boyars
Beckett, Samuel (1962 [1958]) *Malone Dies*, London: Penguin
Beckett, Samuel (1976 [1953]) *Watt*, London: John Calder
Bergonzi, Bernard (1968) 'Thoughts on the Personality Explosion' in B. Bergonzi (ed.), *Innovations*, London: Macmillan: 185–99
Bergonzi, Bernard (1970) *The Situation of the Novel*, London: Macmillan
Bradbury, Malcolm (ed.) (1987) *The Penguin Book of Modern Short Stories*, New York: Viking Penguin
Bradbury, Malcolm (ed.) (1990) *The Novel Today: Contemporary Writers on Modern Fiction*, London: Fontana
Burns, Alan and Sugnet, Charles (1981) *The Imagination on Trial*, London: Allison and Busby

---

29 'Disintegration' acknowledges its social concerns: 'Didactic, too, social comment on teaching, to draw attention, too, to improve' (AA 176).

Burns, Alan (1997) 'Two Chapters from a Book Provisionally Entitled "Human Like the Rest of Us: A Life of B. S. Johnson"', *The Review of Contemporary Fiction* 17 (2): 155–79

Coe, Jonathan (1999) 'Introduction' to B. S. Johnson, *The Unfortunates*, London: Picador

Coe, Jonathan (2004) *Like a Fiery Elephant: The Story of B. S. Johnson*, London: Picador

Figes, Eva (1985) 'B. S. Johnson', *Review of Contemporary Fiction* 5 (2): 70–1

Foucault, Michel (1979) 'What Is an Author?' in Josue V. Harari (ed.), *Textual Strategies*, London: Methuen: 141–60

Genette, Gérard (1997) *Paratexts: Thresholds of Interpretation*, Cambridge: Cambridge University Press

Ghose, Zulfikar (1985) 'Bryan', *Review of Contemporary Fiction* 5 (2): 23–34

Gibson, Andrew (1999) *Postmodernity, Ethics and the Novel: From Leavis to Levinas*, London: Routledge

Hassam, Andrew (1986) 'True Novel or Autobiography? The Case of B. S. Johnson's *Trawl*, *Prose Studies* 9 (1): 62–72

Hassam, Andrew (1988) 'Literary Explorations: The Fictive Sea Journals of William Golding, Robert Nye, B. S. Johnson and Malcolm Lowry', *Ariel* 19 (3): 29–46.

Hassam, Andrew (1993) *Writing and Reality: A Study of Modern British Diary Fiction*, Westport, Connecticut: Greenwood Press

Johnson, B. S. (1963) *Travelling People*, London: Constable

Johnson, B. S. (1964) *Albert Angelo*, London: Constable; (1987) New York: New Directions; (2004) London: Picador

Johnson, B. S. (1966) *Trawl*, London: Secker and Warburg; Panther (London, 1968); (2004) London: Picador

Johnson, B. S. (1969) *The Unfortunates*, London: Secker and Warburg; (1999) London: Picador

Johnson, B. S. (1971) *House Mother Normal*, London: Collins; (1984) Newcastle: Bloodaxe; (2004) London: Picador

Johnson, B. S. (1973a) *Christy Malry's Own Double-Entry*, London: Collins; (1984) London: King Penguin; (2001) London: Picador

Johnson, B. S. (1973b) *Aren't You Rather Young to be Writing Your Memoirs?*, London: Hutchinson

Kanaganayakam, C. (1985) 'Artifice and Paradise in B. S. Johnson's *Travelling People*', *Review of Contemporary Fiction* 5 (2): 87–93

Kelman, James (1989) *A Disaffection*, London: Secker and Warburg

Kennedy, Alan (1974) *The Protean Self: Dramatic Action in Contemporary Fiction*, New York: Columbia University Press

Levitt, Morton P. (1981) 'The Novels of B. S. Johnson: Against the War Against Joyce', *Modern Fiction Studies* 27 (4): 571–86

Levitt, Morton P. (1985) 'B. S. Johnson', *The Dictionary of Literary Biography: British Novelists since 1960*, Detroit: Bruccoli Clark, 14: 438–45

McHale, Brian (1987) *Postmodernist Fiction*, New York: Methuen

Mackrell, Judith (1985) 'B. S. Johnson and the British Experimental Tradition: an Introduction', *Review of Contemporary Fiction* 5 (2): 42–64

Murdoch, Iris (1954) *Under the Net*, New York: Viking

O'Brien, Flann ([1939] 1967) *At Swim-Two-Birds*, London: Penguin

Ommundsen, Wenche (1986) *Self-conscious Fiction and Literary Theory: David Lodge, B. S. Johnson and John Fowles*, PhD thesis, University of Melbourne

Pacey, Philip (1974) 'I on Behalf of Us: B. S. Johnson 1933–1973', *Stand* 15 (2): 19–26

Parrinder, Patrick (1977) 'Pilgrim's Progress: The Novels of B. S. Johnson (1933–73)', *Critical Quarterly* 19 (2): 45–59

Pope, Alexander (1968) *Miscellanies: The Last Volume: Peri Bathous or, Martin Scriblerus His Treatise of the Art of Sinking in Poetry*, New York: Russell and Russell

Rimmon-Kenan, Shlomith (1977) *The Concept of Ambiguity – The Example of James*, Chicago: University of Chicago Press

Rimmon-Kenan, Shlomith (1983) *Narrative Fiction; Contemporary Poetics*, London: Routledge

Ryf, Robert S. (1977) 'B. S. Johnson and the Frontiers of Fiction', *Critique* 19 (1): 58–74

Saporta, Marc (1962) *Composition No. 1*, Paris: Éditions du Seuil

Sterne, Laurence (1985) *The Life and Opinions of Tristram Shandy*, London: Penguin Classics

Tew, Philip (1998) 'Contextualizing B. S. Johnson (1933–1973): the British Novel's Forgotten Voice of Protest', *The Anachronist*, Budapest: 165–92

Tew, Philip (2001) *B. S. Johnson: A Critical Reading*, Manchester: Manchester University Press

Tew, Philip (2002) 'B. S. Johnson', *Review of Contemporary Fiction*, 12 (1): 7–58

Thielemans, Johan (1985) '*Albert Angelo* or B. S. Johnson's Paradigm of Truth', *Review of Contemporary Fiction*, 5 (2): 81–7

Tredell, Nicholas (1985)'The Truths of Lying: *Albert Angelo*', *Review of Contemporary Fiction*, 5 (2): 64–70

Tredell, Nicholas (2000) *Fighting Fictions: The Novels of B. S. Johnson*, Nottingham: Pauper's Press

Vonnegut, Kurt (1970) *Slaughterhouse Five*, London: Cape

Waugh, Patricia (1984) *Metafiction*, London: Methuen

Waugh, Patricia (1995) *Harvest of the Sixties: English Literature and its Background 1960–1990*, Oxford: Oxford University Press

White, Glyn (1999) 'Recalling the Facts: Taking Action in the Matter of B. S. Johnson's *Albert Angelo*', *Hungarian Journal of English and American Studies* 5 (2): 143–62

CHAPTER 7

'Some languages are more visible than others': Christine Brooke-Rose's *Thru*

learning how to become a parasite upon a text nobody reads passed on from generation to generation ... (*Thru* 163)

There is a significant parallel to be seen between the literary career of Christine Brooke-Rose and that of B. S. Johnson. Since the mid-1960s both have been regarded as 'experimental' novelists. Unfortunately Brooke-Rose suffers even more than Johnson from this label. In fact she has said that being a female experimental writer makes the role doubly (or trebly) difficult (1989, 1991b). One major difficulty is that she is very often mentioned in the same breath as Johnson, lumped in with and somehow spoken for by him. Brooke-Rose will be frustrated to appear to be linked with him here, even in separate chapters, and with good reason for these are very different writers.[1] Unlike Johnson, Brooke-Rose has had sustained success as academic critic and theorist. Her major critical works, *A Grammar of Metaphor* (1958), *A ZBC of Ezra Pound* (1971), *A Rhetoric of the Unreal* (1981), *Stories, Theories and Things* (1991b) and most recently *Invisible Author* (2002), have gained her a formidable reputation.

Unfortunately, perception of Brooke-Rose as a critic and an avant-garde writer seems to have only made it more difficult for her novels to get a hearing. A brief survey of indexes will indicate this. In *Possibilities: Essays on the State of the Novel* (1973) Malcolm Bradbury explains: 'and [when] in different ways writers like ... B. S. Johnson, and Christine Brooke-Rose attempted to distil a debate and an aesthetic speculativeness, they too got little close reading' (259). Typically, however, no close reading follows and this is Brooke-Rose's only mention in the book. *The Contemporary English Novel* (Bradbury 1979) is a state-of-the-novel anthology of eight essays in which no fewer than three have a critical run-in with Johnson. In contrast, although her name appears four times (thrice as a novelist, once as a critic), Brooke-Rose is never, it seems, someone who is actually read. Elaine Showalter's *A Literature of Their Own: British Women Novelists from Brontë to Lessing* (1977) makes no mention of her at all. Andrzej Gasiorek's *Post-War British Fiction* (1995) mentions her and quotes her, along with Johnson, in order to define

---

1 Tew (2001: 139–40) makes clear the illogic of trying to link their work closely.

an 'experimentalist' position, but then proceeds to consign both authors to an extremist fringe so that a middle ground of authors more closely engaged in dialogue with realism can be reclaimed. Even Lorna Sage's major survey of female writers, *Women in the House of Fiction* (1992), does no more than quote Brooke-Rose (as critic) once, though the recent collection *Moments of Truth* (2001) makes amends.

Whether it is as part of a list in a casual survey of modern literature or a more detailed study Brooke-Rose, the 'experimental' author, seems to have achieved an ongoing escape from the mainstream critical canon. As we have argued, Johnson makes a conspicuous target and perhaps it is not surprising that hostile critics prefer to attack the perceived experimentalist position in the person or work of Johnson. Brooke-Rose and her novels are much more elusive.

Brooke-Rose's literary career to date can be roughly divided into four periods, of which the first three each consist of four novels each. The first sequence (from 1957) consists of largely realistic novels in which the author discovered what aspects of writing did and did not appeal to her. These novels were superseded, and eventually repudiated (at least partially), during a sequence of increasing experimentation (1964–68): *Out, Such, Between* and ultimately *Thru* (anthologised in 1986b). The third sequence was linked by punning titles and science-fiction elements: *Amalgamemnon* (1984), *Xorandor* (1986a), *Verbivore* (1990) and *Textermination* (1991a). Most recently Brooke-Rose has added a particularly individualistic memoir, *Remake* (1996a), and two fascinating novels: *Next* (1998a), about the homeless in London, and *Subscript* (2000), narrating evolution from within. The sheer invention that Brooke-Rose has shown, her unwillingness to stay still and repeat herself and the fact that she is still around to defend her fresh and challenging novels all make it much more difficult for criticism to fix an attitude towards this writer.

Despite the idiosyncrasy of her career there is no certainty that Christine Brooke-Rose, the novelist, is destined for a place on the margins of literature as experimental and (therefore) unread. Critical interest in her work is steady. Sarah Birch's monograph *Christine Brooke-Rose and Contemporary Fiction* (1994) was followed by Friedman and Martin's collection of essays on her novels, *Utterly Other Discourse* (1995), and Judy Little's *The Experimental Self: Dialogic Subjectivity in Woolf, Pym and Brooke-Rose* (1996). Entries in the *Cambridge Guide to Women's Writing* (Sage 1999) on Brooke-Rose, *Thru* and *Textermination* place her within a tradition and, individually or in anthology, most of the author's later novels remain available.

Thru (1975)

My particular interest in Brooke-Rose's work is *Thru* (1975).[2] The graphic surface of this novel is disrupted more frequently than any other text analysed in depth in this book, but these disruptions are only one aspect of its unconventionality. *Thru* is a highly complex novel, and one that provides numerous problems for commentators. In the recent compilation on Brooke-Rose, *Utterly Other Discourse*, there are five essays that give *Thru* more than passing attention. Three of these manage to quote the concluding lines of the novel which combine the word 'text' and the title. This manoeuvre no doubt helps bring some sense of closure, or boundedness, to the critical project, and reflects the difficulty critics have in finding an approach that will be able to accommodate all the textual games, diagrams and timetables and deceptive narrative levels that occur in *Thru*.[3]

More than any other of her novels, *Thru* is responsible for the perception of Brooke-Rose as a difficult writer. In the introduction to an important interview with the author, made at the time of *Thru*'s publication, Keith Cohen and David Hayman write (having mentioned her lack of an American publisher), that '*Thru* ... may well spark a long deserved recognition, within all the English speaking world, of Christine Brooke-Rose's unique and rewarding talent' (1976: 3). With hindsight these words have an ironic aspect: if anything, *Thru* sparked an opposite result.

Significantly – in terms of both writing and reception of the novel – the author was not in Britain, or the English-speaking world, while she wrote *Thru*, but was a teacher of structuralist narratology at the University of Paris at Vincennes. Such associations with continental academia and theory ensured that the novel received a hostile critical reception in Britain. While there had been those for and against Brooke-Rose's previous novels among reviewers, *Thru* convinced the majority that the author had 'gone too far'. The very mention of literary theory seems to have had the critics sharpening their knives:

> it is very brave of Miss Brooke-Rose to apply certain European strategies to the indigenous product, but like a great many Europeanisms they have a faded date-stamp upon them. The English have missed that particular development of modernism but it is too late to imitate it: we must go beyond it. (Ackroyd 1975: 52)

In this particular article Brooke-Rose is further accused of 'magpie scholarship' and looking for 'an easy academic lay' by quoting Barthes, and *Thru* itself is said to

2 The original page layouts are also used in Brooke-Rose (1986b). The page numbers are, however, different. The formula to convert references from the original edition into references to the *Omnibus* is to add 578 (or + 580 – 2).
3 *Thru*'s mass of signification will more than justify our exclusion of all but minor references to Brooke-Rose's other fiction.

exhibit 'clumsiness and obviousness' (ibid.).[4] This particular example of cultural xenophobia attempts to dismiss the author and text in approximately the following way: *Thru* is experimental like French novels (e.g. those by Maurice Roche and Raymond Queneau), it uses French theory (Derrida, Lacan, Barthes), therefore it is both un-English and imitative, in the worst literary sense. None of this indicates the slightest inclination to get to grips with the text itself, only to reject what it is believed to stand for. Such lazy, knee-jerk criticism when faced with the difficulty of *Thru* was typical (see Reyes 1995: 55–6). We get the sense that the book has been no more than scanned for French names and the blurb glanced at. The piece by C. J. Driver (1975: 20) in *The Guardian* certainly seems to have gone no further than the blurb, quoting it at length, before flicking through in search of something ('some hilarious dialogue') which the critic feels able to comment upon, however superficially. *Thru* is not an example of 'the pallid nature of most Anglo-Saxon experimentalism' (Ackroyd 1975: 52) but shows it at its strongest.

British reviewers of the 1970s had largely been raised on a diet of postwar realism so perhaps their overall hostility is not surprising, but the bad grace with which these reviewers confronted the unfamiliar (and foreign) was instructive for *Thru*'s author. Looking back, quite pragmatically, Brooke-Rose has said: 'I did realise that I had probably, career-wise as they say, done myself a lot of harm because I really was dismissed as completely potty, doing surrealistic tricks and typography and so on' (Friedman and Fuchs 1995: 36). *Thru* marked the beginning of a nine-year hiatus in her fiction-writing career.

Even academic writers have had difficulty accepting *Thru*. Patricia Waugh, for example, draws a line in the sand, this far and no further, to suggest that *Thru* is a limit text of postmodernism (1984: 147–8). Brian McHale assigns to it 'the full postmodernist repertoire of destabilising strategies' and describes it as 'a text of radical ontological hesitation: a paradigmatic postmodern novel' (1995: 200). But whether *Thru* is the epitome of postmodernism or of deconstructive fiction, the novel itself still needs to be read. Pigeonholing texts can only be the most basic response since it ignores individuality and specificity. As Brooke-Rose has complained: 'In many studies of "postmodernism", the mere naming of a feature (device, strategy, topos) seems sufficient, followed, at best, with one or a few examples, at worst with a list of names' (1991b: 211). In the texts which deal with *Thru* it is noticeable that though the novel's graphic devices, the varied diagrammatic and acrostic alterations to conventional page layout, are often mentioned as examples of difficulty, instability and general experimentalism, no one seems keen to analyse them with any real degree of closeness. Even McHale, who has spent some time studying Brooke-Rose, does little with them and they are not specified in his catalogue of the 'destabilising strategies' used in *Thru*:

---

4 We might take 'obviousness' as a criticism of the visual qualities of the text, the implication being that the reviewer could have used the medium in this way but chose not to on account of its vulgar 'obvious' quality.

---

self-contradiction; the placing of episodes or descriptions 'under erasure'; so-called 'strange loops'; *trompe-l'oeil* effects, such as 'demoting' an event, character, or object to a lower narrative level or, conversely, 'promoting' one to a higher level; *mise en abîme*; irresolution or hesitation between mutually exclusive alternative scenarios; and so on. (1995: 200)[5]

In her recent thesis on Brooke-Rose Heather Reyes clearly regards the graphic elements of *Thru* as a problem, attracting attention to the novel but obscuring its content:

in general surveys of the period, it is usually *Thru* which is given the most attention and is sometimes the only one of her novels mentioned. This is certainly the result of startling typography, yet it seems unfair that the text should be promoted as representative of Brooke-Rose's work. Despite frequent citings, it is perhaps the novel which has received the least illuminating criticism, its surface 'difference' (the typographical play) seeming to steal the limelight and receiving attention out of all proportion to its contribution to the total work. (1998: 239)

By contrast I believe the typographical play on *Thru*'s graphic surface makes a crucial contribution to the novel. Reyes's attitude is a reaction to the way that graphic elements of *Thru* have been extracted and displayed in lieu of actual criticism. McHale, for example, 'quotes' an entire iconically designed page in *Postmodernist Fiction* (1987: 185). Morton P. Levitt uses the same page (among other excerpts) to illustrate his entry on Brooke-Rose in *The Dictionary of Literary Biography: British Novelists since 1960* (1985: 126). Since these pages are among the most difficult and enigmatic in the text, especially when taken out of context, the effect is to promote *Thru*'s 'unreadability'. But the appropriate response to these deficiencies demands that we do not try to go around the graphic devices or diminish them, but rather tackle them head-on as part of the text. Reyes's attempt to de-emphasise and sideline the graphic surface of *Thru* becomes statistical: 'In fact, out of one hundred and sixty-two pages only 39 are highly visual, roughly thirty have some visual element, while 93 have no visual element whatsoever' (1998: 242). This is simply misguided for at the very least it implies that a conventional page of text is by some means non-visual. Even if we were to fill out the implications of this understatement, Reyes's census is rather short-sighted and, furthermore, does not acknowledge that the text's rejection of speech marks and any of the recognised substitutes (dashes, italics, caps) is a visual device (or absence of device), one which refuses the conventional privileging of speech throughout.[6] *Thru*'s graphic play is not, in Reyes's view, typical of Brooke-Rose's oeuvre, but I would argue that there is a point at which Brooke-Rose's conceptual play becomes

---

5 Some graphic devices could be accommodated under McHale's *trompe-l'oeil* heading.
6 *Out, Such* and *Between* (1986b) use Joycean introductory dashes instead of speech marks, while *Thru* and her later works do away even with this.

graphic. Furthermore *Next* (1998a; published after Reyes had written) involves considerable graphic play, from the iconic depiction of a homeless person on page 1, to the wandering prose accompanying characters' ramblings across the city throughout the text. Reyes's attitude is particularly odd because having statistically dismissed the graphic elements of *Thru*, she seems willing to engage with them at a conceptual level: 'the opening, closing and often recurring references to the driving mirror do underline the *idea* of the visual in the text' (1998: 242).

This reaction is, I think, motivated by the fact that Reyes has no answer to Patricia Waugh's negative assessment of graphic devices in *Metafiction*, and has accepted this part of her argument. The example Waugh chooses to demonstrate the 'naive imitative fallacy' is taken from Johnson's *See the Old Lady Decently* (1975) which she describes as his most successful novel. However, the example, Poem Two on page 59, is rather shallowly read. It is a concrete poem in which the repeated word 'mammarytit' is sculpted into the profile of a breast, and from this evidence Waugh draws as much as could be expected: 'The concrete form allows Johnson to focus simultaneously on the female shape, its biological maternal function, the idea of the Virgin Mary, the infantile phonetic representation of the word "mother" and the demotic term for the breast' (1984: 98–9). But this poem is not simply a concrete poem we can attach to some of the themes of the novel; it is part of a series of numbered poems within the novel (which the subtitled structure of the text invites us to link). Poem Five on page 128 returns to this image, composing this time with the repeated word 'breast'. However, two lines are are blank but for the strewn letters 'n' and 'nc'. These letters represent the growing cancer in the maternal breast (Johnson's mother had died of this), and their positioning in the image throws new light on the single capitalised 'M' in 'mamMary' in Poem Two. To see such devices as a failure or regression of textual representation, rather than an extension of it, is limiting. Nevertheless, Reyes attempts to rescue Brooke-Rose from such accusations: 'we can see his [Johnson's] tendency to fall into what Patricia Waugh has called the "naive imitative fallacy" which is very far from Brooke-Rose's method' (1998: 255). Such defensive eagerness to distance Brooke-Rose from Johnson effectively brings out their differences: 'Unlike Johnson's mimeticism, her use of the visual is sophisticated, complex, ludic, deconstructive' (1998: 256). But ultimately the rejection of the graphic surface leads away from Reyes's overall intent, which is to demonstrate the ethical rather than the self-reflexive in Brooke-Rose's postmodern work.

We must be careful not to allow the clear presence of 'destabilising' techniques in this text to exclude from our interpretation those other elements which might do something other than contribute to its self-reflexivity. Though it is true that *Thru* revels in play at its graphic surface, this disruption is not necessarily an alternative to representation. Once we escape the critical dead end of seeing postmodernism as 'merely self-reflexive' (to paraphrase Brooke-Rose (1997)) we may be able to see the ways in which Reyes, by very different methods, has shown that Brooke-Rose's texts 'engage with the social and political realities of the modern world in what is clearly an ethical project' (1998: 22).

The importance of *Thru* in Brooke-Rose's career remains particularly apparent in conversations with the author. Originally *Thru* was to have been called 'Textermination', but this title was discarded under the mistaken belief that it had already been used by William Burroughs, and only eventually came to be used for the final text of Brooke-Rose's third sequence of novels (1991a). I mention this to suggest that *Thru* was in some way a climax for its author. She has described it as 'a very special sort of unreadable book' (Friedman and Fuchs 1995: 36) and as 'a novel about the theory of the novel, a fiction about fictionality, a non-narrative about narrativity, a text about intertextuality' (Brooke-Rose 1996c: 104). Within one paragraph of discussion of *Thru* with Ellen J. Friedman and Miriam Fuchs (1995) we can read no fewer than six variations on 'I had to/needed to write it'. Clearly some sort of compulsion seems to have been involved at the time, and in her last critical book *Invisible Author* (2002) Brooke-Rose states that *Thru* is both 'my favourite' (17) and 'my most original text, whatever its faults' (107).

Recent seminars (1995) and publications (1997, 2002) by Brooke-Rose are an attempt to return critics to a text which holds such a significant place in her career as a novelist. Written in summer vacations from teaching at Vincennes (1971–73), *Thru* may be seen as an attempt to try to resolve the tensions between being a writer of fiction and becoming deeply involved with literary theory as a teacher. The result is that *Thru* both applies and plays with post-structuralist theory (and several other varieties). Most analyses of *Thru* show how the novel uses literary theory to deconstruct literary conventions, but they underplay the other side of the equation in which fiction acts upon literary theory and poetics become poeticised. It will have already been noted that *Thru* is not assimilable to conventional realism, but, by setting itself in academic environments in which both literary theory and creative writing are taught as part of everyday life, the novel establishes – at least partly – a mimetic domain for their hybridisation.

Thru may seem to be as complex as possible, verbally and visually, but some of the more obviously unconventional narrative sequences, particularly those involving distortions of the graphic surface, can be demonstrated to be representational in intent, and, I contend, in effect, too. It is important therefore to recognise that aspects of *Thru*'s complexity are motivated by representation, and that the novel uses the representational medium of printed language in new ways – some verbal, some graphic – to this end.

Our awareness of the graphic surface will allow us to continue where previous critics have become entangled in theoretical traps, and we will find that the terms 'graphic device' and 'graphic mimesis' are useful tools for navigating our way through such difficulties (see also White 2002). In fact I would go so far as to say they are essential in dealing critically with this particularly complex text. Our purpose here is thus to include in our interpretation the graphic elements of *Thru* which are neglected, misinterpreted or ignored by the majority of studies, but it is not to try and redress the balance by concentrating on the graphic to the exclusion of the other elements. Instead, we shall show how graphic devices introduce, develop and synthesise important elements in the narrative economy of *Thru* using the word 'economy' in the sense of 'system of interrelationship' but also in the sense of 'efficiency' because so much of this novel is doing double-duty.

The retro-visor

Thru's combined use of visual and verbal can be seen in the use of the 'driving-mirror' with which the novel begins and which most commentators rightly note as a highly significant motif. By the end of page 1 the driving-mirror has become 'le rétro viseur' (a broken version of the French equivalent) and the idea will continue

Through the driving-mirror four eyes stare back
two of them in their proper   place
Now right on
Q   ask us

to de   V   elop   foot on gas
how m(any   how)   eyes?

four   two
of them   correct

on either side ▽   of the
nose   the other

two   ⚠   O danger
slow   down

eXact   replicas

nearer the hairline further up the brow but dimmed as in a glass tarnished by the close-cropped mat of hair they peer through

The mat of hair is khaki, growing a bit too low on the brow the nose too big.

Who speaks?

le rétro   viseur   (some   languages
      more   visible than   others)

Figure 7.1: The text of page one of *Thru*.

to be played with and punned upon in different arrangements throughout the text. For convenience we shall use a hybrid form and generally refer this motif as 'the retro-visor'.

The first page, which introduces the image of the retro-visor, combines visual and verbal play: and it is through this combination that the motif has considerable significance for the way the reader must negotiate *Thru* (see Figure 7.1)

The indented edge of the first paragraph soon falls apart into widely spaced fragments, groupings of three words at most, occasionally reforming into unpunctuated two-line groupings. This spacing acts on the reader in a number of ways. Potentially it is a deterrent, but at the very least it operates as a warning to 'read carefully'. This is further suggested by the capitalised letters 'Q' and 'V' standing for *qui vive* for 'who goes there?' and the associated idea of being 'on the *qui vive*', i.e. awake and alert, as well as the reference *quod vide*, 'which see'. The shape of the 'v' then goes on to develop into a pair of triangles. The second of these triangular icons on the page seems to represent a road warning signs for the driver ('O danger slow down').

These triangles may also be an attempt to represent figuratively the nose of the driver in the mirror, the fragments of text on either side representing the accompanying eyes (there are 'four eyes' for each 'nose'). This suggestion of graphic mimesis is backed up in later recurrences of the retro-visor image which describe the nose in reflection as 'a fraction iconic' (*Thru* 120, hereafter *T*). The visual elements introduced here; the warning sign, the nose as abstract portrait and the rectangle shape, will all function potently later in the text.

It is important to repeat that we are dealing with the *combination* of visual and verbal images here. In a recent essay on the beginning of *Thru* Brooke-Rose describes the triangles within the text as 'a nose, then a danger signal, not a symbol' (1997: 232). Her brief dispute with a symbolic interpretation, itself based on Joyce, concludes: 'If I was thinking of anyone in this opening it was … Yeats' "I made it out of a mouthful of air," which to me had always suggested intercepting words, dragging them down through the brain and onto paper to form a text' (ibid. (see also 2002: 184)). I am not suggesting that this authorial statement explains the text here, but I think it does acknowledge, in the transport of words from brain to paper, the mental *and* the physical presence of words. They reach the reader in the reverse order, shifting from physical to mental, but share the same properties being equally subject to change, mutation, manipulation. Both physical and mental words are language, both reach the same place, the reader, and reading involves both. Throughout this chapter we shall be probing the question of how they combine to produce the interest and complexity of *Thru*.

The driving-mirror recurs throughout the novel bringing with it a group of related phrases. On page 4 we read:

> She shifts the mirror to her rearward glance. It doesn't
> work for her the mistress of the moment of sudden
> isolation at not seeing back to the black magician who
> fantastically juggles luminous hoops in the retro-rec-
> tangular hey put my mirror back.
>
> So it needs adjusting.

This cluster of phrases introduces the black magician (the recumbent road surface which becomes a sexual fantasy and a dream lover at various stages in the text), the dancing hoops (reflected headlights that provide graphic motifs for revolutionary debates) and the rectangle (the shape of the retro-visor, of the paragraph itself and of the traditional classroom and the timetable). However, the most significant phrase in this passage relates to the *use* of the retro-visor: 'So it needs adjusting' (see also *T* 32).

The sense of an ongoing process which the metaphor of the retro-visor *and its adjustment* offer is a vital parallel to the process by which the reader reads. The dispute in the quotation above, over the use of the mirror ('hey put my mirror back'), may be interpreted at different narrative levels. The passage may be understood mimetically as a dispute between characters and/or metatextually as a dispute between narrators, but there is another possibility since equally present in the vehicle of the text, at least during reading, is the figure of the reader, the implied or, as Brooke-Rose prefers, the encoded reader, whose relationship (and thus whose dispute) is with the text itself. The relation of driver and retro-visor, moving and looking forward and seeing what has been passed, can be likened to the hypothesising of the reader as he or she reads this or any other text. It seems that every kind of hypothesis the reader might make 'needs adjusting' frequently in *Thru*. The reader must glance behind every time a new intertextual reference is passed and must often make major adjustments when the anonymity of narrator or other ambiguities about a particular section of the text are foregrounded.

The visual/verbal double significance of the retro-visor leads us to try and divine what might motivate its usage. Looking back more than twenty years to the writing of *Thru* Christine Brooke-Rose regards the concept of the retro-visor as a metaphor for the changing relationship of the author to her text, movement forward in time changing the view of what lies behind.[7] But there are also a number of alternative critical models to choose from.

In his essay '*Thru* the Looking Glass' Hanjo Berressem offers a Lacanian parallel to the use of the retro-visor (1995: 104–5). In Lacan, looking to the future is a way to access the past within the unconscious (see Lacan 1980: 292–325). In *Reading for the Plot* (1985) Peter Brooks develops (via Lacan) a dynamic which parallels this in his discussion of the relationship of narrative to time. The

---

7 Brooke-Rose in response to a question from the author (1995).

traditional framing of narrative in the past tense – while it is ongoing for the reader – is something touched on in *Thru*: 'The present tense does not exist Armel, even as I write and your eyes move into the future from left to right' (*T* 52). Subsequently this idea interested Brooke-Rose to the extent that *Amalgamemnon* is written entirely in the future tense. Brooks concludes: 'If the past is to be read as the present, it is a curious present that we know to be past in relation to a future we know to be already in place, already in wait for us to reach it. Perhaps we would do better to speak of the *anticipation of retrospection* as our chief tool in making sense of narrative, the master trope of its strange logic' (1985: 23, Brooks's italics). Although Brooks's examples mainly come from the nineteenth century, this is not to say that the 'anticipation of retrospection' does not operate in contemporary texts, and even ones that might be aware of it, such as *Thru*. Brooke-Rose (2002: 130–55) claims that since *Out* (1964) she has been writing in the 'narratorless present tense' (2002: 153) a mode picked up from Robbe-Grillet and pursued by writing from inside characters. This mode contributes to *Thru*'s 'naive' mimesis, which we will discuss further later, but is manifested in the novel through the driving-mirror which shows how the past is accessed only through the present.

The textual motifs generated by the retro-visor, and particularly their visual equivalents, recur across *Thru*. Though many of these motifs originate in intertexts, it is their repetition and recycling within this text that are significant here, not the intertexts themselves; *Thru*'s narrative digressions act as intertexts with each other. Tracking every one down within the text would involve virtually rewriting the whole text. Annagret Maack puts it like this: 'By means of varying repetitions, *Thru* creates connections between textual passages ... They create the coherence of the text' (1995: 135). This is the principle to which we must adjust in order to negotiate our way through *Thru*.

In Maack's reading the retro-visor 'becomes the metaphor for the creation of a new text out of old ones, elucidates the reference back to literary quotations, and explains the relation of this text to earlier ones' (1995: 133). We can extend Maack's idea of intertextuality to Barthes's use of the 'rétroviseur' in reference to the plurality of texts: 'if literature and painting are no longer held in hierarchical reflection, one being the *rear-view mirror* for the other, why maintain them any longer as objects at once united and separate, in short, *classed together*? ... Why not forgo the plurality of the "arts" in order to affirm more powerfully the plurality of "texts"?' (1975: 56). Yet in his version it seems that the rear-view mirror holds the two elements in a stable relation, while our impressions from *Thru* show the retro-visor not explaining but destabilising relationships with other texts. The device is unstable because it involves both the graphic representation of a literal (or narrative) situation and a metaphor of the type used by Barthes. Juxtaposition of conceptual and graphic motifs increases instability and potency of this text. Furthermore it shows how *Thru* moves to broaden the plurality of texts by adding what might be supposed to be a metalanguage: criticism. Thus the novel includes both Barthes and structuralism, expressing an intertextual awareness in structuralist terminology: 'generating a text which in effect is a dialogue with all preceding texts, a death and a birth dialectically involved with one another' (*T* 43), and what is most revealing and difficult about reading *Thru* is precisely to do with the way that intertextual motifs are woven together, played with, punned with and accumulated. As Roger Fowler says, intertextuality in *Thru* 'takes the form of a fragmentary kind of allusiveness: the book constantly quotes bits of pre-existing language, imitates established styles of writing. It is a patchwork of references and jokes' (1989: 124). But this is the first, semantic, stage of something we shall be noting with particular reference to the graphic surface: the inclusion of critical prose in the narrative, or, more broadly, of poetics in poetry.

The text's awareness of its own intertextuality is supported by the alteration of the graphic surface as, for example, when two 'footnotes' appear on page 45. They occur at the top of the page following 'See Bibliography*' at the bottom of page 44, and are both in a smaller typesize than the main text. The first asterisked note lists twenty names as diverse as 'Eliot Snoopy Hegel' under the title 'retrogradiens' (which we might interpret as walking backwards, 'into past time' (*OED*)). The second double-asterisked note reproduces the names of the first adding around eighty more under the title 'retroprogradiens' (which we can take as walking backwards to go forwards). This list includes, in no obvious order, critics, theoreticians, linguists, authors, and real and fictional characters including those from *Thru*. The first among them is 'The retrovizor': the method by which we recognise references from outside, and also the way we recognise them inside.

In this way *Thru* would seem to fulfil the concept of textual construction which Derrida draws out in 'Structure, Sign and Play in the Discourse of the Human Sciences': 'If one calls *bricolage* the necessity of borrowing one's concepts from the text of a heritage which is more or less coherent or ruined, it must be said that every discourse is *bricoleur*' (1988: 115).[8] Furthermore, the retro-visor and its principle could be seen to be suggested by deconstruction: it is possible to think of *Thru* as 'drawing the figure of a quadrangle complicated by the structure of a very strange mirror. A mirror which ... does indeed come to stand as a source, like an echo that would somehow precede the origin it seems to answer' (1981: 323). Another Derridean concept, the 'hymen', also becomes 'screen and mirror' so that: 'As soon as a mirror is interposed in some way, the simple opposition between activity and passivity, between production and the product, or between all concepts in -er and all concepts in -ed (signifier/signified, imitator/imitated, structure/structured, etc.), becomes impracticable' (ibid.: 224). *Thru*'s retro-visor effect reminds us that reading is not a simple linear process in which one thing produces another, but the product of multiple and complex oppositions and balances within text. The retrovisor is indeed 'a very strange mirror', but it is so for its own ends, as we shall see.

---

8 *Bricoleur* is male-gendered, but *Thru*'s bricolage is not so.

'Naive' mimesis

Thru is about a relationship between academics, Armel and Larissa, working at different (probably American) universities, involved in teaching creative writing and literary theory, and their particular classes of students (see Brooke-Rose 2002: 64). In this situation where storytelling and theory are equally at home, discussion taking place within classes about narratives in progress and parallel theoretical concerns seems interchangeable with, and inextricable from, the narrative 'proper'. Similarly we find that literary theory features in the speech, thoughts, dreams and personal writings of the central characters. The representation of this milieu causes problems for academic readers because their repertoire of tools (the languages of literary theory, narratology, structuralism, poststructuralism and psychoanalytic criticism) is utilised and poeticised by *Thru*. A significant point, largely ignored by those writers who see nothing but self-reflexivity in this text, or take its theoretical content at face value, is that the presence of such language in this fictional situation can be mimetic as easily as it can be self-reflexive.

Similarly, the graphic disruptions in this novel can offer a direct kind of mimesis. On page 27, the sequence beginning 'Once upon a time laid out in rectangles into which you enter as into a room saying once upon a time the author had supreme authority' offers us a significant demonstration of simple graphic mimesis. This is a classroom scene and the subject of the lesson, with its subtitle, appears upside-down, supplementing the conventionally oriented text. These upside-down lines are mimetic because the inverted text is the most direct and straightforward way of indicating that the teacher is reading what a student in the first row is writing, i.e. a record of his lecture. The inverted text indicates we are receiving this scene quite closely from the teacher's point of view in a literal way.

What he (male gender indicates that Armel is the teacher here) spells is stretched, letter by letter as each is formed in the act of speaking – 'n a r r a t i o n' – and his dialogue is emphasised and contrasted by bold type in the following line 'you see not **narrator** for the reasons just given' (28, bold in original). We are

Take Homer written down in the first row whose **moi** in

1)Homer—moi in 1st line

the first line by way of invocation to the muse is the only instance of the subject-emitter addressing his discourse to the young beardless Marx in the third row taking no notes staring through the phonic signifiers

with riveting eyes that break the chain asunder yet he is omniscient, from a modern viewpoint since he tells us things that Odysseus doesn't know

Fig. 7.2: Text from pages 27–8 of *Thru*

simultaneously receiving both his dialogue and his vision. These overlap in the text, without signal, twice to comic effect on pages 27–8 (Figure 7.2).

Whereas in *Albert Angelo* tutorial speech and thought are broken into separate columns here they overlap or interpenetrate without warning. I believe that the teacher's speech and thoughts may be separated in the following way:

> Take Homer *written down in the first row* whose moi in the first line by way of invocation to the muse is the only instance of the subject-emitter addressing his discourse *to the young beardless Marx in the third row taking no notes staring* through the phonic signifiers *with riveting eyes that break the chain asunder* yet he is omniscient, from a modern viewpoint since he tells us things that Odysseus doesn't know.

Clearly Homer does not address himself to Ali ('the young beardless Marx') as we might be led to believe on first reading the undifferentiated text, but the crossover of tutorial dialogue to tutorial perception produces this amusing effect. It works again as we return to the external tutorial discourse where it now appears that the onlooking student is omniscient.

This crossover device, while initially confusing for the reader, can be accounted for as mimetic: this overlap is a textual representation of the tutor's awareness while teaching. It is possible to have thoughts and observations while speaking; in fact we continue to absorb vast amounts of data through our senses while we speak. Conventional Realist mimesis offers a selective representation of reality while *Thru*, in parts, this section being one, offers a more complex and inclusive version of reality, concentrating on representing in language everything that is actually perceived (or thought) in language.

Let us take a relatively simple example. On page 11 the arched phrase 'across the bridge in the scintillating foreign city' clearly uses a concrete poetic. We receive two impressions, that of shape and that of travel. Firstly, the shaped text mimics that of a hump-back bridge on the page. Secondly, during our reading of the shaped text our left-to-right habit of reading is utilised to give the impression of travel.

As Brooke-Rose says, we can see the phrase 'typographically miming the bridge' (1997: 248). However, this device still strikes us as outside of the normal run of the text because we suddenly 'see' the bridge and the travel over it from the side as though, to use a film metaphor, the director has cut to a different view. The reading experience of hearing the characters' dialogue has, up until this point, given us the impression of travelling in the car *with* the characters. This distancing effect suggests that this graphic device takes us *outside* normal textual perceptions. However, we can reinstall this device as mimesis of a more abstract and conceptual kind: depending on which (if any) occupant of the car the reader assigns the narration to, the arch may be their internal impression of travel, or another possibility is that this device relates to the sexual shenanigans ('manual foreplay' according to Brooke-Rose) in the car, as a kind of post-orgasmic sigh. This may in turn be undercut by possible double meanings in the question and answer in the line immediately under 'the bridge': 'did you? / No I didn't'.

This kind of representational use of the graphic surface might be regarded as 'naive mimesis' in the sense that it assumes a desire for mimesis over consideration for accessible literary conventions. In her interview with Cohen and Hayman, Brooke-Rose counters such objections: 'All right, people will say, "How do you expect your reader to follow this [kind of writing]?" But I'm surprised that readers find this difficult. They all live like this' (1976: 15–16). Living requires a deciphering of immediate experience and it is this ongoing process that *Thru* seems to me to be attempting to represent. As such the novel is clearly in agreement with Barthes's idea, first laid out in *S/Z*, that the writerly or *scriptible* novel is preferable to the *lisible*, readerly one which provides easy, conventional, 'classical' Realism (1975: 4–5). By preference this is Brooke-Rose's mode of reading as well as writing, and *Thru* is by far her most unrestrained example of it (see Brooke-Rose 2002: 108). The writerly text requires some effort from the reader to complete it. Inferences, implications and options are the marks of writerly texts rather than statements, explications and solutions. *Thru* takes this to extremes by keeping almost everything up in the air for the reader, including some fundamental questions about the source of the text.

'Who speaks?'

One of *Thru*'s most frequent refrains (often metamorphosed into other languages) first appears at the bottom of page 1: 'Who speaks?' An answer could be made on a variety of levels: character, narrator, author, reader, text. As potential speakers all these are suspects, and the relationship between them is brought to the forefront of the reader's attention by the use of this phrase. A check of the retro-visor will tell us that 'who speaks' comes from Barthes (1975: 41) and before him Lacan (1980 [1966]: 299).[9]

The question 'who speaks' is not only *asked* by *Thru* but *dramatised*, appealing to the reader to engage in the hermeneutic task of answering it. Typically, *Thru* never makes it simple to identify the speaker from one paragraph to the next; the question 'who speaks?' often appears at just those moments when the reader wonders most. This text is in fact booby-trapped since, just as it seems to become clear who speaks, we are forced to revise our answer. In this way *Thru* forces the reader's writerly text to stay 'being written', not allowing it to become decided, finalised, dead.

To demonstrate what we mean by 'booby-trapped' let us return to the phrase 'who speaks', treating it as a 'simple' question encountered during reading. Who does speak (or narrate) the first page of the novel, for example? It is very difficult to

---

9 The translators of Barthes and Lacan give us 'Who is speaking?' rather than 'who speaks?' Brooke-Rose, reading both in the French, translated the phrase in her own way for intertextual usage in *Thru*. See Brooke-Rose 2002: 66.

say, if we are not to go in search of Brooke-Rose herself through the author function, but there are clues. On page 2 the second arrangement of this query is followed by a guess as to the identity of the speaker (writer): 'which whoever speaks (Nourennin?) calls too low'.

On page 5, against the right margin this name recurs with the line under it 'To be discussed'. This straightforward graphic device places what we have just read as a piece of writing by Ali Nourennin, 'the beardless Marx', who turns out to be a particularly precocious member of the creative writing course. The strong effect produced is that the reader must retrospectively re-evaluate what he or she has just read because it is suddenly attributable to a particular character within the text. Our assumption from the beginning that (in the absence of any other information) the scene in the car was being narrated directly, either by one of the participants or by a third person, has to be abandoned when we realise that the section is mediated by another author and another reader. This 'demotion' of the first section of the novel also implies that the effect leaves us at a higher narrative level. In other words we might feel logocentrically closer to the 'true centre' of the text, but in practice all we can say is that we are somehow closer, not necessarily spatially, to information that will be more valuable during our reading. This device acts as a demonstration – or perhaps an exposure – of the retro-visor operation of reading and is repeated several times later on in the novel, often accomplished with the use of graphic devices.

Yet even with the attribution of the first sequence to a named character *Thru* does not let us rest, for we have not quite answered the question 'Who speaks?' during this excerpt. Ali Nourennin cannot be the whole answer because whoever surmises '(Nourennin?)' is also speaking and, logically, operating at some narrative level between Nourennin and the reader. This voice would seem to belong to an intermediate reader through whose consciousness we receive Nourennin's text. It would be possible to argue that the bracketed question is a self-reflexive device within Nourennin's work, but as such it would still point to an intermediate intended 'reader' of the piece who had some prior knowledge of its author's identity. The implication is that this is the teacher of the creative writing group but, since on first reading this narrator is unnamed and ungendered, it remains difficult to tell.

This demoting device, which forces us to re-evaluate our hypotheses about the narration of the text, produces the effect of having the carpet pulled from under our feet and makes us particularly wary of it happening again, compounding the feeling of uncertainty and defamiliarisation generated by the exploded text of page 1. We may proceed more cautiously as a result of it, yet readerly wariness is no help. Our physically linear reading of the text, and the constantly hypothesising process of reading, makes us vulnerable to such devices again and again and again.

There are several other sections of *Thru* which appear to be the product of the creative writing class in a similar way to the novel's first few pages. The graphic surface adds extra emphasis in these later examples, when sequences conclude with 'handwritten' grades (see *T* 34–5, 48, 73–4). The presentation of parts of the text as 'to be discussed', marked, or graded, is significant. Whether these sequences are 'heard' or 'read' in the text, they are all read by the reader, who is always making his or her own hypotheses. In this way readerly evaluation of the text is kept to the fore without being settled. For example, on page 33 there is a list of student names with various grades attributed as '(Portraits by Dr. Santores)'. This suggests, continuing from the epistolary 'Dear Larissa' on page 26, that we are still in Armel's class. The grading is punned with in structuralist and linguistic terms, the students' role being to receive 'grades of presence/absence competence/performance', which take the place of the class's register and marks for work handed in.

The answer to the question 'who speaks?' on page 33 is thus given to us as Dr Santores. But as we proceed, on to pages 34 to 35, the situation becomes more complex once again. The grading of students or characters continues with an institutional portrait of Saroja Chaitwantee. This table continues into the text below it, the paragraph being concluded with a reproduced handwritten mark and comment: 'B+ *a little static – this exercise demanded a narrative link*'. At first this seems like a method of undercutting the narrative again, but there is no fracture here; we are still focalised with the tutor Armel: the reports and comments do not straightforwardly relate to the text above them in the sense that they would if what they followed was work by Saroja. Nor, in the two examples on page 35, do the sections between the handwritten marks for Peter Brandt and Ali Nourennin actually 'belong' to them, in the sense of fictionally having been authored by them. Instead, these short sections reflect both tutorial thoughts *and* student writing, as in the lesson on Homer. The printed sections between the handwritten marks amount to a *reflection on* the content of the work the students have produced which is then summarised and graded in the handwritten comments by the tutor. This combination of thought and writing is more obvious in the Peter Brandt section. The handwritten marks are not, therefore, a direct representation of what might appear at the end of the marked piece of work but a representation of the writing and thinking of them, both simultaneously; an example of a very complex mimesis.

Conventional narration is stripped away and replaced with something not less but *more* representational; a technique Brooke-Rose has described as 'absolutely objective narration' (1998b: 5). This new 'un-narrated' situation depends on the reader to hold it together, and in this experience of constructing meaning from complex, contradictory signals the reader is closer to his or her own everyday experience. Thus *Thru* attempts mimetic representation of a quite complex (fictional) reality, constructed to include the experience of ambiguity. Whether or not the reader comes to this realisation, the text has done its work. Barthes's version of the 'reality effect' of Realism is superseded here. No longer is reality the inclusion of superfluous detail; *Thru* includes the *consideration* of that detail. The effect might be called 'metatextual mimesis'; it goes further than the readerly attempt to see meaning or meaningless-ness in textual detail and involves the interpretative experience of ambiguity, unresolvability and necessary pragmatic solutions to such difficulties (see White 2002).

Scrapped chapters

The sense of provisionality which *Thru* maintains in its readers with regard to who speaks extends further still. The presence and value of passages of text and of characters who appear throughout the novel are called into question. No character, from *Thru* or its intertexts, escapes evaluation, including Larissa. The creative writing class discuss her destruction over pages 150–5. Their concluding vote is never made explicit, although in the ultimate marked section at the end '(Portraits by the Student Body)' (*T* 159–63) she is graded with an 'x', and, after the vote, does not otherwise appear by name in the closing pages. Armel too gets an 'x' following the argument that 'the phallus man should simply be fizzled out' (*T* 153).

This would seem to give precedence to the class's narrative over all the others, and with all the talk of revolution and the inclusion of the word 'REVOLUTION' itself capitalised and emboldened but reading backwards and upwards within the acrostic polyglyph just after the final grading, there is a logic to this. However, there are other elements which militate against the class's precedence, for example: 'Oh keep them out of it ...', which calls into doubt the source of the final 'portraits', and the final page which reveals that 'the institution of unlearning has been closed down by an obituary act of authority due to textual disturbances' (*T* 164). The university (home of the classroom and many other scenes), the narrative, the text, are all closing down and 'the students have dispersed' (163). Playfully punning with the language of student revolution, *Thru* manages an official grading of all its students or characters, then turns out all the lights. The last ones to leave are 'You^n', the second-person reader(s), placed in the night-driving car that the main characters, Armel and Larissa, arrived in. Because of this association it is also possible to say that the tutorial narrator drives away and the novel closes neatly, not in terms of story or plot but in terms of narrative construction and graphic symmetry.

Such symmetry seems possible only because the text has 'edited' itself, judged performances and (paradoxically) 'decided' to reject some parts of itself. For example, Julia's section of the class narrative (*T* 74–5) is separated off from the classroom discussion that follows it by an extra space between the lines. On this occasion the tutor's comments are in dialogue: 'Hmmm. That's interesting Julia, you've used the given elements very well and introduced new ones' (*T* 75). This leads us to believe that this 'text' is read to the class. The next piece, explicitly read jointly by Salvatore and Julia, is dialogue pre-written and voiced by characters other than those from whose mouths the argumentative encounter purports to come. Unlike the marked sections and even Julia's own piece which immediately precedes it, we read Salvatore's piece within the classroom scene knowing it is a fictional scene set within another. This dominance of the classroom scene over Salvo's narrative is emphasised in a number of ways. The tutor comments prematurely, and Salvo has to correct his work as he's going along:

Hmmm. That's
I haven't finished. And the hoops reiterate set circles of dialogue like why
Armel I want to understand it's so against your own well I am Italian no sorry I
meant to cross that out Well I can't explain. (T 77–8)

Then Salvo's reference to six hours at the end of his section is given graphic
representation by the very literal timetable containing six hours. This doesn't seem
to come from him, nor, since the discussion carries on without reference to it, from
other class members or even the narrating tutor. As a result the low level of Salvo's
narrative is made particularly clear. Finally, after the section has been discussed, it
is put to a vote, and is rejected:

Shall we accept this instalment or let someone else have another go?
Let's put it to the vote shall we. Those for. You can vote too Salvatore. Those
against. Abstentions. Any refusals? A show of hands in the secret ballet of the I
upon the sacred belly of Democracy okay then I'm sorry Salvatore, who would
like to take it up from where Julia left off? Renata. Right. Then Saroja. Fine. (T 79)

Once this occurs it is not just a case of a section of narrative being demoted by its
attribution to a character, but a 'democratic' rejection of the sequence in its
entirety. This is rather like the jury being instructed to disregard a particular remark
made in court. The instruction comes too late. Perhaps it is even more difficult for
the reader to disregard the scene he or she has just read because it is experienced as
print and not, as it is within the 'reality' of the class, dialogue. The reader can return
again and again to the 'unaccepted' section. It does not go away. ~~Like Derrida's sous
rature it remains under the crossing out.~~ The will of the characters, their vote, has
no authority over the book and equally, because our interaction is with the graphic
surface, we, the readers, refuse to concede to the text the ability to reject, and so
limit, aspects of itself.

The same is true of critics: Sarah Birch's useful analysis identifies the feminist
impulse accurately in the text but while catching references to Cixous and Irigaray
she strays into parts of the text which are, in the context of the novel, romantic and
provisional. One of her key examples – 'stop this hysterical rewriting of history' (see
1994: 101) – is taken particularly from Salvatore's rejected section of the class
narrative. This does not devalue what Birch says but simply shows that ultimately
Birch relies on statements made in most 'novelistic' sections of the Armel and
Larissa romance, as we all do. The book is used by the critic as an artefact to
understand the internal world it creates. A sense of the fixed graphic surface is
vitally necessary for us to comprehend such an unstable text as *Thru*. Ultimately,
this novel leads us into diametrical opposition to McHale's view that an awareness
of the graphic surface is destabilising.

Tables and diagrams

One of the most noticeable elements of *Thru* is the way it appears to anchor itself in criticism and theory, particularly the graphic elements employed in these disciplines (see also White 2002). Brooke-Rose's own critical book *The Rhetoric of the Unreal* includes a considerable number of charts, tables and diagrams but their similarity to those in *Thru* is almost entirely visual. Though *Thru* might be taken, at first glance, for a critical work, its tabular and diagrammatic information is reinterpreted through the retro-visor and often turns out to be obfuscating rather than elucidating, as it should be in the conventionally helpful critical text. The re-presentation, in skewed and ironic ways, of literary theory is an important element in *Thru* and seems to be part of an agenda in which the novel opposes the work of literary and linguistic theorists; their inclusion is certainly not neutral or unguardedly enthusiastic as some initial critics seemed to believe.

Thru's treatment of theoretical concepts and diagrams argues against the alternative representation of texts (alternative to text itself) in diagrams and tables. Such devices are reductive and absurd, as shown by the rendering of narrative as variously convoluted lines in *Tristram Shandy* (Sterne 1985: 453–4; 1997: 391–2). Tristram's ideal, the cabbage planter's line, is a diagrammatic ideal for an undiagrammatic medium. It is a parody of the critical dominance over the text and Brooke-Rose wholly rejects such dominance too: 'a method of analysis should not pursue the mirage of a universal grammar (of poetry, of narrative, of text), but be infinitely self-subversive, like the text itself, infinitely flexible to the text, a merely operational metalanguage and easily replaceable' (1976: 9).

Thru includes a reproduction of a critical reproduction of a Renaissance table showing obsessive rhetorical classification (*T* 23) to introduce the concept of rhetoric. Furthering this, *Thru* 101–2 has an academic timetable, which, as well as having the regular timetable features such as day and time, has a box for 'Century' and on different days of the week, in different centuries, seven-session academic days are set up. The subjects which appear in adjacent boxes in this timetable make satirical comparisons. In the tertia session, 'Grammatica' of the thirteenth century is paralleled by 'Initiation to Generative Grammar' in the twentieth, and 'Language as a subversion of society' from the twentieth century is simply 'Rhetorica' in the thirteenth. The idea that 'subjects have to be continually reinvented' appears immediately above the timetable. The difference between the ancient discipline and modern literary theory seems to be simply one of terminology.

The arrangement of text into tables is a recurrent motif in *Thru*. The text lower down page 2 is arranged into four columns. It seems fairly clear there is no potentially mimetic basis for these divisions but there is apparently some logic to them. Reading the contents of the individual columns we find various themes (not coherent sentences) some of which suggest a table of grammar. The left-hand column, beginning 'O capital!' contains references to capital punishment and capital cities. The slenderest right-hand column catalogues pronouns: 'your / your /

your / his / Whose? / Who / us'. The third column concentrates on literary references: 'life story', 'sentence', 'purple passages' and even Burns's 'red red rose'. The undecidability of the second column remains. The concluding word to the sequence is capitalised and broken up into the four columns: 'SIN TAG MA TRICKS'. This punning link of syntagm to sin and tricks signals the difficulty of the readerly attempt to find a coherent organising principle to the arrangement of text fragments into columns, based on grammar or reference, in other words on paradigmatic 'vertical' connections. The effect of the alteration to the conventional graphic surface, breaking the syntagmatic chain of sentence following sentence, is a graphic demonstration of paradigmatic and syntagmatic interpretation placed in opposition to one another.

This sequence also satirises a linguistic approach to writing. In *Linguistics and the Novel* Roger Fowler explains concisely Chomsky's concept of deep and surface structures:

> Surface structure is the observable, or the expressive, layer of a sentence; most concretely, sound or written symbol; somewhat more abstractly, syntax: word- and phrase-order. Deep structure is the abstract content of the sentence: the *structure of meaning* which is being expressed. We experience surface structure directly, but retrieve deep structure, or meaning, only by a complex act of decoding. (1989: 6)

Fowler goes on to discuss the properties of 'surface structure': '*Linearity* is one such property – sentences, but not their meanings, which are abstract, move from left to right in space and time, shifting the reader's attention along and sometimes impeding it' (ibid.). Robert L. Caserio argues that this second clause is dominant in this novel: 'The curious aspect of *Thru* is the way it makes one feel that the free-for-all thruway of the text can become a roadblock' (1988: 294). What happens to the concrete surface structure, our graphic surface, on pages 2 and 3 of *Thru*, is that it abandons linearity and arranges its written symbols on other axes and by other criteria, including linguistic categories. But because syntax in some measure survives in this arrangement there remains another deep structure through the combinations of words. This parodies the transformational grammarians' dissection of language by breaking their rule about having no disjunction at the level of deep structure. A narrative utterance may be broken down into propositions, predicates and roles but narrative survives this trial. It even, in the case of *Thru*, finds ways to transcend it.

On page 4 the text is broken into columns again, laid out in four columns of sections two lines wide, immediately below the words 'To be discussed'. The 'paragraph' describes a classroom scene and is another example of 'naive mimesis', the layout of the text representing the layout of the classroom: 'a roomful of ... rectangular tables'. There is also a visual pun here; the arrangement of the text in the shape of tables here mimics the tabular arrangement of the university timetable, such as we see on page 21, where classes are fitted into ruled boxes. The teacher occupies 'timetable space' as well as the physical (textual) space of a room. The arbitrary nature of both arrangements is brought out by the way words have to be broken across columns, or table entries, for example; 'time   table'. Another classroom sequence begins: 'Once upon a time laid out in rectangles into which you enter as into a room' (T 27). The fairy-tale introduction is now the imposed limitation of the timetable, enclosing the protagonist. Here we see the dimensions of time and space being demonstrated graphically. The purest example of this is on page 78 in the timetable that simply places each hour, from 2300 to 0500 in a separate box, but that in its turn becomes another idea to play with. There are a whole series of timetables throughout the text, each with its own twist on the subject. The novel's play with timetables is tied to the concept of academic structure. In the following examples text and image both attempt to 'contain' time and space.

Over pages 104–5 there is a timetable with a Greek flavour, counting days in ten and keeping Socratic hours. In this case the contents of the table seem relatively homogeneous, the idea seeming simply to put a longer temporal perspective on the academic structure. But there is something exceptional about these pages. The timetable actually forms a barrier: the text on the left-hand page does not skip over and ignore the table when it reaches it but instead is continued at the top of the right-hand page. The text from there moves across to the lower segment of the left-hand page which feeds into the lower section of the right-hand page. In other words the text for these two pages begins and ends at the conventional points but does something very unusual in the middle. The graphic surface of recto *and* verso has been conceived together as a double-page spread, which is extremely unusual even in this context. The use of the timetable as a barrier seems to have a metaphoric meaning. The surrounding text is particularly politically oriented:

> The timetable structures society but destroys the family which structures society, each tale-bearer pressured into his story in order that the hero's quest may proceed. But as we saw the motivation may well be reversed, the timetable structuring the family but destroying society which structures the family.

The references to 'tale-bearer' and 'hero's quest' are drawn from the work of Vladimir Propp who, in his book *Morphology of the Folk Tale* (1928, first translated 1958), rigidly defined what was possible in that form of narrative and was taken up as a starting point by later narrative theorists. Propp's view of narrative is extremely linear:

> Theft cannot take place before the door is forced. Insofar as the tale is concerned, it has its own entirely particular and specific laws. The sequence of events … is strictly uniform. Freedom within this sequence is restricted by very narrow limits which can be exactly formulated. (1979: 22)

Such critical rigidity is, as we have seen, anathema to Brooke-Rose, and in *Thru* it is seen to have a gendered agenda.

On page 90 we find 'a six-hour nightly timetable' for every day of the week which follows on from a direct satire of Propp interwoven with Eliot's 'Prufrock', homing in on the sexual theme of the narrative exchange. The timetable is the device by which 'The two pleasures, the pleasure in your textual act and the curiosity, should be skilfully balanced'. The timetable itself contains a wealth of sexual puns made with academic, particularly psychoanalytical, jargon. The dialectic of desire, beloved of Lacan, appears every night between one and two o'clock except on 'Sated Day' when the male creator traditionally rests from his labours. This timetable could occupy the space left by the twentieth/thirteenth-century timetable after which it is noted 'The hours between completa and laudes may be spent in heterotextuality. There has been a complete reform in genital organisation' (T 102). The rigid timetables of medieval monasticism are invoked here, and the governing of the academic sex-life seems to be a pastiche of Tommaso Campanella's *City of the Sun: A Poetical Dialogue* (1981), a seventeenth-century utopian text which regulates the sex-lives of its citizens by astrological means.

The point about timetables is essentially about enclosure, politically and gender motivated, particularly the male urge to place things in a box and thus control them. There is a serious point here about who makes the timetables, who controls time and space and sex. This is tied to the satire of the diagrammatic impulse; that which can be placed into a diagram, be boxed, is thus controlled. *Thru* fights for narrative which can't be so easily contained. What happens to critical theory here shows that narrative is quite capable of imposing itself on method, and destabilising any schema that attempts to encompass it.

Acrostic pages

The case against linearity in criticism, narrative theory and reading itself is further developed by a series of pages in *Thru* on which the graphic surface is used to present text that can be read in a number of directions. Page 6 of *Thru* has a full-page acrostic arrangement of this kind. Here the eye (of the reader?) is thematised, the word 'eye' appearing ten times. We also come across 'beam' and 'mote' relating to the New Testament proverb about taking the beam out of one's own eye before looking for the speck in another's. References are also made to the blinding in *King Lear* and Bataille's *The Story of the Eye* (see Figure 7.3).

I think we would be unwise to search for some iconic or representational motif to this page. The fragmentation of the text is the symptom of horizontal words being arranged to allow other words to be read downwards through them. Within the horizontal text various letters are highlighted by being capitalised agrammatically. These letters are also given typographic emphasis by being set in bold type which differentiates them from the two merely capitalised 'I's in the arrangement. In the first half of the page the acrostic, downwards-reading, words all relate to textual study: STORY, MYSTERY, TEXT, ENIGMA, ARCHITRACE,

```
              never                    the      lesS
              this is                           noT
                                                nO
                                  (My)
         the                      h Y s T e R y  of The
                                                          Eye
  becAuse I would noT                 S e  E thY      cRuel   Nails
  boaRish                                              fAngs
                          pluck  ouT                        hIs
                pooR old         (E    Xtract)       (Cruel
     Cruel       nAils)   uPon          These        eyEs of
     tHine
     I'll set     (C      R u El                            fanGs)
                  my     foOt  Poo R old eyes
     These       eyEs        hIs  eYes
  pooR old eyes
  beAm                                                        Mote
     Cruel              fanGs
     Eyes                cRuel                                fAngs
                        boArish
                       ·bea M
                          Moat
                          Etc
                       alreaDy       (all read eye)

                       naIls
                        Nails

                     upon These
                  eyes of tHine I'll
                        sEt

                 the re Mote   sTone
                 Wide   Eyes   wEt?
                 pArch  Ment  waX
                 arXi   stOne      Trace
                        dRy
                       papYrus
                   eye 'S
```

blue lacuna of learning
and unlearning a text within a text passed on from
generation to generation of an increasing vastness that
nevertheless dwindles to an elite initiated to a text no-
one else will read by means maybe of the flick of a
switch for the overhead projector and diagrams drawn
into a boxed screen to the right of the desk with a
spirit-loaded pen thus not losing eye-contact.

Figure 7.3: The intersection of *Thru* pages 6 (acrostic) and 7 (normal)

TRACE.[10] The lower half of the page arranges a central column of letters that aligns between two separate beginnings that bracket together. Thus we have 'pro/ epigrammed in the memory's'. 'Gramm' means 'what is written', and an epigram is a witty, pointed or antithetical saying, so these elements have the sense of being built-in (to the text) and memorable (in the mind), but exactly what is programmed or epigrammed can only be whichever of the foregoing vertical words we choose. MEMORY'S is flanked by WAX and TEXT, bringing to mind Freud's comparison of the memory with the mystic writing pad (see Derrida 1978). But this is only part of another theme: that of writing itself. Stone, parchment, wax and papyrus are also included in the horizontal arrangement. The concept of writing itself is taken back to Egyptian wax tablets and on page 7 there is a whimsical lisping poem about 'bithy little Thoth', the Ibis-headed god who, in mythology, brought writing to the Egyptians. The story of Thoth is told also by Plato in his *Phaedrus*, where it is placed in the mouth of Socrates who uses it to illustrate the disadvantages inherent in the medium of writing. His argument is that Thoth's gift, offered as a 'medicine' for 'memory and wisdom', 'will produce forgetfulness' and 'a show of wisdom without the reality' (1946: 104–5). In this way the words flanking 'memory' become alternatives for it.

This nexus of tale-telling is analysed in considerable detail by Derrida in *Dissemination*, and it is from here that *Thru* picks up these threads. Derrida explains that, because of the classical concept of the ideal original, 'writing appears to Plato (and after him to all of philosophy, which is as such constituted by this gesture) as that process of redoubling in which we are fatally (en)trained: the supplement of a supplement, the signifier of a signifier, the representative of a representative' (1981: 109). But what seems to have interested Brooke-Rose most is Derrida's concept of 'the play of writing' (ibid.: 95). This combines with another trope from the classical source: the idea of the pipe-player, or, as *Thru* has it, the flute-player, which comes from *The Symposium* where Socrates' philosophic style is compared to the bewitching flute-playing of the satyr, Marsyas (Plato 1951: 100–1). This is reflected in the iconic text arranged as 'dancing hoops' on pages 40 and particularly 41 where circular text springing from a classroom political debate reads: 'marx on division of labour / plato said no society could exist unless we were all flute players / each capable of being a flute player'. The direct implication satirises Plato's ideal society, advocated in his *Republic*, which requires all its citizens to be male philosophers, but – in the context of *Thru* – we might be able to equate flute-playing and narrating.

Wax tablets, the form in which the Old Testament may originally have been written, are suggestively introduced on page 3 when we read of the 'WHORE of Babel ... Cramping HIS styl   us', the capitalisation of HIS suggesting that a male deity is referred to, linking the story of Thoth and Ammon with the Judaeo-

---

10   The last two words come from Derrida: the idea of writing as a 'trace' rather than a 'presence' from 1981: 155; 'Architrace' in the sense of 'original trace' from 1978: 196, 213, 229.

Christian God. The stylus is his phallic pen, suggesting also the pen-is. Thus the Whore of Babel seems to shrivel the phallus and ruin the ability to write. Her move to Babel from Babylon further suggests an association with a multiplicity of languages, spoken rather than written. The democratisation of flute-playing and the opposition to the single phallo-cratic narrator both fit with the shifting structure of the text which we have already identified.

Yet these words flanking 'MEMORY'S' do not complete the sentence. That leads straight into 'blue lacuna of learning and unlearning' which runs horizontally at the top of page 7 (Figure 7.3) (see also Brooke-Rose 1997: 244, 2002: 80).

What is going on here? The axis of the text of page 6 seems quite clearly to be split with words reading horizontally and vertically. What we find, as readers attempting to deal with this, is – with the help of the lead-in from page 5 – that our way out of this fragmented text is to read down. This is what allows us to get back to the more familiarly orientated page 7.

What sense we are to make of the words that bridge the division is perhaps even more difficult to fathom. If we take on board the 'blue lacuna' as a pun on 'blue lagoon' we have a suggestion of idyllic gaps in learning, but what do they relate to? The 'blue lacuna' can also be linked to the intertextual motif of 'the blue guitar' taken from Wallace Stevens's poem 'The Man with the Blue Guitar'. In this poem the guitarist is accused:

> They said, 'You have a blue guitar,
> You do not play things as they are.'
>
> The man replied, 'Things as they are
> Are changed upon the blue guitar' (1965: 52)

Can we take, therefore, 'the blue lacuna' as the gap between reality and its representation (in poetry for Stevens, in prose for Brooke-Rose)? This would allow us to take the learning and unlearning to refer to expectations of mimesis: the conventions learned that need to be unlearned in order to take on board *Thru*'s new 'naive' mimesis.

This process may be combined with the elements which compose page 5: the history of writing and the history of narrative (the myths about Thoth and the Ten Commandments are, of course, narrative). These elements are brought into the university classroom for an elite few to study despite the fact that the trace and architraces of narrative live on in all and are vitally important to our mental processes. This latter point is Peter Brooks's thesis in *Reading for the Plot*. He argues that narrative – or plotting – is basic 'to our very articulation of experience in general' (1985: xi). *Thru* shows this without minimising the complexity of that experience. Nor does this novel neglect the physical form of that articulation (text). In fact *Thru*'s play with acrostic text further focuses attention on the most basic unit of text: the letter.

Individual letters as signifiers

Thru's acrostic play foregrounds the importance of the letter which may be read more than once, on different axes. Several letters in the acrostic on page 6 and in the circular devices ('dancing hoops') on pages 40–1 serve double-duty. In other examples, such as the arrangement on page 12 (clearly echoed on 113), and the polyglyph device on page 21 (and similarly on 163), letters do more than this, being readable from multiple axes; vertical, horizontal, diagonal, circular.[11] The best known polyglyph is the Sator square which includes the Latin words *rotas*, *opera*, *tenet*, *arepo* and *sator* readable vertically and horizontally, backwards and upwards. *Thru*'s examples are less perfect but more interesting, connecting and involving the text that introduces and follows them.

Certain letters can be even more heavily loaded with meaning. 'X', for example, recurs as such on several occasions with a variety of functions arranged around its axes (*T* 12, 20, 49, 89, 112, 117). This is because it is used to symbolise a particular diagram by theoretician A. J. Greimas. On pages 55–6 *Thru* actually quotes a whole page of Greimas '(by kind permission of the author)' ending in his diagram.[12] As we can see in the third section of page 12 there are special readings of 'I' and 'U' as well as X. Elsewhere 'O' for Other and zero is privileged. These motifs, characters as characters, are significant. They form the components of jokes about the deep structure of language (or interpretations of language) versus textuality.

The graphic 'X' motif, for example, recurs throughout the text. In his essay '*Thru* the Looking Glass' Hanjo Berressem makes a psychoanalytical and linguistic parallel to the retro-visor, arguing that *Thru* juxtaposes *langue*, which operates from the beginning of the sentence to its end, and *parole*, which works from end to beginning. From this Berressem develops an analysis of *Thru*'s 'chiastic' leitmotif, gathering Greimas diagram references to illustrate his point. But Berressem's keen-eyed post-structuralist approach to the prominence of this motif is ultimately problematical. He writes of *Thru*: 'Because of its fundamental playfulness and openness, a structural analysis of the text is virtually impossible. In Greimasian terms, the text is "hopelessly" heterological and defined by an "abysmally" complex isotopia' (1995: 113). This implies that we should, in the end, be able to make a structural analysis when, in fact, *Thru*'s treatment of Greimas's and others' theoretical schemes about the novel reverses this relationship and analyses structuralism. In a recent essay Brooke-Rose asks:

> what is the epistemological status of … a structuralist diagram of contraries and
> contradictories from elementary logic, used by Greimas over twenty years ago

---

11 The term 'polyglyph' comes from Harris (1995: 118–19).
12 The original appearance of the diagram seems to have been in Greimas and Rastier (1968). The diagram is also used in Brooke-Rose 1981: 391. In correspondence (1998b: 5) Brooke-Rose has pointed out that the Greimas 'X' also includes Lacan's 'Z' from Lacan 1980: 193.

---

in his narrative grammar? As a representation of a supposed narrative structure, it is a fiction, a theory about narrative movements, to be verified and proved, at least for simple tales. As a rectangle on a page, it is an object, a visual fact. (1996b: 13)

To put it simply, Berressem takes the use of the Greimas diagram in *Thru* too seriously. In *Stories, Theories and Things* Brooke-Rose describes her first encounter with the diagram as one which 'made me laugh out loud' (1991b: 237). In that example the diagram's contraries and contradictories dealt with sexual relations under the following four terms: matrimonial (prescribed), normal (non-forbidden), non-matrimonial (non-prescribed), and abnormal (forbidden). This was followed by two more examples which 'allow for sixteen different kinds of sexual relationships – surely a poor generating model' (1991b: 238). Here Brooke-Rose is making a pun on 'generating' in terms of sexuality, procreation, which relates to the playful call for 'genital reorganisation' in *Thru* (punning on Freud's term 'genital organisation'). It is this usage that seems to have inspired the Greimas diagram's 'eternal quadrangle' role in the novel. In the centre of *Thru* (83) Greimas's diagram is laid out in Larissa's dialogue, and its inherent sexism exposed. In Reyes' *Delectable Metarealism* this is taken to be the ultimate 'meaning' of the Greimas diagram in *Thru* (1998: 271). I would tend to regard this use of it as the prime one only in the sense that it is from this initial reaction that the text begins finding new applications for it; sexual, psychological, literary and graphic.

Greimas's diagram also introduces other significant points relating to the way in which the terms around the diagram are summarised or represented by individual letters. We have seen how we must negotiate our way across the exploded acrostic pages of *Thru* at the level of character, but these characters can have their own significance outside the fact that they are part of a word. As in Greimas's diagram they can 'stand for' something.

Hang it all we have the story of an △ 
O but is not incompetent performance a non-disjunction at level of deep structure? I me if it be possible despite non-equivalence to rewrite I as O and O as I

Figure 7.4: Multiple signification of the letter 'I' from *Thru* 7

On page 7 when we have the cue of 'audio-visual' and 'overhead projector' we can identify a pedagogic narrator (see Figure 7.4). The I in the triangle seems to be both a signal and a warning of (about) first-person narration, followed by a statement of intent, or perhaps an attempt, to write the self as other and the other as self. This idea, expressed by rewriting one letter as another, comes from Chomskyan linguistics or transformational grammar. Transformations allow the rewriting of surface but not deep structure. There can be no disjunctions at the level of deep structure, and therefore it is impossible to rewrite subject as object, or S as O. *Thru* tackles this on page 43: 'a neater and more cryptic formula where S for subject somehow via S^1 (S^n) is rewritten as O for Object, o^1, o^2, o^n'. The 'somehow' is important. The marking of the terms here suggests the method will be that of the Greimas box. Yet in a sense *Thru* rewrites subject as object on page 1 where the retro-visor becomes le viseur. There, with the invocation of the French *viser* (to aim), the I in the triangle becomes a target. Rewriting 'I as O and O as I' is a similar, and larger, project within the text, and an attempt at a psychological impossibility according to Lacan.

The problems we have been experiencing identifying exactly who speaks spring from such attempts to exchange O and I. On page 8 are two alternative lists of characters inventing other characters, each containing another, like a Russian doll. Ultimately, however, I believe that the identification left undetermined throughout the text reduces to the relationship between Armel and Larissa.[13] With the additional inventions of the class one of these two, or possibly both, is inventing the other based on a shared fictional 'past' that we, the readers, have no access to. Later we are told: 'It follows therefore that if Larissa invents Armel inventing Larissa, Armel also invents Larissa inventing Armel' (*T* 108). Deciding which character is the source of the others is, given the structure of the novel, an impossible task, yet on page 7 the tutor offers a method with a version of Greimas's narratological diagram. Here instead of reformulating Propp's character functions the diagram arranges four 'I's. Like the capital I and the capital O this diagrammatic X becomes a textual motif occurring for the first time within a word immediately below: 'teXthattaway'. This motif forms a parody of linearity, a four-way split. Implicit in it is the idea of deception from western movie cliché. It suggests that the reader may find himself or herself engaged in a pursuit of narratorial identity, for ever pointed in a new direction by Greimas's diagram, at every point given a new prompt by the text, 'they went thattaway', but never actually catching them.

The graphic surface allows letters to signify beyond their role in a given word, beyond their contribution to the semantics of several words, and ultimately individually. In *Thru* deconstructive terms are put literally into practice and, once the text starts signifying in this way, it seems, to bowdlerise deconstructive terminology, there is no stopping it.[14]

---

13 Compare R. D. Laing's (1967: 45) definition of psychotherapy: 'an obstinate attempt of two people to recover the wholeness of being human through the relationship between them.'
14 The bowdlerisation here is mine. The Rev. Thomas Bowdler cut the sexual elements in his edition of Shakespeare. *Thru* actually does the opposite with deconstruction as its subject, importing the issue of sex and gender, and showing the gender biases within it.

The vertical text

Thru is not merely using the graphic surface to expand the potentialities of fiction, it goes further in that it questions the basic conventions of the language, in particular our habit of reading English (and other European languages) from left to right: 'This structure is generated by recursivity rules which in English tend to be to the right, as in French, whereas Japanese favours recursivity to the left' (*T* 99–100). Once Brooke-Rose has questioned the conventional recursivity of normal English reading she is free to challenge it. Many commentators note the acrostic layouts with the vertical readings we have discussed above but there are many more that no one has spotted and Brooke-Rose has only recently started pointing out in exasperation.

This defiant strand begins at the bottom of page 2 where we have previously noted the paradigmatic rearrangement of the graphic surface. In the left-hand column, reading the capitals of the capital cities downwards, we find the word 'BRAIN'. The first letters of the third column 'below' are also capitalised, spelling 'WHICH'. This forms our introduction to checking the first letters of lines for extra textual 'clues', diachronic units of meaning that no narratological vocabulary had, or indeed has, been developed for. These vertical readings occur in the first letters of the ranged-right text almost continually from the bottom of page 2 until page 20. They also appear at the end of the novel, and occasionally in short sections in between providing an extra, literally paradigmatic, reading of the text.

Awareness of this vertical text requires attention to the page at the level of character, and takes us back to the stopping-on-a-sixpence precision of 'YOU ARE HERE' seen inserted in Roman Jakobson's diagram of linguistic communication reproduced on page 51 and recurring on 117 where it halts the reader at an 'O' in the centre of a large-scale Greimas 'X' with 'O' and 'I' arranged at the corners. The fact that when we stop reading on a particular page we return to that page, a particular paragraph, a particular sentence, a particular capital letter, indicates that, however much we read normally by recognising words as units on the page, we can and do occasionally navigate ourselves across the graphic space of a page by character. When Brooke-Rose (literally) capitalises on this in her acrostics we have to focus more closely, but this seems to happen only when we are left stranded by the text in white space. If we are allowed to return to our regular recursive reading habits we are quite happy. In normally oriented text, letters are not privileged and, unlike in poetry, the lines have no grammatical value. A quotation from a text, even if it separates and indents a long quotation, pays no attention to the line breaks of the original text unless it is a poem in verse. *Thru* wholly betrays this automatism. In this text it is not an irrelevant hypothesis to look for words which we can read downwards through the horizontal text. This extra level of reading hidden in the graphic surface does not, therefore, alert us to the materiality of the page of text; instead, it slips by us, even if we are on the look out for such materiality, because the only thing that separates this vertical reading of the text from our usual reading is the expected direction of travel for the eye, in other words, our conventions of reading.

In his examination of prose which inhabits the spatial dimensions of the page usually reserved for poets, McHale, having listed a number of authors using blank horizontal space, including Johnson (1971) and Gray (1984), moves on to the potential of vertical and diagonal space (naturally, in his view, to be used to foreground the materiality of the book). He lists *Thru* here as providing examples of diagonal and vertical texts, but he is referring to the blatantly acrostic pages (e.g. *T* 6) rather than to the vertical readings possible in pages which seem dominated by conventionally arranged left-to-right reading text. McHale clearly misses these possible readings during his discussion of the horizontal variances at work within *Thru*: 'Horizontal space can be foregrounded … by tampering with the margins. Thus … in Christine Brooke-Rose's *Thru* (1975), the text is sometimes justified only at the left margin, like poetry, sometimes only at the right, and sometimes at both margins' (1987: 183).

In his eagerness to spot spatial signification leading to exposure of the materiality of the text, McHale fails to look at what the varying margins and justification in *Thru* might actually be caused by. Those ranged-right pages he refers to are the first twenty where we can read down the left-hand margin. The bulk of the text is conventionally justified across the page with a few exceptions (for example we can read 'My death he the truth through Hasty SWItch of siGnifiers and sO ON' down the left hand margins of 119–20). But it is at the end of the novel where we encounter the pages McHale describes as 'justified … only at the right hand margin'. These pages are in fact so arranged as to allow us to read down the *right-hand* margin, from the lower part of page 157 until the elaborate grading of all the characters and writers who are mentioned in the text which begins on page 159. This vertical reading runs: 'exeunt narrators with a swift Switch of signifiers no more i superimposing'. Such vertical texts can make important contributions to our reading of the text.

We might well ask ourselves: who speaks here? But what this line of text suggests, by its virtual invisibility and its readability, is the presence *and* absence of the author. Though not endowed with a proper name, we find a figure, *literally* in this case, 'marking off the edges of the text, revealing, or at least characterising, its mode of being' (Foucault 1979: 147).

The words of the vertical text seem to be a combination of Freudian and structuralist language. The vertical text running from pages 2 to 5 reads: 'BRAIN WHICH creates death she the truth ever escaping through swift switch of signifiers'. The latter half of this could describe the way in which a complete elucidation of *Thru* manages to stay just beyond our reach, but it doesn't give us the information we need to ever be one jump ahead of the text. The 'hidden' acrostics are not to be regarded as a secret key that explains the novel. In fact they ask as many questions as they provide answers; for example, the acrostic on page 9 asks us

'What is Larissa doing now or Veronica?' Their significance is in the way that they relate to the horizontal text on the pages which 'carry' them.

For example, from the last three lines of page 9 to the beginning of the double column on page 13, the vertical text reads: 'TWo white thighs DO it two White legs wo you dadDY bitcH YOU TIT BITCH you got IT ALL wrong.' This acts as a kind of sexual 'subtext' which supplements the erotically charged horizontal text over these pages and the more visible emboldened and capitalised text reading down within the acrostic layout over pages 10 and 11: 'EXPECTED GESTURE / NO MYSTERY WELL I WANT HER CUNT.'

Brooke-Rose suggests that this vertical text contains the hidden, but conscious, thoughts of characters when in 'Is Self-Reflexivity Mere?' she states that the driver of the car 'has been thinking (down the left margin)' (1997: 248). This would make the vertical text, at least partly, another use of the graphic surface intended to enhance the mimetic complexity of the text. As such it is a highly successful device producing a 'simultaneity that we all experience but which sequential language can't achieve except with adverbs like "meanwhile" or "later"' (ibid.: 240 (see also 2002: 74)). Unfortunately the success remains relatively formal since, even though vertical and horizontal texts fully co-exist in the same place, they can never actually coincide because they can never be read simultaneously.

I would like to suggest that the hidden (yet simultaneous) vertical text might in some way function as the 'unconscious' of the horizontal text. There is evidence to support this over pages 15 and 16 where we can read a German vertical text: 'wo Es war Soll Ich werden.' This is a key phrase from Freud, usually translated literally 'Where Id (it) was shall Ego (I) come to be'. Might the vertical text then be a statement of textual 'ego', i.e. comprehensible text, arriving where previously there had only been the unconscious play of letters in vertical relation to one another? In *Reading for the Plot* Peter Brooks looks at the importance of Freud's phrase:

> What man can be depends on the uncertain relation of the conscious subject to the unconscious. 'Wo Es War Soll Ich Werden:' the famous dictum is traditionally, and optimistically, translated, "Where Id was shall Ego come to be,' but it may rather signify a never ending struggle of the ego to coincide with and master that otherness within that drives the subject in obscure ways. And the telling of the history of this struggle is always a hypothetical construction. (1985: 284)

This might suggest a less optimistic reading of the arrival of the ego in that it has only a slight foothold, one vertical line in any page of potential vertical readings. Furthermore, as we have already mentioned, though vertical and horizontal texts co-exist in the same place, they can never actually coincide. Therefore conflict between ego and id, between comprehensible and incomprehensible, between horizontal and vertical text remains. This conflict could be summarised as one between I (ego) and Other (id) and can be seen to be of great importance elsewhere in the vertical text.

In the closing of the initial sequence of vertical text on page 20 (see Figure 7.5) we find further support for this parallel for that which cannot be united. This an important arrangement in which the vertical text combines with the signification of individual letters and theory, in the form of the Greimas diagram. The vertical text on this page reads 'IN ORDER TO stop this stop'. But there is an additional vertical text where 'IN ORDER TO' is repeated on the right-hand edge of the top part of the page, reading from bottom to top. This Greimas diagram superimposed over the first rectangle of text points to one 'I', two 'O's and an 'I' in a triangle as on page 1. The textual content of this rectangle unites major textual themes: the overhead projector, the spirit-loaded pen, the four eyes from the retro-visor. It combines linguistics and psychoanalysis in 'floating up every 90 minutes or sO To surface structure from deep level dreamlessness'. Most importantly of all it involves the reader in a sexual exchange: 'Diagonals meeting In O On which I enters O and Envelopes contraries contradictories'.

In the box with a switch for the overhead projector tO
Note and a spirit-loaded pen, thus not loosing eye-contacT
Or some still making love perhaps four eyes crossed foR
Riveting limbs, M or Y, opening crossing pentapod or ninE
Diagonals meeting In   On which I enters O anD
Envelopes contraries contradictories subalterns as a staR
Rivets form substance floating up every 90 minutes or sO
To surface structure from deep level dreamlessness dowN
Over under electroded lids for a shared cigarette.

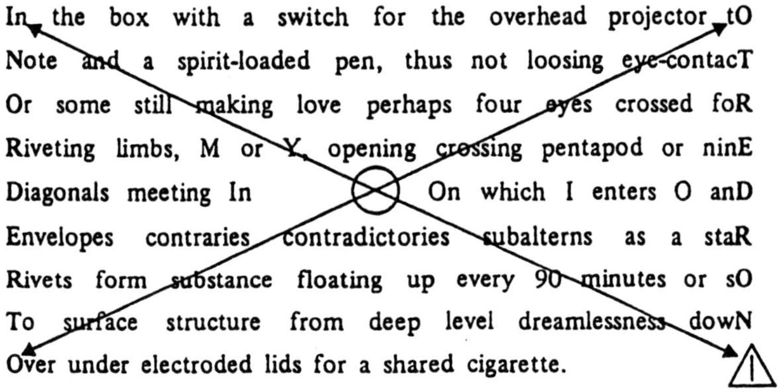

Figure 7.5: Nexus of graphic devices and vertical text on *Thru* 20

At the centre of the Greimas diagram on page 20 (Figure 7.5), overlaying the point of crossover, is a large 'O' (compare *T* 117). This 'O', this other, I suggest, is the reader, the intersection of all the complexities of character and narration as the text attempts to rewrite its 'O' as 'I'. The central 'O' separates the capital I in 'In' and the capital 'O' in 'On', but it ultimately unites them. And every graphic disruption appears 'IN ORDER TO' make this possible.

Below the section with the overwritten X we find that the warning sign is supplemented by two more triangular signs ahead. The first of these is made out of a 'Y', the second is simply an iconic shape, but both signify by their different orientation not a warning but 'STOP', or at the very least 'Give Way'. Finally, opposite the vertical text that demands 'stop this stop this', reading down the right-hand margin we find the last piece of vertical text of the opening sequence repeating the call from the faculty meetings for 'order now order'. For a time the coherent vertical text will be 'repressed'.

Try as it might, the medium of literature cannot rewrite O as I, or unite O and I, representing writer and reader. In realising this limitation *Thru* may be said to be far more 'self-aware' than other texts, yet that does not stop the text doing its utmost to prolong and intensify that contact which *is* possible.

Textuality and sexuality

In the previous sections we have seen how attribution of narration is problematised in *Thru*, with narrators seemingly interchangeable, and how readerly hypotheses about the narrative are kept provisional. We have also seen 'O' and 'I', other and subject, moved towards interchange. The intersection of these two thrusts of the text is bound up with the issue of gender, but to a distinct objective; that of the re-equilibration of male and female, text and reader. How is this 'genital reorganisation' to be accomplished? By what Derrida calls the 'baffling economy of seduction' (1981: 226). Or, as *Thru* puts it: 'within the grammar of that narrative the roles can be interchanged and textasy multiplied until punctually at a fixed hour all the forged orgy ceases' (*T* 87).

In *Reading for the Plot* Peter Brooks argues against narratological paradigmatic readings, in favour of readings that take into account the human psychological need for narrative. Brooks mentions twice: 'Susan Sontag argued some years ago, we need an erotics of art' and offers his contribution in this study described 'more soberly, [as] a reading of our compulsions to read' (1985: 36 and xv). Brooke-Rose, too, is aware of 'the human need for fictions' (1991b: 175) but, according to Brooks, such 'erotics' – depending heavily on the reader's involvement – traditionally hinge on plot. *Thru* contradicts this. There is very little clear action in *Thru*, but there are mysteries which are clearly emphasised: whose are the eyes in the driving-mirror? Who is narrating? And most explicitly, 'Who speaks?' *Thru* keeps us guessing and guessing; it relies on our need to know. This reading of *Thru* parallels the dynamic of the sexual relationship in the text; the play between 'the vulgar desire to know', in the sense of gain definite information but also in the carnal, biblical sense, and the frequent advice given in the book 'never let yourself be fully known' (*T* 54, 89,135, 146, applied to both men and women).

Brooke-Rose's conclusion to her essay 'Illiterations', written fifteen years after *Thru*, puts the relationship between reader and text in sexual terms:

> it would surely be a good thing if more men learned to read as women …, so that the bisexual effort, which they have metaphorically appropriated at one end, should not remain so wholly on the woman's side at the other. Both should read as both, just as both write as both. (1989: 68)

That male readers can read as female and female readers can read as male requires the text itself to be bisexual. *Thru* achieves this state by the way it almost continually refuses to allow its narrative sections to be attributed to a gendered narrator during reading. Decisions on the gender of the narrators are left to the reader with the proviso that if we could fix gender in one part of the text then it would necessarily cross over, Greimas-like, in the next, because the main contenders for the role of narrator at any one time are usually of opposite sexes (see Little 1996: 129).

Emma Kafelanos's study of *Thru*, which she titles 'Textasy' (1980), draws out the sexual thread of the narrative, concentrating on the relationship between Armel and Larissa (and between them and their respective lovers) at whichever narrative level they operate. She explains how their close relationship works on an explicitly metatextual level in the novel:

> the four eyes in the rearview mirror generate the two main narrators of the novel, a man and a woman, Armel Santores and Larissa Toren. As another character in the novel discovers, 'the names are anagrams. Except for ME in hers and I in his' (p.69). That is, the two names have eleven letters in common. These eleven letters plus the two letters in the word 'me' form the name Armel Santores; the same eleven letters plus the letter 'I' form Larissa Toren. (1980: 44)

The combined textual/sexual puns of *Thru* generate some irony here, and generation can be both grammatical and reproductive. We might also add, as Damien Grant notes, that the eleven letters that Armel and Larissa have in common can make 'narrate loss' (1995: 119). This relates to what Kafelanos goes on to show: that it is impossible for us to distinguish Armel and Larissa as narrators (in other words decide who speaks). However, Kafelanos explains the interchangeability of narrators in the following way: 'Larissa and Armel both are clearly aspects of the author'. To justify this Kafelanos uses Brooke-Rose's interview with Cohen and Hayman, in which the author mentions talking to herself as 'je' and 'tu' in French (1976: 17), and concludes that *Thru* is 'a generative fantasy' of 'fictional creation' because 'Just as the two pairs of eyes in the opening image are the reflection of one person, Larissa and Armel together (the one intellectual, the other emotional) seem to form one complete human being, perhaps in many respects Brooke-Rose herself' (1980: 46, 45).

Kafelanos's work is interesting and helpful in the way it focuses on the sexual theme but she is mistaken, I think, in taking the generative relationship to be between two sides of Brooke-Rose herself, so naturalising the text through author psychology. This is not to dismiss Kafelanos's argument – undoubtedly a split within the author, Brooke-Rose the novelist and Brooke-Rose the theorist, played a significant part in the composition of *Thru* (see Brooke-Rose 1991 and 2002) – but I do not really think this is what *Thru* presents to us.

The sexual links in *Thru* do not remain just between characters. At the top of the textual hierarchy there is another romance going on, which parallels that of the main characters. In it two characters occupy the same space, like Armel and Larissa; these are writer and reader: 'the reader is the writer and the writer the reader' (*T* 30). This is something echoed by Brooke-Rose in her interview with Cohen and Hayman. Her attitude shifts, seemingly, in two pages of reported dialogue from 'you do not in fact think of the reader' to 'I think the reader is me, as I write' to 'It's not just solipsism, there is a reader out there' (1976: 16–17). Brooke-Rose's final pronouncement on the subject is: 'I think the reader is that, it's a *je/tu*' (1976:17). In fact it is an earlier version of this last statement – when Brooke-Rose admits she talks to herself as 'je' and 'tu' – that Kafelanos uses as a way of linking Armel and Larissa with Brooke-Rose. As Brooks argues, there is an 'erotics' of text that involves the reader, but unfortunately Kafelanos's argument – which would otherwise support Brooks – denies the importance of the reader in the erotic economy of *Thru*.

The relationship of the reader to the inanimate text always tends towards the personal or intimate according to Roger Fowler:

> Narrative discourse is created out of the interaction of the culture's conventions, the author's expressive deployment of these conventions as they are coded in language, and the reader's activity in releasing meaning from the text. The co-operative process is not *personal*, in that it does not depend on the private feelings of writer or reader, nor *impersonal* in that human beings are vitally involved, but *intersubjective*, a communicative act calling on shared values. (1989: 81, italics original)

Fowler's formulation does tend to make the process sound cosy. Perhaps it would be more appropriate to *Thru*'s revolutionary content and historical context to suggest shared 'experience' through the communication of individuals or shared 'suspension of common sense' (see Laing 1967: 15–16 and Brown 1959: ix). The nature of collaboration between writer/reader and reader/writer in *Thru* is implicit within the acrostic of page 112 from which we take Figure 7.6. This arrangement suggests a collaborative effort addressed to the first person singular, but this is not, as Kafelanos suggests, the self of the author in a masturbatory arrangement but something that involves the reader crucially. Or, as Joseph Francis Pestino puts it: 'Brooke-Rose's analogy makes this writer/reader bond even more intimate, almost hermaphroditic' (1986: 181). Here the text writes itself in and simultaneously denies itself. The text includes '(I)', but this character is also part of 'EX(I)T'. The exit via the horizontal word 'Thattaway' sends us off again, through the text, continuing to try and solve its seductive mysteries with only the most ambiguous directions to follow.

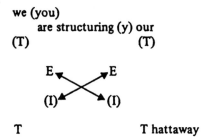

Figure 7.6: Diagram of collaborative structure of text from *Thru* 112

The 'untrustworthy nature of the role of the narrator' which Kafelanos is quick to pick up is especially so for the characters who are being narrated. But this feeling of untrustworthiness is always shared, at a metatextual level, by the reader. For example, let us take the following quotation: 'Whoever invented you is the absently unreliable narrator or the unreliably absent narrator or you in love with him who is in love with the implied author who is in love with himself and therefore absent in the nature of things' (T 96).[15] This, as seems apparent from how high it manages to climb in terms of literary levels (from character to implied author), is the voice of a textual entity of some 'authority', in more than one sense. Yet at the same time the male gendering of all the figures in this chain, rather than suggesting 'homo-textuality', may simply mean this chain is theoretical – implied by a character at a lower level. The reader, unable to locate the voice, which in its hypothesising parodies his or her own, simply does not know who speaks or who to trust. Knowing exactly where we stand remains impossible in *Thru*, but the connecter in this chain – love – attaches together the unreliable, the absent and the implied.

In this way *Thru* works towards a male/female unification, the collision that will create a bisexual re-equilibration and join the separate genders. The fourth column on pages 2–3 shows this progression towards unification in microcosm: 'your / your / your / his / Whose? / Who / us.' We can also read a progression in the vertical text. In the first section there is 'she the truth ever escaping Through Swift Switch of Signifiers'. On page 119 it is 'he the truth through Hasty Switch of Signifiers and so on'. Finally the right-justified text of the final section tells us 'exeunt narrators with a swift Switch of signifiers no more i superimposing' (157–9). This sequence suggests the passage through different gendered narrations which at the approach-ing end of the text will finally leave the reader, the text's 'O', free of the text's 'i'.

The vertical text also makes other contributions. We read: 'What is she in a Name is sHe an IotAboo Echo' (16–17). I do not think the capital 'H' in 'sHe' is accidental. Here is a pronoun that contains male within female by the use of the graphic surface. The combination word 'iotaboo' combines 'iota' as in 'it does not matter one iota' and 'taboo' such as the incest prohibition discussed by Lévi-Strauss and deconstructed by Derrida. But the important point about this word is the combination of 'Io'; the 'I' and the 'O' for 'other' (also Italian for 'I' and the name of the nymph raped by Zeus in the form of a bull). The co-presence of these elements is what is taboo, linguistically, grammatically and psychologically. When *Thru* uses the erotics of the text explicitly it attempts to create a situation in which there is a place for a male 'I', a female 'O', a female 'I' and a male 'O'. Realising, however, that even in a gender re-equilibrating Greimas diagram the diagram interposes itself between its terms rather than uniting them, *Thru* attempts to accomplish its aim by creating an aporia in which the x is removed and the relationship between the terms is undecidable or, to put it another way, retains its mystery.

---

15 And, almost word for word 137–8. Kafelanos (1980: 45) quotes the first part from 96.

We cannot escape *Thru*'s unreliability and ambiguity, or naturalise it by uniting Armel and Larissa as aspects of Brooke-Rose as Kafelanos does. Armel and Larissa are bound together in the text where we will not find a real author, only a conceptual, implied one. Similarly it is not possible for us to unite Armel and Larissa in the reader. The couple remain in the text and it is there that they provide a parallel for the relationship of writer to reader. This second ungendered pair are not, of course, a couple, but we may be able to say that, in the same way that Armel and Larissa are 'a poem', writer and reader may be joined together through the erotics of text in this novel. Although we are aware that in the endlessly deferred pleasure of the text they will never be united, there remains a consolation, too, because they cannot be separated either.

In *Thru* Christine Brooke-Rose challenges the reader with the most sustained disruption of the graphic surface in all the texts we have studied. Such conscious complexity has led to the critical conceit that self-reflexivity is *Thru*'s objective, an idea that colours most interpretations of this text. We have argued that the purpose of *Thru*'s self-reflexivity must also be considered. With the concept of critical rhetoric and the inclusion of critical diagrams, *Thru*'s self-reflexivity demonstrates that critical control of narrative is itself a fiction. By poeticising poetics *Thru* shows narrative dominating and confounding criticism, proving that it is inherently the stronger of the two. But *Thru*'s unconventional narrative delivers something more representational too; it uses the graphic surface directly to create a metatextual mimesis in the mind of the reader. The end result is a metatextual text/reader romance which combines issues of textuality and sexuality and demands literary gender re-equilibration.

References

Ackroyd, Peter (1975) 'Modernist?', *The Spectator*, 235 (7672): 52.
Barthes, Roland (1975) *S/Z*, London: Jonathan Cape (translated by Richard Miller)
Berressem, Hanjo (1995) 'Thru the Looking Glass: A Journey into the Universe of Discourse' in Ellen J. Friedman and Richard Martin (eds), *Utterly Other Discourse*, Normal, Illinois: Dalkey Archive: 104–16
Birch, Sarah (1994) *Christine Brooke-Rose and Contemporary Fiction*, Oxford: Clarendon
Bradbury, Malcolm (1973) *Possibilities: Essays on the State of the Novel*, Oxford: Oxford University Press
Bradbury, Malcolm and Palmer, David (eds) (1979) *The Contemporary English Novel*, London: Arnold
Brooke-Rose, Christine (1958) *A Grammar of Metaphor*, London: Secker and Warburg,
Brooke-Rose, Christine (1971) *A ZBC of Ezra Pound*, London: Faber
Brooke-Rose, Christine (1975) *Thru*, London: Hamish Hamilton
Brooke-Rose, Christine (1976) *A Structural Analysis of Pound's Usura Canto: Jakobson's Method Extended and Applied to Free Verse*, The Hague: Mouton
Brooke-Rose, Christine (1981) *A Rhetoric of the Unreal: Studies in Narrative and Structure, Especially of the Fantastic*, Cambridge: Cambridge University Press
Brooke-Rose, Christine (1984) *Amalgamemnon*, Manchester: Carcanet
Brooke-Rose, Christine (1986a) *Xorandor*, Manchester: Carcanet

Brooke-Rose, Christine (1986b) *The Christine Brooke-Rose Omnibus: Out Such Between Thru*, Manchester: Carcanet
Brooke-Rose, Christine (1989) 'Illiterations' in Elleen J. Friedman and Miriam Fuchs (eds), *Breaking the Sequence*, Princeton: Princeton University Press: 55–71
Brooke-Rose, Christine (1990) *Verbivore*, Manchester: Carcanet
Brooke-Rose, Christine (1991a) *Textermination*, Manchester: Carcanet
Brooke-Rose, Christine (1991b) *Stories, Theories and Things*, Cambridge: Cambridge University Press
Brooke-Rose, Christine (1995) Seminar on *Thru* at the University of East Anglia
Brooke-Rose, Christine (1996a) *Remake*, Manchester: Carcanet
Brooke-Rose, Christine (1996b) 'Remaking', *European English Messenger* 5 (2): 12–17
Brooke-Rose, Christine (1996c) 'Splitlitcrit', *Narrative* 4 (1): 93–107
Brooke-Rose, Christine (1997) 'Is Self-Reflexivity Mere?', *Quarterly West* Winter 1996–7: 230–65
Brooke-Rose, Christine (1998a) *Next*, Manchester: Carcanet
Brooke-Rose, Christine (1998b) Letter to the author (4 February 1998)
Brooke-Rose, Christine (2000) *Subscript*, Manchester: Carcanet
Brooke-Rose, Christine (2002) *Invisible Author: Last Essays*, Colombus: Ohio State University Press
Brooks, Peter (1985) *Reading for the Plot: Design and Intention in Narrative*, New York: Vintage
Brown, Norman O. (1959) *Life Against Death: The Psychoanalytical Meaning of History*, Connecticut: Wesleyan University Press
Campanella, Tommaso (1981) *City of the Sun: A Poetical Dialogue*, Berkeley: University of California Press (translated by Daniel J. Donno)
Caserio, Robert L. (1988) 'Mobility and Masochism: Christine Brooke-Rose and J. G. Ballard', *Novel*, Winter: 292–311
Cohen, Keith and Hayman, David (1976) 'An Interview with Christine Brooke-Rose', *Contemporary Literature* 17: 1–23
Derrida, Jacques (1988) 'Structure, Sign and Play in the Discourse of the Human Sciences' in D. Lodge (ed.), *Modern Criticism and Theory*, London: Longman: 107–23
Derrida, Jacques (1978) *Writing and Difference*, London: Routledge and Kegan Paul
Derrida, Jacques (1981) *Dissemination*, Chicago: University of Chicago Press
Driver, C. J. (1975) 'Text and Context', *The Guardian*, 113 (3): 20
Foucault, Michel (1979) 'What Is an Author?' in Josue V. Harari (ed.), *Textual Strategies*, London: Methuen: 141–60
Fowler, Roger (1989) *Linguistics and the Novel*, Routledge: London
Friedman, Ellen J. and Fuchs, Miriam (1995) 'A Conversation with Christine Brooke-Rose' in Ellen J. Friedman and Richard Martin (eds), *Utterly Other Discourse*, Normal, Illinois: Dalkey Archive: 29–37
Friedman, Ellen J. and Martin, Richard (eds) (1995) *Utterly Other Discourse*, Normal, Illinois: Dalkey Archive
Gasiorek, Andrzej (1995) *Post-War British Fiction: Realism and After*, London: Arnold
Grant, Damien (1995) 'The Emperor's New Clothes: Narrative Anxiety in *Thru*' in Ellen J. Friedman and Richard Martin (eds), *Utterly Other Discourse*, Normal, Illinois: Dalkey Archive: 117–29
Gray, Alasdair (1984) *Unlikely Stories, Mostly*, London: Penguin
Greimas A. J. and Rastier, François (1968) 'The Interaction of Semiological Constraints', *Yale French Studies* 41: 86–105
Harris, Roy (1995) *Signs of Writing*, London: Routledge
Johnson, B. S. (1971) *House Mother Normal*, London: Collins
Johnson, B. S. (1975) *See the Old Lady Decently*, New York: Viking
Kafelanos, Emma (1980) 'Textasy: Christine Brooke-Rose's *Thru*', *International Fiction Review* 7 (1): 43–6.
Lacan, Jacques (1980 [1966]) *Écrits: A Selection*, London: Routledge
Laing, R. D. (1967) *The Politics of Experience and The Bird of Paradise*, Harmondsworth: Penguin
Levitt, Morton P. (1985) 'Christine Brooke-Rose' in *The Dictionary of Literary Biography: British Novelists since 1960* 14: 124–9

Little, Judy (1996) *The Experimental Self: Dialogic Subjectivity in Woolf, Pym and Brooke-Rose*, Carbondale: Southern Illinois University Press

Maack, Annagret (1995) 'Narrative Techniques in *Thru* and *Amalgamemnon*' in Ellen J. Friedman and Richard Martin (eds), *Utterly Other Discourse*, Normal, Illinois: Dalkey Archive: 130–42

McHale, Brian (1987) *Postmodernist Fiction*, New York: Methuen

McHale, Brian (1995) 'The Postmodernism(s) of Christine Brooke-Rose' in Ellen J. Friedman and Richard Martin (eds), *Utterly Other Discourse*, Normal, Illinois: Dalkey Archive: 192–213

Pestino, Joseph Francis (1986) *The Reader/Writer Affair; Instigating Repertoire in the Experimental Fiction of Susan Sontag, Walter Abish, Rejean Ducharme, Paul West and Christine Brooke-Rose*, PhD thesis, Pennsylvania State University

Plato (1946) *Phaedrus* in *Four Dialogues of Plato* (translated by John Stuart Mill), London: Watts

Plato (1951) *The Symposium*, London: Penguin Classics (translated by Walter Hamilton)

Propp, Vladimir (1979) *Morphology of the Folk Tale*, Austin: University of Texas Press (translated by L. Scott)

Reyes, Heather (1995) 'The British and Their "Fixions", the French and their Factions' in Ellen J. Friedman and Richard Martin (eds), *Utterly Other Discourse*, Normal, Illinois: Dalkey Archive: 52–63

Reyes, Heather (1998) *Delectable Metarealism / Ethical Experiments: Re-reading Christine Brooke-Rose*, PhD thesis, Birkbeck, London

Sage, Lorna (1992) *Women in The House of Fiction: Postwar Women Novelists*, London: Routledge

Sage, Lorna (ed.) (1999) *Cambridge Guide to Women's Writing*, Cambridge: Cambridge University Press

Sage, Lorna (2001) *Moments of Truth: Twelve Twentieth Century Women Writers*, London: 4th Estate

Showalter, Elaine (1977) *A Literature of Their Own: British Women Novelists from Brontë to Lessing*, Princeton: Princeton University Press

Sterne, Laurence (1985 [1759–67]) *The Life and Opinions of Tristram Shandy, Gentleman*, London: Penguin Classics; (1997) London: Penguin Classics

Stevens, Wallace (1965) *Selected Poems*, London: Faber

Tew, Philip (2001) *B. S. Johnson: A Critical Reading*, Manchester: Manchester University Press

Waugh, Patricia (1984) *Metafiction: The Theory and Practice of Self-Conscious Fiction*, London: Methuen

White, Glyn (2002) ' "YOU ARE HERE": Reading and Representation in Christine Brooke-Rose's *Thru*', *Poetics Today* 23 (4): 611–31

CHAPTER 8

Alasdair Gray: 'Maker of books'

Critical interest in the work of Alasdair Gray has consistently exceeded that in Johnson or Brooke-Rose. Since Gray's first novel, *Lanark: A Life in Four Books* (1981) there have been three critical works devoted to him, and no survey of contemporary Scottish literature is complete without an essay on some aspect of his work. In fact a wider awareness of Scottish writing followed the publication of *Lanark*, and Gray's success has helped, inspired and influenced the works of James Kelman, Iain Banks, Agnes Owens, Janice Galloway and Irvine Welsh and others (see Williamson 2002: 182).

Since *Lanark* Gray has published five more novels: *1982, Janine* (1984), *The Fall of Kelvin Walker* (1985), *McGrotty and Ludmilla* (1990a), *Something Leather* (1990b), *Poor Things* (1992), and *A History Maker* (1994). There have also been five volumes of short stories, a sixth shared with James Kelman and Agnes Owens, a volume of poetry, a short autobiography, two versions of a polemic, a play and the mammoth *The Book of Prefaces* (2000) edited by Gray. Almost all of these works are designed and illustrated by Gray, with graphic and typographic devices used in most of the fiction and more traditional graphic material appearing throughout in the form of illustrated frontispieces and title pages. Phil Moores's (2002) bibliography usefully records the details of Gray's various volumes and shows why Gray is justified in describing himself as a 'maker of books' (Gray 1990c: 140), and John Sutherland states that: 'Where other novelists write fiction Gray creates books' (1996: 22a).

The presence of the book in prose fiction is fully acknowledged by Gray, and this attitude greatly widens the effects that he can produce, the levels he can generate and the perspectives he can create without ceding power or control to illustrator typesetter or publisher. 'Work as if you were in the early days of a better nation' – the phrase is stamped on the hard covers of several of Gray's books – illustrates perfectly his recognition of the book as artefact. Such embossed or metalled designs form one aspect of his work that cannot be carried over from hardback to paperback, and no other novelist has done more to utilise this surface, which is usually seen as the bookbinder's province. Illustrated designs and, more often, phrases are repeated on Gray's hard covers but their exact nature is unpredictable. The hardback of *Mavis*

Belfrage: A Romantic Novel (1996) repeats the title on the spine and features the motto 'Independence' on front and back covers but underneath two small boxes of text tell us: 'I CALL THIS BOOK A NOVEL SINCE MOST READERS PREFER LONG STORIES TO SHORT / UNDER THE PAPER JACKET I ADMIT THIS BOOK SHOULD BE CALLED – TEACHERS: 6 SHORT TALES'. The 'I', just like the 'goodbyes' that are the last words to be read in (almost) all Gray's texts, claims the entire book for the author as his own product.

However, while nearly always noted and praised, even in negative reviews, Gray's illustrations and design mean something only supplementary to the texts' inherent literary originality for most critics. For the casual critic the role of typography and design are usually simply explained by Gray's past employment as an artist, while more ambitious critical work on Gray tends to produce separate essays on his different areas of endeavour. The collection *The Arts of Alasdair Gray* (Crawford and Nairn 1991) through its title, cover and interior illustrations recognises the importance of Gray's art to his writing but perpetuates the division of writer and artist by having one essay 'Alasdair Gray, Visual Artist' (Oliver 1991: 22–36) stay with Gray's fine art output and then allowing the other essays to concentrate on Gray as a man of letters alone. The most recent collection, *Alasdair Gray: Critical Appreciations and a Bibliography* (Moores 2002) contains a lively essay 'Art for the Earlier Days of a Better Nation' (King 2002: 93–121) which recognises Gray's work as designer and illustrator, but only in order to argue that his artistic talents would be better employed on large-scale murals. It remains true that Gray's combination of skills as designer, artist *and* writer are never united in critical work on him, despite the fact that his work features illustration, text and typography as though they were all part of the same palette and equally valid within the compass of the term 'book'. My project here is to show how the whole of this palette is readable and I shall be discussing how the graphic devices and illustrations function within Gray's fiction. This will necessarily require disentangling or developing some existing interpretations and misinterpretations. I will attempt to do so using *Lanark* as an example.

Although *Lanark* and many of Gray's other texts contain large sections of writing that may be described as traditionally representational, Gray is con- sistently labelled as a postmodernist writer.[1] This brings him international attention despite the fact that the author himself has made clear on several occasions his dissatisfaction with the term; 'I have never found a definition of postmodernism that gave me a distinct idea of it' (Axelrod 1995: 111). This

---

1 Gray's realistic mode can be seen in Jock McLeish's central confession in *1982 Janine*, 'Report to the Trustees of the Bellahouston Travelling Scholarship' in *Lean Tales* (1985), *The Fall of Kelvin Walker*, much of *Something Leather*, 'Houses and Small Labour Parties' in *Ten Tales Tall and True* (1993) and the tales contained in *Mavis Belfrage; A Romantic Novel* (1996) and *The Ends of Our Tethers* (2003).

kind of carping is unlikely to get him out from under the label, as other writers have found, particularly when it seems the product of an international consensus.[2] However, the critical amorphousness of the term 'postmodernist' isn't very productive. The most common misinterpretation of the graphic devices in Gray's novels is that they are signifiers of postmodernist play (whether this is seen as positive or problematic) and nothing more. This is an easy way for critics to move past them, but the perpetuation of such facile responses seriously undervalues devices which are a fully functioning aspect of Gray's work. Typography, graphic devices and illustrations are vital to *Lanark*; they tie its dual narrative to craft and visionary traditions going back to Blake and beyond him to the first flowering of the printed book in the Renaissance, and newly articulate these traditions in a late twentieth-century historical context. The result is a novel that shows a breadth of use of the graphic surface but which is not to be critically judged or characterised by it.

Lanark: A Life in Four Books (1981)

Lanark, a large (561 pages) and complex novel, has been included in discussions of Scottish literature, urban writing, science fiction and postmodernism. The last of these terms is most problematic, especially if we follow Fredric Jameson's description of postmodernism as 'an alarming and pathological symptom of a society that has become incapable of dealing with time and history' (1983: 117). While Gray's work shows many stylistic indications of postmodernism, not least a playful tone, he is very far from being 'incapable of dealing with time and history'. The themes of *Lanark* are in fact time, history and politics to the extent that, in some of the novel's literalised metaphors, time becomes the currency of politics. That the city of Unthank has lost track of its time and history is the very weakness that allows its enemies to plot its destruction. Such large-scale awareness of history and time is contrasted by Duncan Thaw's arguments with his father in which he contends that the world needs 'a memory and a conscience' (*Lanark*, hereafter *L*, 296; all editions in English use the same pagination). Thaw sees the past as a reminder of wrongs that cannot, and should not, be forgotten: 'the past ... is the only inevitable part of the universe. No government, no force, no God can make what has been not have been. The past is eternal and every day our abortions fall into it: love affairs we bungled, homes we damaged, children we couldn't be kind to' (*L* 337).

The reasons why the novel's emphasis on time and history may drop into

---

2 There is published work on Gray from Germany, where all Gray's work has been translated, Italy, France, Spain, the United States of America and Canada.

the background of critical studies of this novel are familiar by now (see Chapter 4): stylistic evidence of postmodernism is taken as evidence of a particular outlook incompatible with dealing with time and history. At some point all reviewers and commentators have to confront the fact that *Lanark* is a novel that 'even looks different' (Murray and Tait 1984: 219), and such responses recur. For example, Randall Stevenson notes Gray's involvement in the packaging of his texts and argues that this is typical of 'postmodernism's ludic urge to take fiction and imaginative play beyond their usual limits. Gray also achieves this in another way, by including in his novels so many icons and drawings, complexly related to a text which is itself often transformed by alterations of typeface or unconventional typographical layout' (1991: 55). But Stevenson chooses not to (or is unable to) interrogate or explain the complex relationships between text and form that he acknowledges here. Our objective in this chapter is to do so, and, through this examination, to draw out how the use of the graphic surface in *Lanark* both reflects and binds together the self-reflexive and political elements of the text. Understanding what may be frequently identified as simply ludic allows us to see how the use of the graphic surface is capable of creating thought-provoking perspectives and dynamic contexts for the reader which are essential in interpreting the artefact *Lanark* fully. In order to read *Lanark* in its own terms, not as a demonstration of other concerns, we must pay attention to its typography, page layout, illustrations and unusual structure.

Perhaps *Lanark*'s most striking device is the unconventional non-numerical, ordering of the four books of the subtitle. The books appear in the sequence 3, 1, 2, 4.[3] This arrangement is clearly accomplished through graphic means. It is announced on the elaborate Table of Contents, and supported by separate title pages for each (*L* 1, 119, 221, 355). While this might be passed off as simply a device to 'foreground the order of reading' (McHale 1987: 193) its key role is in complicating the relationship between the central character(s), Duncan Thaw and Lanark, who would otherwise seem to develop, one into the other, in the numerical ordering of the books.

This can be illustrated through a chronologically arranged version of story, or *fabula,* of the novel which is summarised in the recollections of the central character, three chapters from the end (*L* 517–18). Because of the ordering of the books the reader has previously had a very different perspective, having read these events in a greatly fragmented way. We can best show how plot, or *sjuzhet,* differs from *fabula* in *Lanark* if we insert into our quotation the numbers of the chapters (which *are* numerically presented throughout, 1–44) in which the events referred to occur:

---

3 Even the four-volume edition (2001) preserved the order by having Volume 1 contain Book 3, Volume 2, Book 1 etc.

First he had been a child [12–14], then a schoolboy [15–20], then his mother died [19]. He became a student [21–7], tried to work as a painter [27–9] and became very ill [26, 29–30]. He hung uselessly round cafés for a time [1–6], then took a job in an institute [8]. He got mixed up with a woman there [9–11], lost the job [10], then went on to live in a badly governed place [31–4] where his son was born [37]. The woman and child left him [39], and for no very clear reason he had been sent on a mission to some sort of assembly [39–40]. This had been hard at first [40–1], then easy, because he was suddenly a famous man with important papers in his briefcase [41]. Women loved him [41]. He had been granted an unexpected holiday with Sandy, then something cold had stung his cheek [41]

Complicating the issue still further is the fact that Lanark's rude awakening, and this reevaluation of his life appear at the end of chapter 41, but take place after the events described in the first half of chapter 42. *Lanark's* blatant presentation of *sjuzhet* over *fabula* is seen by critics as either as a prompt to try and make sense of the text in a more traditional way or as a postmodern rejection of traditional form. Both these responses need to be examined.

In 'Private Confession and Public Satire in the Fiction of Alasdair Gray' Douglas Gifford seeks to unify the lives of Thaw and Lanark and find a traditional realistic 'explanation' for the text's non-numerical arrangement.[4] His attempt thus 'begins' with Book One, but in the attempt to 'read the events of Book Three and integrate them easily into the 'realism' of Books One and Two' Gifford discovers a contradiction or paradox: 'Either Lanark is a flawed personality with whose hallucinations we sympathise or he's a trustworthy guide through a sick society' (1987: 112). The strain which this paradox puts on Gifford's hypothesis becomes too much during the course of Book Four which 'awakens the reader's questioning with a vengeance' and eventually 'throws the reader's holistic awareness of the novel into total disarray' (1987: 113). In other words, Gifford's attempt to understand Books Three and Four as hallucinations of a sick Thaw simply won't stand up. As Penny Smith says: 'the text as a whole strains against such consistency' (1995: 117). The text does allow us to see Lanark's adventures as Thaw's literary afterlife; one which allegorically demonstrates the sociopolitical structures that dictated Thaw's failure to find happiness. The author figure in the Epilogue, Nastler, plainly promotes something similar: '"The Thaw narrative shows a man dying because he is bad at loving. It is enclosed by your narrative which shows civilization collapsing for the same reason"' (*L* 484). The epilogue's annotator also suggests a precedent in Flann O'Brien's *The Third Policeman* (*L* 490).

---

4 This essay informs 'Author's Postscript Completed by Douglas Gifford' in the Canongate Classics edition of Gray's *Unlikely Stories, Mostly* (1997).

Gifford, however, is not interested in Nastler but is determined to seek Gray, the author, through the text rather than to deal with the text in itself. Gifford's belief (1987: 102) that in his fiction 'Gray ... essentially performs a recurrent act of personal confession, which is simultaneously disowned and denied by its context of trickery, allegory, or other formalisation' has some biographical validity (Gray shares with Thaw a wartime childhood and an art school education) yet by taking this for authorial intention Gifford fails the text. By seeing so much of the text as 'trickery, allegory, or other formalisation' that obscures autobiography, Gifford ignores or downplays much of what is so distinctive about the novel.

Gifford does recognise that there are larger perspectives to *Lanark* when he describes it as an attempt to 'make the private nightmare of a flawed human, a human nevertheless of intelligence and sensitivity, into the global nightmare of the human race' (1987: 111).[5] However when he continues: 'He [Gray] wants to combine therapeutic autobiography with satiric social analysis' there is a problem. Such autobiography as there is in *Lanark* is simply a part of the fictional biography of the central character and is subsumed by narrative: it is the interpretation made by the reader that is important. When Lanark is being built up as a viable delegate to the international conference in Provan, Sludden comments on Lanark's attempt to write (which he at first encouraged then dismissed) during their time in the Elite café: 'Lanark, to his credit, produced one of the finest fragments of autobiographical prose *and* social commentary it has been my privilege to criticize' (*L* 464, emphasis in original). Lanark's writing (chapter 3) was only the first of these; it is Sludden who notes its political potential (when it is convenient for him to do so). The social commentary and the politics of the novel are the reader's to construct as metatext on the basis of the text as a whole. Our interest in *Lanark* cannot be what we might be able to glimpse of the author (though this is a metatext we habitually construct), but must be what we can make of the relationship, created by the novel's discourse, of the central character and his environment, in relation to our own circumstances.

In 'Is Eating People Really Wrong? Dining with Alasdair Gray' George Donaldson and Alison Lee take Thaw/Lanark as one life but examine the significance of its fractured *fabula* and what effect this might create for the reader. Significantly Donaldson and Lee place *Lanark* in the genre of *bildungsroman* in which:

> the hero's errors educate him or her until his or her personal knowledge of order accords with that of the reader or narrator. The moment of resolution in such a novel is therefore also a guarantee of political order, for the hero's discovery of what the reader and narrator already know at

---

5 I agree with Gifford's contention (113) that in these terms *1982, Janine* is 'Gray's masterpiece'.

once restores the hero to the knowledgeable community, while substantiating that community's knowledge. (Donaldson and Lee 1995: 158)

Lanark, however, is something more than a *bildungsroman*. The Thaw narrative alone covers the more typical span of that form. *Lanark: A Life in Four Books* extends its narrative to offer a full fictional biography; it does not stop with the suicide that closes Duncan Thaw's *bildungsroman* but continues into Lanark's adulthood and old age. Arnold van Gennep's study of cultural rituals *The Rites of Passage* suggests a typical sequence that might be undergone in a full life: 'rites of pregnancy and delivery ... rites at adoption, puberty, initiation, marriage, enthronement, ordination, sacrifice, and funeral rites' (van Gennep 1960: 182–3). Nevertheless, Donaldson and Lee's point about the disruption of readerly expectations holds good, as does the significance of the relationship between these expectations and the society within which they are perceived. All the transitions of Lanark's life are consistently thwarted or undercut as he fails to integrate into his society. In this way the non-chronological *sjuzhet* of *Lanark* becomes politically motivated:

> *Lanark*'s ... subversion of these ingrained expectations directs the reader to question the character of the power that enables this order to appear natural. The question itself is largely political but its expression is formal, for the novel begins not by posing a question about how a hegemony naturalizes itself but rather by inverting some conventions of narrative power and authority. Here, the reader is not discursively superior to Lanark; time is not linear and so experience seems less obviously a journey towards a self-evident, pre-existing destination. The power of form to create and maintain authority and the formal means through which that same authority may be undermined are at the paradoxical heart of *Lanark*. (1995: 158–9)

This process, this calling into question of authority, is properly linked to the reader here. By placing Thaw's life between sections of Lanark's, the progress of the life is disrupted and the non-chronological structuring of *Lanark* exposes a good deal more than just the conventional structure of the *bildungsroman*, carrying the text into conflict with the conventions of the larger society in which it is written. The way that this functions is partly, as Donaldson and Lee argue, to do with the expectations of genre but more particularly to do with context established within the text. This is where the two 'halves' of the text come into play, play in more than the ludic sense, beyond one half simply mirroring the other.

While he is at odds with other members of his society, the central character undertakes three quests to try and make his own existence meaningful; the first occupies Duncan Thaw's adolescent life, the second takes place when Lanark and Rima are a couple, and the third Lanark undertakes for the sake of his son Alexander and Greater Unthank. His quests for meaning are at once rejections of conventional values and replacements from within; i.e. his own versions of them. Only Lanark's quest for sunlight is not an abject failure, though that success is pitifully brief.

The combination of disrupted chronology and disrupted literary form is important because the structure doubles it: lives and quests are thwarted in the text just as the non-numerical structure disrupts our generic expectations. Marie Odile Pittin argues that what holds the four books of *Lanark* together is 'a complex network of cross-references, be they thematic, structural or formal. These act upon both plots in turn, thus attributing a third meaning to the whole' (1996: 199). The reader is the repository for such ambiguities created in the rub between contradictory (but not mutually exclusive) information supplied by the text. Thus the comments about time in Books One and Two have a resonance for the reader who reaches them by way of Book Three that they would not possess if the link were made in reverse, but chronological, order. Similarly, instead of dragonhide representing Thaw's eczema (if the books appeared in Gifford's preferred order), we have the dragonhide disease already established in Book Three and can note that Thaw's eczema is like (but not equivalent to) it. Cairns Craig terms the two characters 'hypotypes of one another, a hypotype being an empty "type", one whose significance is unknowable until it is fulfilled and completed by another narrative' (1999: 182). Such metatextual readings may not be reduced to strictly allegorical correspondences nor confined to a general overview: they operate between the two main narratives to create perspectives and context for each other as Stephen Bernstein argues: 'That the two lives are conjoined is the subtitle's point, leading most readers to look for ways in which these two lives might comment upon one another' (1999: 36). The characters inhabit different but significantly similar worlds, in which there is one location that links all the books of *Lanark*: the Necropolis (see Bernstein 40–4). Together the lives of Thaw and Lanark produce an amalgam; interdependent during reading, they are parallels *and* continuations of each other. This reflective space between versions, accounts and viewpoints appears in the majority of Gray's other novels; *A History Maker, Something Leather* and *Poor Things*. It is created by establishing different perspectives from which to view the narrative. In *Lanark* this is the task of the Prologue.

The Prologue (*L* 107–17) occupies the crossover point or hinge between the Lanark and Thaw narratives. It contains the auto-narration of the life of the oracle, once a financier only interested in the certainties offered by numbers ('Compared with his phone number our closest friend is shifty and treacherous' *L* 108) who fades out of existence to become a disembodied voice. The oracle's role is to tell Lanark (and the reader) the story of Thaw in what forms Books One and Two. This arrangement creates a situation where the

Prologue can announce Books One and Two as an origin to Book Three yet simultaneously present them as a continuation of Book Three's narrative. In this scheme the narrative circumstances established in the Prologue, with Rima and Lanark listening to the oracle, continue as metanarrative throughout Books One and Two. Thus, although the oracle's tale within the Prologue might seem fairly self-contained, it establishes a narrative situation in which the interrelationship of Thaw and Lanark is exposed from multiple perspectives.

The relatively ambiguous status of the oracle makes reducing or rationalising the relationship between the character Lanark and the oracle's narration of Thaw's life more difficult than if their stories were simply placed side by side. When first detected, the voice of the oracle is 'sexless and eager but on an odd unemphatic note, as if its words could never be printed between quotation marks' (L 104). At one level this justifies a typographical necessity; otherwise, by convention, every paragraph of Books One and Two would need to begin with quotation marks. At another level we can account for it as an example of mimesis, since when the oracle speaks his 'voice sounded so far inside the head that the story seemed less narrated than remembered' (L 117). The removal of quotation marks from the oracle allows his narrative to be seen as an auto-narrated memory of life as Thaw which is actually drawn out of Lanark. Yet no matter how close we get to Lanark's thoughts we are always told them rather than receiving them direct or by free indirect discourse.

We can see this distancing at the bottom of page 186 when Thaw's asthmatic breathing crisis is rendered as a stream of incoherent words and gasps that conveys a breathlessness to the reader. The effect is simply achieved with a lack of punctuation:

> He clenched his fists against his chest and dragged breath into it with a gargling sound. Fear became panic and broke his mind into string of gibbering half-thoughts that would not form: I can't you are I won't it does it will drowning in no no no no air I can't you are it does ... (L 186, ellipsis in original)

The framing of this directly mimetic effect, the way that the unpunctuated clause follows colon and narrated explanation, keeps Duncan's experience in the safely distanced third person.

Even so, the oracle seems sometimes to function more like a medium than a narrator. His voice changes in regard to the subject of its narration: when it begins Thaw's story it is 'in the voice of a precocious child', while when telling his own it is a 'male, pompous elderly voice' (L 104, 105). Later it is clear that Rima has heard something entirely different since she says: 'In the first place the oracle was a woman, not a man. In the second place her story was about me' (L 357). This information implies that the reader has thus only been receiving what Lanark heard, and this puts them closer to him than the more conventional mimetic assumption that the reader is merely listening in from a distance.

Discovering that Rima has heard something different from Lanark and ourselves is likely to get us checking back to see if Rima didn't at some stage comment on Thaw's story. There is an 'Interlude', featuring Lanark, the oracle and Rima, between these two books (*L* 259) which the contents pages tell us is 'to remind us that Thaw's story exists within the hull of Lanark's'. We are nudged in a similar way when Lanark interrupts the oracle at the beginning of the last chapter of Book Two (*L* 350–1). However, in none of these pauses does Rima say anything that is not attributable to her hearing her own story. Janice Galloway argues that: 'Gray's writing … is informed by a democratic urge that does not sell women short: he knows our version of the story is different, possibly even opposed, but of equal force' (1995: 195). The significance of other voices, such as the one Rima hears, but which are largely 'inaudible' to readers and central character, might seem negligible, but it is important in reminding the reader of 'hidden' voices at work in this text structuring it and focusing it. A closer examination of the novel's graphic surface will allow us to discover more of these voices later, but the Prologue is also a mechanism for delivering the Thaw narrative within Lanark's, and through this device *Lanark* generates powerful metatexts from their interrelationship. A significant role is played in this generation by the graphic surface and by the physical book which literally bind Lanark and Thaw together. The worlds of Thaw and Lanark are built of the same materials.

The graphic surface of Lanark

Lanark is a text which is emphatically conveyed to us by the typographical unity of a book. It is this physical medium as much as anything which places the Thaw/Lanark narratives side by side. In discussing the typography of *Lanark* it is necessary to point out that it was first published by Canongate of Edinburgh, a small publishing house, which accepted Gray's offer to design the book and its cover (see Axelrod 1995: 114). The technology of photo-typesetting means that subsequent editions by different publishers, even if of slightly different size, use the same pages settings to print from. Thus the choice of typeface, Garamond, and the proportions of the text area in all British editions originate with Gray (see also Craig 1999: 191–2).

We shall now pay specific attention to the typographic consistency of the text, noting that this consistency applies equally to the fantasy and realistic narratives. Across the novel several general conventions are followed but there is also an extensive system of internal conventions using italics, bold type, capitalisation and various combinations thereof. Additionally we shall see alterations to typesize, changes of typeface and rearrangement of page layout all used to enhance the representational 'vocabulary' of the typography in *Lanark*.

Emphasis

The most basic level of typographic variety within the text, and the most straightforward, is the conventional italicisation of the titles of books in *Lanark*. We can see examples on page 52: '*Oor Wullie's Annual for 1938 … No Orchids for Miss Blandish … The Holy War*' and again for Mr Thaw's reference works on page 160. Song titles are similarly treated on page 187.

Italics are also used, as is relatively common in fiction, to emphasise particular words or phrases which are stressed during speech. *Lanark* features this device throughout the text, for example, '*daylight*' (*L* 4), '*days*' (*L* 5), '*you*' (*L* 412). This emphasis operates as a cue for understanding the lines, but also suggests that an actual spoken voice is being mimed by the printed dialogue. Italics also indicate when foreign languages are used (e.g. *L* 407).

Capitals are sometimes used, like italics, for emphasis of speech but with the added connotation of artificiality. This may be in terms of inappropriateness as when young Duncan Thaw attempts to refer to the authority of the 'ENCYCLOPAEDIA' in his dispute with the midden-rakers (*L* 127). In the circumstances its status as an 'unnatural' book-learned word is made clear and earns Thaw nothing but ridicule. A near parallel to this occurs when Lanark is about to take on the mantle of Provost and he is interviewed by Sludden's tame journalists:

> 'I wonder if Provost Lanark would care to say something quotable about what he is going to *do* at the Provan assembly.'
> After thinking for a while Lanark said boldly, 'I will try to tell the truth.'
> 'Couldn't you make it more emphatic?' said the reckless man. 'Couldn't you say, "Come hell or high water I will tell the world the TRUTH"?' (*L* 464–5)

In this case the capitalised word is as hollow as 'ENCYCLOPAEDIA' but it is ironic because so is the strength of the 'TRUTH' Lanark is taking to the assembly. He will not be heard; no one is interested in the dossiers on the suffering of the working classes, only in the mineral wealth that there might be under Unthank. On page 547 the Multan admits that Lanark speaks the truth but also understands that the word and what it stands for have no power, because 'three or four big boys run the whole show'. So in this way typography, the capitalised emphasis, signifies how hollow the word is. As the Multan says, 'Words by themselves are no good', and this is true however large we might write them, or however loudly we might say them.

While academic conventions dictate that indents without quotation marks will be used for lengthy quotations, *Lanark* keeps the quotation marks and uses bold type to indicate spoken quoted material as, for example, when Lanark reads from *The Holy War* (*L* 82), and from *No Orchids for Miss Blandish* (*L* 83). When the words are only read, as for example the passage from Hume (*L* 161), there are no quotation marks, only the bold type. Since the typefaces of these sources are unlikely to be in bold in any edition, the bold text is not representationally motivated and the use of this type clearly emphasises the borrowed status of these words.

Bold type is used in a second way in *Lanark,* to indicate something about volume. During the performance of Brown's Lugworm Casanovas (*L* 403–4) amplified voice and, to some extent music, is rendered in bold. The music is capitalised too ('**BAWAM**'). Similarly on page 446 a loudspeaker message is rendered in emboldened small caps which indicate its artificially increased volume but tonal constriction.

Extended speech which is *not* dialogue is rendered differently again. There are two examples where it is double-indented, Sludden's broadcast on pages 448–53 and Monboddo's speech to the conference on pages 537–46, and one where it is centred and in italics, the robotic secretary's minutes on page 551. These devices function to emphasise the different form of these discourses; the difference between dialogue and monologue. The blank space may be seen to invite our commentary, or, more directly, to represent that which is excluded by such monologic discourse.

So far our examples have mainly indicated a hierarchy of discourses within *Lanark,* but we have already seen elements that have an impact upon the expressive range of the text, particularly in representing sound (speech emphasis, music volume). These might be extended if we think that spoken quotations, and foreign words also sound different to the normal run of speech. However, the representational vocabulary of typography in *Lanark* expands further as we begin to consider *visual* motivations for typographic choices.

Evidence

In interview Gray has pointed out that the italic is 'a type based on hand-writing rather than Roman chiselling' (Axelrod 1995: 111). *Lanark,* like the majority of other novels, is in roman face rather than italics. Roman text, named after the inscriptions of the longest-lived European empire, is the writing of the state and governs that of the individual. Within this context sustained italics indicate handwriting.[6] Our first example is the beginning of Lanark's short autobiography on page 15: '*The first thing I remember is*'. This eventually forms the beginning of Lanark's short first-person narrative which is to be read in roman text as 'CHAPTER 3. Manuscript'. Other examples of

---

6 Gray uses this distinction throughout his work. In *Poor Things,* for example, the letters which report the central part of the narrative are both rendered throughout in italics (1992: 77–98, 105–89).

handwritten/italic passages within the text are Thaw's prayer (*L* 187), extracts from his diary (*L* 190, 236), his attempts to construct aphorisms (*L* 250), his mother's unsent letter to *Reader's Digest* (*L* 203) and Rima's 'Dear Lanark' letter (*L* 457). This is graphic mimesis: the form of the typography is altered to more clearly represent handwriting, though it remains typography.

Further examples of graphic mimesis include the bold type used to represent the visual appearance of other 'found' text within *Lanark* more accurately than that taken from other books. On page 399 the snatches of mausoleum inscriptions which Lanark reads are emboldened, perhaps to indicate depth of carving:

'... His victorious campaign ...'
'... whose unselfish devotion ...'
'... revered by his students ...'
'... esteemed by his colleagues ...'
'... beloved by all ...'

The pomposity of these inscriptions (removed from specificity) relates to the bourgeois values of those Victorians wealthy enough to build mausoleums. This strand is taken to its limit with the ridiculous commemorative plaque Thaw comes across on his last day:

Upon
THIS SPOT
King Edward
had lunch after stalking
28th August, 1902

This plaque is treated similarly to the mausoleum inscriptions but arranged as though centred on the stone itself. This device further ridicules the content of the plaque by taking it out of context, making page 353 of *Lanark* THIS SPOT where King Edward lunched. Between them these examples form a strong contrast to the memorial of James Nisbet, a presbyterian martyred for refusing the official prayer book in 1684. Part of the 'slipshod verse' on Nisbet's memorial is quoted on page 336:

As Britain lyes in guilt, you see
'Tis asked o reader, art thou free?

We might justify the lack of emboldening for this text by explaining that this is quoted by Thaw in dialogue (i.e. the 'source' is not visual), but equally we might consider the relative status of the inscription makers. Continuing his monologue about Scottish rebels and memorials, Thaw talks about Hardie, Baird and Wilson, three Glasgow weavers executed in 1820 for turning out for the merest suggestion of a general revolution in the panic that followed Peterloo, the accession of George IV and the Cato Street Plot. Thaw suggests that such struggles for enfranchisement and choice were acceded to only when 'the government realised it could give the vote to almost everyone without losing power' (L 337). Yet Nisbet's question still remains. Its contrast to the deeply-incised roman inscriptions of the perished great and good and ruling monarchs is, if we notice it, a telling one.

The use of graphic emphasis to represent a supposed visual source also applies to representations of graffiti. We see this in Drummond's studio (L 283) and in the Cathedral (L 402) and in the streets of Unthank (L 434). That most of these cases are capitalised may be attributed to emphasis, but I think we could equally suggest that capitalisation represents a 'faithful rendering', or a reminder, of the form in which the 'originals' appear. The changes of typeface to something more readable at a distance, for example when the book lays open, gives an effect of graffiti within the text.

Capitalised text is in fact most often used in Lanark to suggest a fictional source by appearing to mimic it. Thus we see the content of posters recorded in capitals: 'YOU HAVEN'T MUCH TIME – PROTEST NOW' (L 42); 'JUST BECAUSE YOU'RE PARANOID DON'T THINK THEY AREN'T PLOTTING AGAINST YOU' (L 519); placards (L 373); and signs of all types. There is a directory of names in the institute (L 64), and signs for 'OUT OF ORDER' (L 92) and 'EXECUTIVE GALLERY' (L 472). Signs for 'INQUIRIES' appear twice (L 205, 435), following an earlier '**ENQUIRIES**' (L 20). There is also a 'faithful' recording of the damaged sign for pedestrian underpass (L 393). In each case the change of form in the type suggests an 'exterior' source, an actual referent, and this applies to both the Thaw and Lanark narratives. By appearing to refer to specific visual qualities, the text bolsters the reference implicit in text.

Finally capitalisation is used to represent (not reproduce) the display typefaces from adverts. The first example is the 'BEAUTY PLUS STAMINA' slogan which accompanies the image of blonde girl in Greek armour advertising 'Amazon Adhesive Shoe Soles' who fascinates Duncan Thaw (L 135). Later, in Book Four (L 432–4, 454), there is a series of adverts both capitalised and emboldened, for example: '**QUICK MONEY IS TIME IN YOUR POCKET – BUY MONEY FASTER FROM THE QUANTUM EXPONENTIAL**'. The typography here is used to create an impression of the 'loud' (in the Information Theory sense *and* brash and capitalistic) environment of Greater Unthank. This gains effect from the arrangement of the type on the page: another poster shows that the 'volume' of advertising is not innocent:

ADVERTISING OVERSTIMULATES,
MISINFORMS,
CORRUPTS.
If you feel this, send your name and address
to the Council Advertising Commission and
receive your free booklet explaining why we
can't do without it.

The centring of this 'ad' takes its textual representation one step further by alluding to a different kind of textual layout. It puts the preceding ads (many but not so individualised) into perspective: a great blur of words and demands that the citizen cannot escape.

The sinister use of advertising comes strongly into play with the 'cryptic names' seen on sides of trucks on Lanark and Rima's way to Unthank. Presented in this way, these names are used to signal the component entities of 'the creature': 'QUANTUM, VOLSTAT, CORTEXIN, ALGOLAGNICS' (*L* 389). These names can be deconstructed. Algolagnics, relates to 'algolagnia' an early term for sadomasochism. Conversation with Timon Kodac of Algolagnics reveals the company's interference in politics (based on Joseph Conrad's *Nostromo*): 'Of course we weren't called Algolagnics then; that was the old Material Interest Corporation. Boy what a gang of pirates *they* were!' (*L* 508). The previous company name would also share an acronym with the Military Industrial Complex. Quantam relates to a company specialising in the sale of time, and their adverts relate very closely to a liberalisation of Benjamin Franklin's metaphorical pronouncement, 'time is money'. Cortexin, a combination of cortex and toxin, make biological components, in particular artificial brain matter. Volstat, suggesting the electrical measurement 'volt', actually combines *vol*, French for steal, with 'state', conjuring Proudhon's dictum, 'all property is theft'. Such interpretation is not what is intended by the advertisers who use the authority implied in the volume and intensity of their typographic form to resist piecemeal interpretation. Later in the text these names hybridise and combine, indicating the confusing hydra-like character of the corporate creature.

As we have repeatedly seen, *Lanark* uses typography to distinguish *and* mime implied sources. This mimetic principle comes into play whenever the textual source of a quotation, fictional or actual, has a typical form markedly different from that of *Lanark* itself. The small size of the type used in the quotation from the *1875 Imperial Gazetteer of Scotland* about the Monkland Canal (*L* 278) is typical of nineteenth-century reference works. Similarly, quotations from newspapers, whether the *Evening News* or *The Glasgow Herald* (*L* 326–8) or the institute's *Western Lobby* (*L* 371–2, 416–17), are given headlines and presented on the page occupying the width of a newspaper column.

There are two examples in *Lanark* where concern for accurate description of fictional printed material has extended to the inclusion of a different typeface. The new typeface is easily identifiable as sans-serif. This more modern typeface is used for the magazine titles Thaw sees in an office during a job interview (*L* 206). The suggestion here is of the alien world of work, of specialist publications, typographically distinct from Thaw's experience which is related to us in a serifed face. A similar feeling of alienation applies in the more significant example of the programme to the conference in Provan (L 474–6). It is, however, an alienation which is in sympathy with the character rather than an alienation for the reader in response to a change of the form of the text. Parts of the sans-serif programme are in bold and capitalised text, and the layout of its pages differs from the conventional layout of the novel. So many altered details seem to reproduce the programme as Lanark might read it, if there was a programme, if there was a conference, if there was a Lanark. Yet typographically the text continues to set evidence before us.

This is pushed a degree further in the 'Epilogue'. To gain access to this chapter Lanark enters a door that looks rather like a chapter opening and finds himself in a room filled with a forest of easels bearing painted images of the room itself. In the room Lanark encounters a character he has been told is a local king but who turns out to be his author, Nastler.[7] The text attempts to show us that Lanark is indeed somehow at a level above himself, one in which he can see where he has been written:

> With a reckless gesture he [Nastler] handed Lanark a paper from the bed. It was covered with childish handwriting and many words were scored out or inserted with little arrows. Much of it seemed to be dialogue but Lanark's eye was caught by a sentence in italics which said: *Much of it seemed to be dialogue but Lanark's eye was caught by a sentence in italics which said:* Lanark gave the paper back asking, 'What's that supposed to prove?' (L 481)

Lanark's reading lights upon a description of his actions and there seems to be an almost perfect equivalence of action and text. Alison Lee states: 'The chapter is, in fact, being created through the very process of reading as is pointedly revealed by [these] lines which both Lanark and the reader read' (1990: 111). The process of reading thus seems for a moment simultaneous with the 'action' in the text. But 'we' do not quite coincide with Lanark. The sentence appears twice: once to describe Lanark's actions; once to describe what he sees (and we recognise) which must be the second appearance of the sentence. This has the result of making our order of reading somehow seem wrong. Though the italicised second sentence seems to be the one he reads, it has to be in his world already for him to read it and therefore somehow precedes him.

There is further oddity here: we are told that the page is handwritten, containing a sentence 'in italics'. Now, as we have seen, italics often represent handwriting, but italics are not handwriting.[8] In handwriting we tend to use

---

7 The name 'Nastler' may be a corruption of Alasdair, with an added suggestion of 'nasty', but it is important to keep in sight that Nastler is only Lanark's author, not *Lanark's* author, Gray.

8 There is a calligraphic italic script and there was an influential movement towards italic handwriting in education from the 1930s (see Sassoon 1999: 71–3, 112–20).

underlining for emphasis. Thus there is a double move towards mimesis here. The italic versions of typefaces are more like handwriting (and, as we have seen, this is reflected in the textual world of *Lanark*), but the handwritten sentence which Lanark reads is already in italics: therefore the italicised sentence imitates its supposed source twice over as handwriting *and* as italics. The text tries to guarantee its own representation here but, since it can't actually deliver handwriting or handwritten italics, it can only really acknowledge that it is at a remove from its own fictional reality.

'And what's that supposed to prove?' Lanark is right to ask.

If this graphic device proves anything it is that *Lanark*, the book, is made of print, and that, however representational, mimetic or realistic the text is, print simply can't reproduce handwriting, childish or otherwise, let alone dialogue.

In the dialogue on pages 484–5 the conjuror explains to Lanark:

> 'Everything you have experienced and are experiencing … is made of one thing.'
> 'Atoms,' said Lanark.
> 'No. Print. Some worlds are made of atoms but yours is made of tiny marks* marching in neat lines, like armies of insects, across pages and pages and pages of white paper.'
>
> *This is a false antithesis. Printed paper has an atomic structure like anything else. 'Words' would have been a better term than 'print' being less definably concrete.

The note attached to the word 'marks' is footnote number 4 in *Lanark*. In it Sidney Workman, the Epilogue's annotator character, misses the point. Print is quite accurate. The atoms which make the print are not of Lanark's world at all. Workman's alternative, 'words', is far too slippery; for words may be print or sound. In fact, the means by which Workman's footnote itself functions depends on print, not words, and the use of the page as a graphic space.

This conclusion moves us to see Lanark's world as one which is entirely print. But Lanark cannot see it and continues to live his life as if it were real. Here is a reminder that reader and character approach the typography that mediates their contact from opposite sides. They are, however, fellow travellers through what it describes and, for the reader, all locations in Lanark's narrative are places in the book, whether they exist in reality or not.

Signs and places

The capitalised rendering of signs which we have seen above extends to the 'EMERGENCY EXIT' notices which Lanark and Rima encounter on the door at the edge of the intercalendrical zone (interior 376, exterior 378, 381). The representation of this sign goes beyond graphic mimesis and effectively constitutes an important textual location. When Lanark and Rima find themselves back at the outside of this door after trying to move away from it they

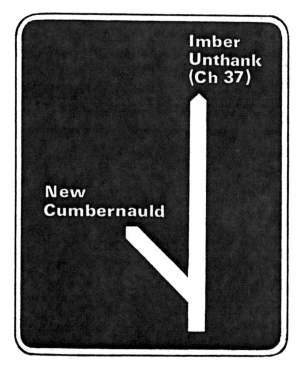

Figure 8.1: Fictional road sign from *Lanark* 385

are disconcerted. The reader, too, experiences a moment of confusion. Although as readers we can turn back to the pair's previous visit to the door to check on the identicality of the signs (or the number of the door), within the linear 'reality' of the narrative we have returned to the same place. Even though as a location the door is multiple for us, as a device it works very well because, like Lanark and Rima, we, too, are confused by the door's reappearance (we have already read past that device). The nature of this effect (a momentary confusion) forms a link (or ties in to the existing link) between the reader and the character, Lanark. The brief confusion created is closer to our experience of 'confusion' than the word 'door' is to what we grasp from that signifier in relation to any specific 'door'. Thus the device functions mimetically at a metatextual level.

The visual representation of signs or notices is taken further with the images of road signs that Lanark and Rima see on the way to Unthank (*L* 385, 391) The presence of the 'road signs' themselves, while exceptional, is, however, clearly mimetically motivated. For example, the first sign is introduced in the following way: 'There was a thirty-foot-high road sign on the grassy verge'. The simple black and white image which follows and its reversed typography (white 'on' black) is as easily and quickly read as real road signs (Figure 8.1). The fact that what appears at first to be a road number on the signs is in fact a chapter reference shows a different aspect of metatextuality here. These images seem to present the reader with the same options which face the characters, yet only Unthank is labelled as associated with a particular chapter. The other directions, 'Imber' and 'New Cumbernauld', are literally nowhere. When Rima's flirtation with the truck driver seems to be leading them to Imber it is disconcerting for the reader. Both the plot and his or her passage through the book seem in jeopardy since the reader is dependent on the character's choice, not their own. Lanark's shout *'We're going to Unthank!'* (389) indicates the certainty of their destination and strengthens his bond with the reader. Chapters work for the reader but not for the characters, and signify much as road numbers do; not in and of themselves but as aids to getting to a destination.

This overview of the text is significant. In the Epilogue the text is hemmed in by the marginal Index of Plagiarisms that purports to reference alphabetically all the authors from whom Gray has plagiarised. I have discussed the complex and spurious entry of criticism into the text in the guise of critic 'Sidney Workman' elsewhere (White 2000). It suffices to say here that critical source-spotting is pointed out as a reflexive bind by the three references within the index that generate an endless loop from 'Black Angus' to 'Macneacail, Aonghas', to 'Nicholson, Angus'. However, the Index is not simply a playful trap for the unwary; to a certain extent *it is what it says it is*. It doesn't provide us with page references to plagiarisms but directs us to them by way of chapter and paragraph. Once we grasp that a paragraph in *Lanark* is that which is separated from the text above and below it by a line space we can find, for example, the blockplag from Hume in 'Chap.16, para.9'. This invitation to revisit the novel in a non-linear way reveals that, while Lanark cannot grasp that his world is contained in a book, there are agencies that know this very well.

The Prologue, discussed earlier, is an important step in the process of making us aware of this voice which is explicitly aware of the graphic surface in *Lanark*. The new voice appears graphically as a difference in page design from the previous chapters. Instead of simply telling us chapter number and title in capitals as they have done up until this point (*L* 108), on left and right hand pages respectively, the bold, lower-case running heads above the text now form descriptive sentences. The appearance of variable running headers in the Prologue requires us to think about the status of this material. In most modern texts such running heads never impinge on our awareness to the extent that we can identify them as a voice: where used they are generally characterless, conventionally recording the name of the author and the title of the book or chapter title. Throughout most of *Lanark* they follow this pattern with chapter number on the left-hand header, and chapter title on right-hand header. But in the Prologue we can read the headers across each double page spread in sequence so that they make up a poem:

> **A Bleak Man Tells Why He Likes Bleakness**
> **It Seems a Strength but Proves a Weakness**
> **When Every Body is Withdrawn**
> **There's Nothing to Fall Back Upon**
> **Returning to His Sensual Birth**
> **A Splendid Body Gives Him Worth**
> **A Reckless Body Gives Him Worth**
> **But Not Enough to Make Him Well**
> **Can Lanark Lead Him Out of Hell?**
> **Can He Help Lanark Out of Hell?**

The relative self-containment of this 'poem' almost counteracts Genette's statement that such paratextual material will 'make sense only to an addressee who is clearly involved in reading the text, for these internal titles presume familiarity with everything that has preceded' (1997: 294). The last two headers do, however, link the Prologue's narrative strongly to Lanark's. Although in the narrative the oracle doesn't actually claim to be in Hell, his existence as a disembodied voice is very much like limbo. In fact, in this regard the oracle resembles Gloopy, in his institute form: his body has been used as food by the institute and his 'voice and feelings and sense of responsibility' have also been 'cannibalised' to provide a voice-operated lift service (L 86).

The use of disembodied voices generated by characters, remnants of characters and narration leads us to speculate on where the additional voice provided by the variable headers comes from. Since the headers refer to the oracle in the third person, it would be difficult to assign them to him. A further piece of evidence that the oracle is subsidiary to the structuring of the text could be the fact that he attempts to start Book One on pages 104–5, but, being interrupted by Lanark and having supplied his own story, he has to repeat them at the beginning of Book One on page 121. However, the oracle does refer the reader back to an earlier part of the text when Thaw journeys over the same countryside: 'Consider him passing along the route described at the start of Book One, Chapter 18 only he dozes most of the way and gets out at Glencoe village' (L 351). This use of the form of the book tends to disrupt our perception that what we are receiving (i.e. a textual account of Thaw's life) is the internalised voice of the oracle working on Lanark's memory – suddenly it has chapters. But Lanark himself doesn't refer to this advice, merely suggesting, after another long sentence describing the hostel where Thaw's father now lives, that the oracle 'Leave out the local colour'. The reference to a specific chapter suggests that the oracle has some metatextual awareness, but perhaps it extends only as far as his own narration. It is clear, however, that for the reader the text has chapters, and that only some privileged characters (in this instance the oracle but also Nastler and Workman in the Epilogue) share this awareness.[9]

I think, turning back to the Table of Contents, that we might be able to suggest that running heads and contents issue from the same source; one that deals in page numbers, chapters and summaries, and which therefore conceives of the narrative as a book. The voice of the Table of Contents page shows us the non-sequential ordering of the books and provides a descriptive sentence about each of the equally displaced Prologue and Epilogue and the Interlude. Its overall knowledge of the text seems complete: it names Thaw and Lanark and the Epilogue's annotator, Sidney Workman, and it would also seem to be responsible for the naming of the chapters.

The amount of control exerted by the Table of Contents and headers is clearly significant. A chapter title such as 'CHAPTER 19: Mrs. Thaw Disappears' indicates how this voice conceives of the book as an overall unit and plays up the subtleties of the links between its sections (the internal books). The voice of the Table of Contents, distanced from the prose, arranges the text, setting up the complexity of the Thaw/Lanark relationship and at the same time presenting a reading experience that works across the whole novel as a complete unit.

The relationship between the narrative and the illustrations which appear in it is a use of the graphic surface we have not yet had to consider.

Illustrations

In *Lanark* there are five illustrated pages: the frontispiece and the title pages to each of the four books. The first critic to pay sustained attention to these elements of the text was Alison Lee in her *Realism and Power: Postmodern British Fiction*, which uses the title page to Book One of *Lanark* as its own cover.

Lee refers particularly to the frontispiece. The imagery of this page includes an industrial city, a female figure eating apples from a tree that seems to grow from her body, a hand reaching from some waves to grasp the sun, a mutated whale (or Leviathan) suckling an embracing human couple, an enigmatically observing female and a self-dissecting male figure resting on a stack of books upon which also sit two skulls with baby angels inside. Lee notes that 'the drawing of a drawing [the self-dissecting man] drawing itself (both of which emanate from an open book which is resting on three other open books) signals the auto-referential structure of the novel' (1990:104).

---

9 The oracle says: 'The only things I'll try to leave out are the repetitions, and I'll probably fail' (105). The insertion of the chapter reference would thus visibly gloss the oracle's inefficiency and might indicate that the Prologue has been edited by another textual voice.

However, the stack of books might also represent the novel's intertextuality (or non-auto-referentiality), or to show that texts allow us to dissect ourselves. I agree with Lee that Gray's illustrations have a distinctive and important part to play in the impact of the novel but I would like to take issue with her statement that 'The illustrated title pages ... exert tremendous control in shaping the way the reader reads the text' (1990: 103–4). I do not believe in 'the tyranny of the visual image as a mimetic device' or that the illustrations affect the reader in a controlling, dominating or enclosing way (1990: 99).

The frontispiece in the paperback edition is different from that in the hardback which Lee uses and reproduces in her book (see Figures 8.2 and 8.3). The difference between the two can be seen most easily by looking at the year placed centrally at the bottom of the image. In the hardback '1981' version the name of the publisher, Canongate, and the place of publishing, Edinburgh, feature prominently. In the paperback editions for Panther and Paladin, both imprints of Collins, the date is 1982 and the publisher details are replaced with the text's subtitle and dedication to Gray's son Andrew. This rearrangement of text within the frontispiece is accompanied by some changes to the form of the leviathan, the background and the juxtaposition of elements. Perhaps the most significant loss is that of the descriptive sentence 'With allegorical titlepages imitating the best precedents'. This statement parallels the idea behind the Index of Plagiarisms in the Epilogue by suggesting that the illustrations are in some measure plagiarised too (as indeed they are).

I would also like to to take issue with Lee's statement that the illustrations in *Lanark* 'have two prose equivalents: the paintings created by Duncan Thaw and described in prose, and the Epilogue which, because of its complex typography, imitates in prose images what the title pages do in visual ones' (1990: 103). I am not convinced that the Epilogue (*L* 479–99) is composed of 'prose images'. If we look at the admittedly complex typography of the Epilogue as blocks of text, it is much less complex than any of the title pages. Even the diagonally fragmented and multiple-voiced 'Ministry of Voices' in *1982, Janine* doesn't get close to the complex imagery of the frontispiece. Essentially this is because, pictorially, typography has no depth. If we look at the Epilogue in terms of the graphic marks at the level of letters then it is more complex, but so would any page of text from the novel. Surely neither of these explains 'prose images'? The term suggests it might refer to semantic images drawn from the text by the reader – the Epilogue has many, mostly conjured by Nastler – but this is not what Lee means either.

The grounds for Lee's assumption that images are somehow 'more real' than text becomes clearer when semantic images are referred to as abstractions:

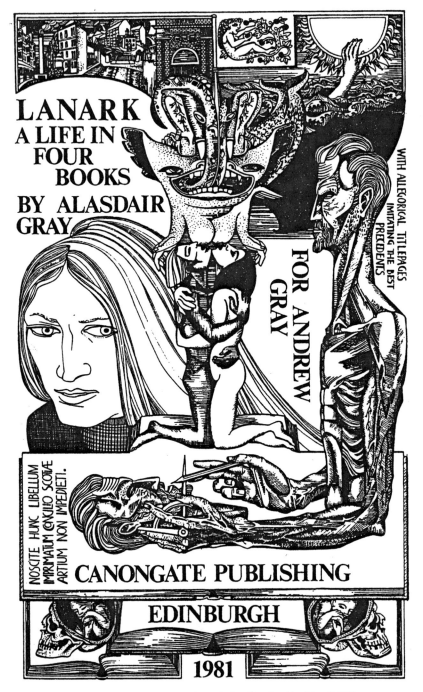

Figure 8.2: Frontispiece to *Lanark*, first (hardback) edition (1981)

Figure 8.3: Frontispiece to *Lanark*, first and subsequent paperback editions (from 1982)

Like the phenomenon of the 'movie of the book' (or worse, the mini-series), these images make abstractions concrete, and in this way encourage a Realist reading of the relationship between the visual images and the prose. They create the illusion of a one-to-one correspondence, as though the images capture an external 'reality' which is then mirrored in prose. Or that, juxtaposed with the prose the illustrations become the 'reality' that language represents. (1990: 107–8)

At its simplest level this is just a sophisticated version of the contemporary prejudice against illustrations in novels, especially those for adults. But clearly Lee believes that prose itself cannot actually represent, or perform mimesis. We may compare the representational situation described here to the complex examples of typographical mimesis we have discussed above. We have suggested that *Lanark* posits a fictional 'reality' which typography can't reproduce but can imitate. But *Lanark*'s prose doesn't imitate its illustrations, nor do the illustrations straightforwardly depict the content of the prose. Lee forgets the vital term 'allegorical' from the frontispiece here (*OED*: 'Description of a subject under the guise of some other subject of aptly suggestive resemblance'). The phrase 'the best precedents' and the use of Latin within the illustrations invoke classical scholarship back as far as the Renaissance or the printed book itself. Lee notes the use of Hobbes's *Leviathan* and the figure of the state as a giant man (which is based on Andrew Crowe's original 1651 frontispiece), but it doesn't seem possible that such allegorical forms (even if the reader has no knowledge of the philosophical references) could be seen to make a 'one-to-one correspondence' with any part of the text. If the reader is to make connections between illustrations and text it is, I think, with an awareness that the interrelation is more complex and less direct than the one Lee suggests.

What can we see in the illustrations that seems to be direct representation? When Gray puts Melancholia and Atlantis on to the globe in the title page for Book Three (Figure 8.4) they are not as Lee suggests 'literalized in images' and provided with 'single meaning, a truth, which is then imposed on the prose' (1990: 109). If we look closely at the globe we see that the lands are a version of a familiar globe and that Africa and Asia are clearly and correctly labelled. Melancholia represents the continent of Europe. The glum, shoeless angel who inhabits this land, sitting behind the Balkans with his feet extending into France, is a figure influenced by Albrecht Dürer's etching 'Melancholia II'. Atlantis is North America and its illustrated occupants, the Statue of Liberty and a stegosaurus, give it a comic historical perspective. The only clues we have (eventually) to this nomenclature being imposed on the prose is in the announcement of the arrival at the Provan assembly of Governor Vonnegut of West Atlantis (*L* 473), which is as likely to suggest an intertextual reference rather than internal correspondence. Similarly, the one

Figure 8.4: Title page for Book Three of *Lanark* (page 1)

sided-discussion a drunken Lanark has with Timon Kodac of South Atlantis (507–8) does provides us with enough intertextual clues to equate South Atlantis with South America but the impact on our reading, if noticed, is liable to be slight. The effect of these palimpsest locations is not to fix meaning for the prose but to show a parallel to the process of map-making (a theme drawn out by Bernstein, 1999: 35–58) referred to in the novel's closing lines:

> **I STARTED MAKING MAPS WHEN I WAS SMALL**
> **SHOWING PLACE, RESOURCES, WHERE THE ENEMY**
> **AND WHERE LOVE LAY. I DID NOT KNOW**
> **TIME ADDS TO LAND. EVENTS DRIFT CONTINUALLY DOWN,**
> **EFFACING LANDMARKS, RAISING THE LEVEL, LIKE SNOW.**
>
> **I HAVE GROWN UP. MY MAPS ARE OUT OF DATE.**
> **THE LAND LIES OVER ME NOW.**
> **I CANNOT MOVE. IT IS TIME TO GO.**

The context in which the globe appears, held aloft by a female 'Magistra Vitae', puts it into a similar perspective as an attempt to balance, to map out, the relationship of the other elements of the image: truth, experience, providence, death, oblivion, good and bad fame. The less than technical map also refers to the Renaissance tradition and the tendency of map makers to fill in areas of ignorance.

On the title page for Book One (Figure 8.5) we might take the faces in the foreground to be those of Thaw, his mother and his sister Ruth, though if we compare Gray's cover for *Lean Tales*, a collaboration with James Kelman and Agnes Owens, it becomes apparent that the male figure is a portrait of a young James Kelman. In the background we see a flooding city that may well be Glasgow since the pillars between which the flood gushes are inscribed with Glasgow's motto 'Let Glasgow Flourish' with the extension 'by Telling the Truth'. Later in the text, when Unthank is flooded, we can retrospectively use the image to associate, or reinforce the textual association of, Glasgow and Unthank, explicitly cued, for example, when Nastler describes Unthank as 'rather like Glasgow' (*L* 483). This illustration literally combines the two narratives, but the scene we are shown, a young Thaw and family in Glasgow during a flood, never happens.

The title page to Book Two (Figure 8.6) shows a large group watching a dissection taking place in classical architecture. We can link this to Thaw's being allowed to draw in the university dissection room and his morbid awareness of human anatomy. But the scene itself is quite closely based on a Renaissance engraving, itself much copied: 'An Anatomical Dissection being carried out by Andreas Vesalius', title page to Vesalius' *De humani corporis fabrica* anatomical manual (1543). As in the case of the borrowings from Dürer's *Melancholia* and the Hobbes mechanickal man frontispiece, the best

Figure 8.5: Title page to *Lanark* Book One (119)

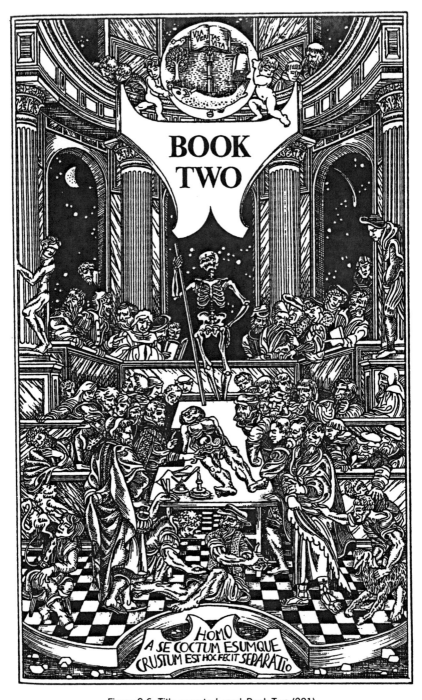

Figure 8.6: Title page to *Lanark* Book Two (221)

precedents are used, but the 'intertexts' are early book engravings rather than texts or textual incidents from *Lanark*.

We might understand the title page of Book Four (Figure 8.7) as a west to east view across the centre of Scotland taking in both Glasgow and Edinburgh and showing above and below the forces which govern that tract of land. Above is the giant crowned figure wielding sword and crook which are labelled symbols of force and persuasion (see also Figure 8.5). The figure is composed of ranks of smaller beings; marching men form the arm carrying the sword, a preacher and many kneeling figures form the arm with the crook. The figure's neck seems to be made of ladies-in-waiting while a circle of bowler-hatted men connects the arms to the head keeping separate the less regimented figures of the lower torso. In the lower section of the page 'force' is represented in four panels which contain respectively a truncheon, police headgear, the army and tanks in the streets. 'Persuasion' is represented by a legal document, academic and legal headgear, the classroom and the industrial production line.

The image of this title page is probably clearer on its own than in its narrative position between the end of Thaw's life and the beginning of Lanark's journey back to Unthank. The forces delineated in the title page are not particularly visible in Thaw's life and the surreal world of Book Four obscures direct references. However, there is a considerable amount of politics involved in Lanark's brief job in 'social stability', his appearance before the Committee, his sudden rise to Lord Provost, his attendance of the Council assembly, and his imprisonment by the police. He also meets grown-up Jimmy MacFee, a mohome producer, and his own grown-up son, Alexander, now an army officer, involved in the battle for Unthank. But it is only retrospectively that we can make such links. The visual information gained from the illustrations doesn't 'happen' in the same way that the prose does and somehow seems to be stored in a different mental archive. The title page illustration certainly does not 'control' or 'shape' our reading because, as readers, we have enough on our plate.

It is at a conceptual, metatextual level that our readings of text and image intersect and we might be able to apply Lee's third and most general option for the link between the two: 'images juxtaposed with prose become the "reality" that language re-presents' (1990: 108). However, I suggest that the only way to equate images and text in *Lanark* is in terms of the word 'context' in its largest sense of 'The connexion or coherence between the parts of a discourse'. All is context or part of the contexture: 'the connected structure or "body" of a literary composition'.

In 'Alasdair Gray, Visual Artist' Cordelia Oliver includes excerpts from an interview in which Gray discusses the division between painting (standing for visual imagery) and writing:

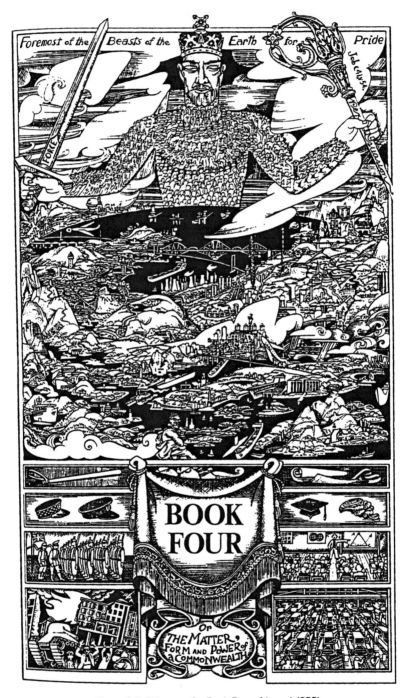

Figure 8.7: Title page for Book Four of *Lanark* (355)

The difference is that writing, or drama for that matter, operates through the medium of time, whereas painting and sculpture operate through the medium of space. But one implies the other, and painting, after all, abides contemplation. (Oliver 1991: 103)

The second sentence seems to be an attempt to minimise the difference implied by the first. Pittin puts it more strongly: 'the visual arts present us with a content that can be identified in a short time span as well as in a non-linear mode, thus virtually annihilating the notion of time' (1996: 203).[10] The contemplation of painting Gray mentions would seem to be non-linear, but then ultimately our understanding of a text is non-linear; we rearrange *sjuzhet* into *fabula*, we construct a chronology for the narrative piecemeal from different parts of the linear text.

Lee's assertion that 'Language ... allows for greater abstraction than do visual images' is correct, but we must bear in mind that this is a difference in degree and not absolute (1990: 109). It is clear that a verbal image of Thaw's mural in the text will be less precise, more open to interpretation, than a visual impression of it. But this is to assume that there is a visual image to which a verbal image of it is secondary, i.e. to fall into a naive realist approach. Conversely it is not so easy to say that a visual image of something which exists in primary form as prose is any more true or accurate than the verbal image. The difference is the perceptual system whereby we apprehend the subject. Because we generally apprehend the world directly through vision we are inclined to take image as closer to 'reality' than prose, but artificial images are secondary modelling systems just like prose. Might we not reach an equally good concept of 'a chest of drawers' through the printed phrase as through an illustration? A black-and-white drawing might specify a number of drawers but a mental visualisation from the words is likely to suggest a colour and a number of drawers in the absence of specific inform-ation. In both cases the information is hardly complete or finalised. We need to take into account that the economy of perception accommodates the economy of representation.

This is something Lee recognises with regard to the verbal representa-tions of Thaw's paintings. Throughout her reactions to these prose images a parallel to the verbal work, the novel itself, is possible: 'Thaw envisions such a multitude of possibilities that he cannot limit himself to a single, finished work. He is constantly re-interpreting and re-working every image that he paints' (1990: 110). And again: 'The mural cannot be conceptualized or cate-gorized and thus cannot be accorded a single authoritative meaning' (1990: 111). But even when Gray offers an image that clearly parallels Thaw's

---

10 The quoted sentence is supplemented with the odd proviso: 'This is an intellectually interesting principle for postmodernism though not literally applicable to fiction writing.'

mural, such as the embracing couple from the Frontispiece who resemble the mural's Adam and Eve, or a reproduction of a similar painting as on the dust cover of volume 3 of the four-volume 2001 edition, or even when we see reproductions of Gray's own mural from Greenhead Church (Oliver 1991: 27), the parallel image does not deliver a single authoritative meaning. Any pictorial image is only 'Thaw's mural' as much as the words 'Thaw's mural' and the description of it are the thing in the prose. Thaw is a fiction, his mural is a fiction and any image we give to his fictional mural is a fiction of our own.

The illustrations in *Lanark* do not exert tremendous 'control' over the reader's interpretation, they simply complicate the issue. They do not explain the prose nor are they explained by it. In the same way that Lanark and Thaw provide a context for each other so do images and text provide contexts for each other. They might be described as mutually illuminating but 'control' is wrong: if one dominates the other, it is the sheer weight of prose that must be more significant, even if a picture is worth a thousand words. We simply cannot 'read' *Lanark* by looking at the pictures. The significance of the illustrations is as much or as little as the individual reader allows them but even then it does not belong to the illustrations themselves but is produced in the interplay in the mind of the reader between prose and image. Like Christine Brooke-Rose's vertical text in *Thru*, *Lanark*'s illustrations are narrative 'continued' by other means, which challenges the reader to synthesise the additional content.

Simultaneous correspondences

In the previous section we have seen that through its individual typographical conventions and exceptional visual devices *Lanark* unites its disjunctions and generates dynamic contextual perspectives for the reader. We have also seen in earlier sections that the novel contains several voices such as the oracle, the Table of Contents and Sidney Workman which also contribute to the perspectives on offer. The coherent graphic surface of the novel presents all these perspectives and viewpoints simultaneously as an array of metatexts for the reader to investigate as best suits them whether it is linear, chronological or intertextual (through the Epilogue). But *Lanark*'s metatextual interplay applies not only to larger units like the books and the characters; it also involves units smaller than the sentence and generates a situation in which *Lanark* is on occasions haunted by itself. In the 'body' of the institute, with its gusting, circular, and circulating corridors, Lanark hears: 'bodiless voices conversing against the clamour' (*L* 64), and fragments of what these bodiless voices say are recorded:

'... glad to see the light in the sky ...'
'... frames were shining on the walls ...'
'... you need certificates ...'
'... camels in Arabia ...'
'... annihilating sweetness ...'

Other such voices in corridors of the institute appear on pages 62 and 72. In a sense the bodiless voices all follow the model of the echoes which Duncan Thaw hears in Glasgow Art School (*L* 213), but the point about these particular bodiless voices is that these lines are spoken elsewhere in the text, with bodies, with context.

Only the first of the fragmented voices in the passage from page 64, quoted above, the last eight words of the regular text (*L* 560), is unattributed prose. The last of the five fragments will be read again as the last words in Book Two, describing the death of Thaw (*L* 354) and is thus narrated by the oracle. In this case there is the possibility of Lanark remembering the 'annihilating sweetness' that closed Thaw's life, but we cannot explain Lanark also hearing the last line of his own life. Since many of the other fragmented lines will appear again, in context, in Books One and Two, the possibility that these fragments represent Lanark remembering life as Thaw remains in play until the very end of the text, but ultimately a linear chronological explanation is refused by this device.

Such echoes don't apply only to the retrospective account of Thaw's life; there is a similar effect linking the teenaged Thaw with Lanark in the intercalendrical zone (see Bernstein 1999: 39). Page 181 describes Thaw convalescing at a hotel in rural Scotland and, from outside, overhearing 'the conversation of two people in an adjacent room. One speaker was excited and raised his voice so much above the steady drone of the other that Thaw almost heard the words: "... ferns and grass what's wonderful about grass ...".' The ellipsis around these words makes them resemble the disembodied voices in the institute corridors and eventually these words recur as dialogue between Lanark and Rima. In fact, in the distorting world of the intercalendrical zone, this dialogue occurs twice. It *happens* on page 384: '"And Rima, here's ferns and grass." / "What's wonderful about grass?"' but it is prefigured on page 381: '"... here's ferns and grass ..." / "What's wonderful about grass?"' These cross-references, minute in the scale of *Lanark*, seem to me to be quite important. They can be seen to indicate a fracturing of time, showing that moments in the lives of Thaw and Lanark are simultaneous. These latter examples cannot be explained as fragmentary memories of the character because by chronological order or by linear development the floating reference precedes the one fixed in the text. These cross-references illustrate that *the whole book* is in some sense simultaneous. Pages 181, 381 and 384 all exist at the same time: we could, if we chose to, read them in any order. This device hints at and allows us to glimpse the simultaneity of *Lanark*, rather than insisting upon it, but such devices are more than a demonstration of the form of the novel: they engage the reader in the problem of interpreting textual phenomena across the novel (outside *fabula* and *sjuzhet*) and, in so doing, demand we seek out and connect the echoing phrases.

Returning to the sequence of phrases between the deaths of Lanark and Thaw, we find that the second fragment '… frames were shining on the walls …' comes from a tale told by blind Mr Coulter about his working life helping his father framing and hanging pictures for the houses of the rich (*L* 172). The frames shine because they are reflecting sunlight, which Lanark searches for in Unthank, and they are only to be seen in such glory because Mr Coulter has opened the front door to allow the light in. Thus briefly the Coulters' work is democratised.

The phrase '… you need certificates …' is spoken by Thaw's father, imploring his son to apply himself to his upcoming secondary education so that he will have an economically sound future. He goes on 'I had no certificates. The best I could become was a machine minder in Laird's box-making factory. During the war of course there was a shortage of men with certificates, and I got a job purely on my abilities' (*L* 147–148). Thaw's impression of such a future is 'absolutely repulsive' yet he conforms to it, and is shortly taking Latin instead of French because of a combination of peer, parental and institutional pressure.

The phrase '… camels in Arabia …' comes from Mrs Thaw's definition of a 'caravan' which, as she tries to explain to her young son, was her childhood vision of the trees atop Cathkin Braes (*L* 131). This is an early glimpse of Duncan's mother as an imaginative person in her own right. Later, through a chance encounter on a bus, she is to be remembered to him by an old friend of hers as 'a wild one', a heartbreaker, taking different men to the opera on successive nights. Finding her sheet music and looking at her wedding photograph, 'Thaw could think of no connection between this lively shop girl full of songs and sexual daring and the stern gaunt woman he remembered' (316). The link between his father's concern for certificates, the crushing of Mrs Thaw's liveliness and Mr Coulter's epiphanic moment of job satisfaction is the economic drudgery of working life, and specifically that required by those who have children to support. Mr and Mrs Thaw's anxieties over the fate of their son are essentially about whether some good will come of their sacrifices, whether their son might be better off than themselves and so avoid their struggle. Thus parental success is (self-) measured in economic terms and both parents are given cause to question this (*L* 136, 194).

The gathering of these phrases, which will require a rereading to track them all down, suggests that we should read them in their 'original' context with especial interest and supply interpretation which the oracle's account does not provide. In other words we are asked, at a metatextual level, to question the values which Duncan Thaw is being made to conform to. Context for such questioning is provided by the world that we find Lanark in. The relationship between the two characters' environments, while ambiguous, is productive especially in economic and historical terms. The council leader, Lord Monboddo, uses the Provan conference to assert that 'There are no villains in history. Pessimists point to Attila and Tamerlane, but these active men liquidated unprofitable states which *needed* a destroyer to release their assets' (*L* 542). Here Monboddo links real-world figures to the history of Unthank's world, making them share a history even as he gives that history his own peculiar gloss. He later admits 'I fear I have angered almost everyone here by a too cynical view of history. I have described it [history] as a growing and spreading of wealth' (*L* 544). This summation does not fit with what Lanark has seen of despair and poverty in Unthank, but then Monboddo's definition of wealth turns out to be 'a surplus of men'. This view of men as economic units rather than individuals reminds us of Mr Thaw's advancement, despite his lack of certificates, when there was a 'shortage of men' during the war. The effect of combining Mr Thaw's naive use of economic terminology and Monboddo's view, which we are meant to understand as cynical, is to remind us of Thaw and Lanark's awareness of the usage this 'surplus of men' is put to. Doing research for his painting of the Last Supper Thaw

> used the underground railway where passengers faced each other in rows and could be examined without seeing to stare. Folk nearer the river were usually gaunter, half a head shorter and had cheaper clothes than folk in the suburbs. He had not seen the connection between physical work, poverty and bad feeding before because he came from Riddrie, an in-between district where tradesmen and petty clerks like his father lived. (*L* 245)

This awareness becomes increasingly a consciousness of the injustice of this situation, which Thaw cannot forgive: 'No kindly future will ever repair a past as vile as ours' (*L* 295).

When Eva Schtzngrm sends Lanark to the Provan conference she includes 'a social report cuffering all the olt ground— no region our size has so much unemployment, uses so much corporal punishment in schools, has so many children cared for by the state, so much alcoholism, so many adults in prison or such a shortage of housing. It is all very olt stuff but people should be reminded' (465). The text does not claim that the same is true of Glasgow, or Scotland, but the parallel between Unthank and Glasgow suggests that these are at least real problems in a real world, and that they are of long standing because such issues are regularly ignored by centralised powers which have no interest in the lives of the working class.

Lanark's name, however, adverts to alternative; a localised, democratic British community: Robert Owen's industrial development at New Lanark that functioned between 1800 and 1828. A forerunner of socialism, Owen wanted to establish self-sufficient communities between five hundred and three thousand in size which would be mainly agrarian but which would possess the most up-to-date machinery and would form unions embracing the world.[11] This enlightened concern for the working classes is clearly anathema to a representative of centralised power such as Monboddo.

While Thaw's father imagines 'a *real* civilization' in 'another couple of centuries' Thaw responds: 'Yah, I'm sick of ordinary people's ability to eat muck and survive. Animals are nobler. A fierce animal will die fighting against insults to its nature, and a meek one will starve to death under them. Only human beings have the hideous versatility to adapt to lovelessness and live and live and live while being exploited and abused by their own kind' (295). The submissive attitude of the oppressed which Thaw condemns is illustrated more clearly in Lanark's interview with the 'maker' MacFee. When Lanark intimates that the present disruptions stem from a council attempt to 'liquidate' Unthank, MacFee responds: 'Christ, that isn't news. We've known that for ages in the shops! "Alright," I said, "Let the place die as long as my weans are spared." But you bastards are really putting the boot in now, aren't you?' (L 454). The idea that ordinary people 'eat muck' for the sake of their children has previously been exemplified by the sacrifices made by the Thaws. And when in his last, suicidal trip, Duncan cannot bring himself to disrupt his father's new life, it is an acknowledgement that he cannot continue to draw on the reserves of the elder generation: 'The quiet interior has a completeness, a calm contented polish, which Thaw feels should not be touched. He can break it, not add to it' (L 351).

'Man is the pie that bakes and eats himself'

It is in the political context outlined above that we may understand the recurrent use of the phrase 'Man is the pie that bakes and eats himself' within *Lanark*. The phrase is clearly voiced three times; once by Monsignor Noakes (L 101), once by Grant the shop steward (L 411), and once by Duncan Thaw in an asthmatic delirium (L 188). In the former two examples the full quotation is 'Man is the pie that bakes and eats himself and the recipe is separation', whereas Duncan's childish version is 'Men are pies that bake and eat themselves, and the recipe is hate'. It appears also as an anonymous fragment in a sequence of 'cross-references' on page 62. Gray's illustration 'Portrait of Lanark author in media res circa 1967' (Figure 8.8) provides some

11 Lanark, county town of Lanarkshire, made a Royal Burgh by David I of Scotland, has strong nationalist credentials, too: it was the home of William Wallace.

PORTRAIT
OF LANARK
AUTHOR
IN MEDIA RES
CIRCA 1967

Man is the lie that before & eats its self,
& the recife is admiration.

Figure 8.8: Alasdair Gray, portrait of Lanark author in media res (1967)

extra-textual support for the significance of the phrase in that this is all that we see 'the author' write (in other words this phrase stands in for the text) and his disembodied head that stares back at him from his writing desk begins to interpret it literally. Coming from at least three different mouths and in several variations, this phrase belongs to none in particular. Instead it colours our reading of the whole novel and plays an important role in defining our perception of the political concerns therein.

This image of auto-cannibalism represents 'man's' struggles with other men to provide for himself. The image is nearly literalized in the institute menu, including Enigma de Filets Congalés, made from the sponges or 'softs' cases. In much the same way, less literally, the institute uses terminal dragonhide cases which explode or 'turn salamander' as energy sources.

The origins of this process are ancient. In *The Marriage of Heaven and Hell* William Blake exposes the process by which the few govern many and justify it.

> The ancient Poets animated all sensible objects
> with Gods or Geniuses, calling them by names and adorning them
> with the properties of woods, rivers, mountains, lakes, cities, nations,
> and whatever their enlarged & numerous senses could perceive.
> And particularly they studied the genius of each
> city & country, placing it under its mental deity.
> Till a system was formed, which some took ad-
> vantage of & enslav'd the vulgar by attempting to
> realize or abstract the mental deities from their
> objects; thus began the Priesthood,
> Choosing forms of worship from poetic tales.
> And at length they pronounced that the Gods
> had orderd such things.
> Thus men forgot that All deities reside in the human breast.
>   (1994 [1790]: 11. Blake's spelling retained)

This thinking, developed from an examination of religion, may be linked to Thaw's doubts about God in Books One and Two. But it may be translated into the more overtly political concerns of Books Three and Four to show how the state (priesthood) co-opts local governments (deities) into a centralised system (national monotheism) which men buy into and so allow themselves to be shackled. Religion for Blake must be a matter of choice; Gods are fictions which human communities should be freely allowed to choose or reject. *Lanark* suggests the same should apply to government, but does not; a significant point in a once-independent nation 'united' with another. Yet the text shows that this only happens because man allows it to happen, because he is duped into supporting his own jailers. This is what Blake refers to in his famous phrase 'mind-forg'd manacles' (1970 [1794]: pl. 46) and it is similarly expressed in a 'proverb of hell': 'Prisons are built with stones of law, brothels with bricks of religion' (1994 [1790]: 8). Without the state control of the law there would be no imprisonment, and without religion's control of sexuality in marriage there would be no prostitution (with its female prisoners). In accepting law and religion as abstract exterior forces over his life man submits himself and his kind to these iniquities. This is the sense in which, in Gray's terms, man 'bakes himself'.

'And the recipe is separation'

The second part of the 'Man is the pie …' quotation appears also in a brief sequence of cross-references from a quiet corridor on page 72: 'the voices here were like whispers in a seashell: "Lilac and laburnum … marble and honey … the recipe is separation"'. These three phrases *do* seem like a recipe, but the separation is between Thaw and female affection. The first phrase comes from the very neutral observation of his street: 'The houses opposite were semi-detached villas with lilacs and a yellow laburnum tree in the gardens' (*L* 197). Yet this is what Duncan sees while he holds the hand of his dying mother once she has become too weak to talk. The second phrase comes from one of several uses of it during the art-school ball where Thaw fatally embarrasses himself by taking seriously the attention of a dancing partner who is simply amusing herself with his naivety (*L* 257–9). There are two types of separation here. The first is death, a separation only because – as we know from Thaw's continuation into Lanark— this may not be a conclusive ending; 'Mrs. Thaw Disappears' rather than dies and it might be Mrs Thaw and his earlier self that Lanark sees through the window in the institute ward on page 75. The second type of separation is sexual in that Duncan has no way of communicating with women his own age, beset as he is with sexual self-consciousness and guilt. The first type of separation is a given of the human condition, but the second is a societal flaw.

The misery of Lanark's personal isolation in Unthank manifests itself in dragonhide. We can see the links between this affliction and Thaw's eczema, but in this defamiliarised form it is more terrifying in that the affected body part seems to belong to a different creature and has only a vaguely subservient attitude. Rather than an allegorical presentation of eczema this dragonhide is a literalized metaphor. The Epilogue makes clear the source on page 496:

> **REICH, WILHELM**
> Book 3. The Dragonhide which
> infects the first six chapters is
> a Difplag of the muscular con-
> striction Reich calls 'armouring.'

For Reich character armour is: 'First, the armoring of the ego against the

outer world and the inner instinctual demands; second, the economic function of absorbing the excess of sexual energy which results from sexual stasis,
or in other words, of keeping this energy from manifesting itself as anxiety'
(1950: 218).[12] The psychological problem is, however, as emotionally
crippling as the developing disease is for dragonhide sufferers in *Lanark*:

> *The plague ridden individual experiences ... an intolerable inhibition; in*
> *order to express itself at all, the impulse first has to break through the armor;*
> *in this process, the original intention and the rational goal get lost. The*
> *result* of the action contains very little of the original, rational intention;
> it reflects the *destructiveness* which had to be mobilized for the
> breakthrough through the armour. (Reich 1950: 263)

We can see this quite clearly in the fiction when Rima, having driven Lanark
away, tries to offer him a coat against the cold but the kindness becomes a
nearly violent act that he cannot accept:

> She said, 'Goodbye, Lanark!' and gripped his arm and led him to the door,
> and pushed him out and slammed it.
>
> He groped his way downstairs. Near the bottom he heard her open the
> door and shout 'Lanark!' He looked back. Something dark and whirling
> came down on his head, heavily enfolding it, and again the door
> slammed. He dragged the thing off and found it was a sheepskin jacket
> with the fleece turned inward. He hung this on the inside knob of the
> bottom door and stepped into the lane and walked away. (*L* 37)

On page 95, when her dragon armour falls away because of Lanark's stub-
born devotion, the first thing Rima says is 'You should have taken that coat. I
didn't want you to be cold.' This is not to say that Gray constructed his
narrative using Reich as a model but that Reich's metaphor was suggestive in
the creation of dragonhide.

Reich also makes clear that '*The sexual crisis of youth is an integral part of*
the crisis of the authoritarian social order' (1969 [1961]: 115). Reich's term
'armouring' replaces Freud's term 'repression' which has political as well as
psychological implications. The following quotation seems especially
applicable to Thaw's life in Glasgow:

> As long as youth was tied to the family, as long as girls, exposed to little
> sexual excitation, were content to wait for the man who eventually would
> take care of them, as long as boys lived in abstinence, masturbation or
> went to prostitutes – so long was there only silent suffering, neurosis or
> sexual brutality ... the sexual needs which strive for liberation are
> hemmed in by the inhibitions acquired through education on the one

---

12 Reich developed this concept metaphorically, too, eventually to the point of literalisation; analysing his
patients for physical signs of a segmented armour.

hand, and by the objections of authoritarian society on the other hand. (1969 [1961]: 114)[13]

The problems of Duncan Thaw – his suffering, his awkwardness, his sadistic fantasies, his self-neglect and tantrums, his delusions of grandeur, self-deprecation and acted stupidity – fit with Reich's analysis of a masochistic personality (1950: 210–47).

Some of these problems – in particular his lurid fantasies and delusions of grandeur – are given full rein when Thaw has become Lanark and in Book Four finds himself involved in politics. After Lanark is made Provost he is given a haircut and he imagines himself 'impressive and statesmanlike. He placed his hands on his hips and said quietly, "When Lord Monboddo says that the council has done its best to help Unthank he is lying to us – or has been lied to by others"' (L 461). However, after his adventures and misadventures at the conference, Lanark finds no other platform to speak these lines but by interrupting Monboddo during his closing address:

> he was appalled to find himself standing and shouting 'EXEXEXEXEXEXEXEX' at the top of his voice. Powys and Odin gripped his wrists, but he wrenched them free and yelled, 'EXCUSE ME! EXCUSE ME! but Lord Monboddo lied when he said all the delegates agreed to manage things through open, honest debates! Or else he has been lied to by other people' (L 547)

This shows what Lanark's visions of grandeur really amount to. Instead of being 'a famous man with important papers in his briefcase' (L 518), his last appearance at the conference is as an infamous drunkard with no information that can save Unthank at all. As well as discrediting his 'statesmanlike' vision, this anticlimax ridicules the youthful fantasies of Duncan Thaw (L 157–8) in which he sees himself as Prime Minister of a small fertile valley in the aftermath of a nuclear war. In this role he is lionised, maintains his socialist principles and refuses to exploit his power. However, the opposite influences govern his sexual fantasies, which take place in a secret Arizona goldmine (158–9) where he exploits and tortures his slave labourers. This binding up of political and psycho-sexual is important in Lanark (and even more important in 1982, Janine). It is as Provost that Lanark is involved in an orgy that brings on his epiphanic vision of Sandy on Ben Rua. None the less it is this seduction that leads to the failure of his mission. As with Thaw's boyish fantasies, one contaminates the other; the demands of the goldmine undermine the republic so that Thaw feels 'a self-contempt so great that it included all his imaginary worlds' (L 159). Both sex and power involve

---

13 Compare the last stanza of Blake's 'London' and the closing chorus of The Marriage of Heaven and Hell (1994 [1790]: 27).

exploitation and while Lanark is sexually seduced the council conducts its corrupt business uninterrupted.

The diseases which afflict the people of Unthank are those of their society's making, and there are other sections of that society who benefit from it, whether directly (Sludden's domination of Gay), or indirectly (the institute). We are left to realise that the 'diseases' suffered by citizens of our own liberal democracy are problems caused by that society: not accidentally but deliberately through the *recipe of separation*, which allows this to happen and is what keeps people from realising what is being done to them. Society cloaks the recipe for separation in its abstraction: the idea that it stands for all of us (according to Hobbes) masking the fact that it only really stands for only some of us, as Blake knew. The diseases are only the effects of the victims 'adapting' to their environment. This is made clear by a telling example given to Thaw by the medical professor who inspects his progress in a ward of Stobhill hospital:

> This patient, gentlemen, is suffering from adaption. Let me give you an example of adaption. A hardworking man of thirty loses his job through no fault of his own. For two or three months he hunts for work but can't find any. His national insurance money runs out and he goes on the dole. In these circumstances his energy and initiative are a burden to him. They make him want to break things and punch people. So instinctively his metabolism lowers itself. He grows slovenly and depressed. A year or two passes, he's offered a job at last and refuses it. Unemployment has become a way of life. He's adapted to it. In the same way people come here with commonplace illnesses which, after an initial improvement, stop responding to treatment. Why? In the absence of other factors we must assume that the patient has adapted to the *hospital itself*. (L 311–12, Gray's emphasis)

In the larger metaphor society itself is a hospital, for everyone in it is sick. What is important for our reading of *Lanark* is the means by which a cure might be achieved. In his final confrontation with Monboddo Lanark says: "'I don't care what happens to most people. All of us over eighteen have been warped into deserving what happens to us. But if your *reason* shows that civilization can only continue by damaging the brains and hearts of most children, then ... your reason and civilization are false and will destroy themselves'" (L 551, Gray's ellipses and emphasis). Similar warnings are seen in the work of Norman O. Brown: 'mankind, unconscious of its real desires and therefore unable to obtain satisfaction, is hostile to life and ready to destroy itself' (1970 [1959]: x (see also Marcuse 1956)).

A reasoning or philosophy different from Monboddo's profit-based macro-vision is what is required. This has more than a glancing significance to *1982, Janine* which features on its hard cover the epigraph: 'Truly the remedy's inside the disease and the meaning of being ill is to bring the eye to the heart'. Gifford (1987: 102) calls this device 'gentle trickery' but we should not downplay its significance simply because other authors do not avail themselves of such possibilities. We might be able to take this phrase as a recipe to 'unbake' the pie. The sentiments expressed in *Janine* parallel those of R. D. Laing: 'the *ordinary* person is a shrivelled desiccated fragment of what a person can be' (1967: 22). Change is needed to provide human beings with the chance of fulfilment, and this type of change has two aspects. The first is personal satisfaction, freedom from the oppressive state. An answer is within Reich's awareness, as the epigraph to his later works states: 'Love, work and knowledge are the well-springs of our life. They should also govern it.' The second aspect is that this freedom must not be gained at the expense of others: though Lanark on Ben Rua experiences the sun he cannot enjoy personal happiness while others suffer. This is expressed by Blake's 'The Human Abstract': 'Pity would be no more, / If we did not make somebody Poor: / And Mercy no more could be, / If all were as happy as we' (1970 [1794]: pl. 47). Overall *Lanark* rejects the idea of individual recognition at the expense of others and advocates collaboration rather than exploitation between individuals.

Gray seems to identify a connection between Blake and Reich; a radical tradition aware of the connection between the political and the psycho-sexual. *Lanark* encodes the discourse of a long, dissenting-visionary tradition as a response to the late twentieth-century realities of social conditioning and globalised capitalism. The presence of this dissenting tradition in *Lanark* is not anachronistic, since it licenses those in the present to write acts of critique and imaginative daring. In fact the tradition is (paradoxically) less stable than postmodern theory which limits any possible radicalism by invoking the fictionality of fiction. The radical tradition is against censorship, state control and, as we find Milton arguing, against poetic convention: 'Truth is compared in Scripture to a streaming fountain; if her waters flow not in perpetual progression, they sicken to a muddy pool of conformity and tradition' (1973 [1644]: 29). But progression requires a knowledge of the past and a broad awareness of the present. Ultimately *Lanark* can be seen to narrate the failure of this tradition against the takeover of the multinational and the occlusion of the collective as an option. The attitude is clear in the instruction on the hard-cover epigraph of *Unlikely Stories, Mostly*, *Poor Things* and the massive *Book of Prefaces*: 'Work as if you were in the early days of a better nation.' The luxury of an embossed or metalled hard cover wasn't available for the first edition of *Lanark* – its success was not assured – but it has become part of Gray's repertoire and one of the delights in the books themselves. *Lanark* has a coherent system for the use of graphic surface structured by a consciousness of tradition and the store of possibilities and inventions which it offers; the graphic surface is simply part of the repertoire of making books.

Lanark's fracturing and doubling of narrative occurs within this context of the coherence of the graphic surface. The text's inherent graphic stability creates a mimetic environment which performs instability as reality and determines that we must relate the text's elements to each other in a non-hierarchical way. We must read Thaw against Lanark, *Lanark* against itself and other texts, the epilogue against the whole, and our own readings against an 'authorial' reading and a 'critical' reading. Each reader experiences and interprets the text in at least some of these contexts, depending on his or her own subjectivity, but with licence to interpret and question, and to relate their reading to the world outside the text and its hierarchies.

In Alasdair Gray's work, especially *Lanark*, a coherent use of graphic surface is structured by a consciousness of literary and craft traditions and what is often seen as postmodern instability is anchored in the making of books. The result is comparable with *Thru*'s metatextual mimesis, and with *Albert Angelo*'s attempt to capture chaos, though it is neither so relentlessly destabilising as the former or so tightly controlled as the latter. I don't wish to suggest that *Lanark* arrives at a happy medium but that, in its own terms, *Lanark* shows how the presence of the book is a key to dealing with literary texts. The book is a technological space, certainly, but belongs to a particular kind of technology with a history and with possibilities far from exhausted. Gray's major novels (and indeed his major critical work *The Book of Prefaces* (2002)) revel in the juxtaposition of different textual voices and ways in which the reader can read the text against itself because of its presence in three dimensions.

References

Axelrod, Mark (1995) 'An Epistolary Interview, Mostly with Alasdair Gray', *Review of Contemporary Fiction* 15 (2): 106–15

Bernstein, Stephen (1999) *Alasdair Gray*, Lewisburg: Bucknell University Press

Blake, William (1970 [1794]) *Songs of Innocence and of Experience*, Oxford: Oxford University Press

Blake, William (1994 [1790]) *The Marriage of Heaven and Hell*, New York: Dover

Brown, Norman O. (1970 [1959]) *Life Against Death: The Psychoanalytical Meaning of History*, Middletown, Connecticut: Wesleyan University Press

Craig, Cairns (1999) *The Modern Scottish Novel: Narrative and the National Imagination*, Edinburgh: Edinburgh University Press

Crawford, Robert and Nairn, Thomas (eds) (1991) *The Arts of Alasdair Gray*, Edinburgh: Edinburgh University Press

Donaldson, George and Lee, Alison (1995) 'Is Eating People Really Wrong? Dining with Alasdair Gray', *Review of Contemporary Fiction* 15 (2): 155–61

Galloway, Janice (1995) 'Different Oracles: Me and Alasdair Gray', *Review of Contemporary Fiction* 15 (2): 193–96

van Gennep, Arnold (1960) *The Rites of Passage*, London: Routledge & Kegan Paul

Genette, Gérard (1997) *Paratexts: Thresholds of Interpretation*, Cambridge: Cambridge University Press

Gifford, Douglas (1987) 'Private Confession and Public Satire in the Fiction of Alasdair Gray', *Chapman* 10 (1–2): 101–16

Gifford, Douglas (1997) 'Author's Postscript Completed by Douglas Gifford' in Alasdair Gray, *Unlikely Stories, Mostly*, Edinburgh: Canongate

Gray, Alasdair (1981) *Lanark, A Life in Four Books*, Edinburgh: Canongate; (1982) St Albans: Granada; (1985) Edinburgh: Canongate (embossed hardback); (1991) London: Picador; (2001) Edinburgh: Canongate (4 volumes); (2002) Edinburgh: Canongate Classics

Gray, Alasdair (1983) *Unlikely Stories, Mostly*, Edinburgh: Canongate; (1997) Edinburgh: Canongate Classics

Gray, Alasdair (1984) *1982, Janine*, London: Cape

Gray, Alasdair (1985a) *The Fall of Kelvin Walker*, Edinburgh: Canongate

Gray, Alasdair (1985b) *Lean Tales*, London: Jonathan Cape (with James Kelman and Agnes Owens)

Gray, Alasdair (1990a) *McGrotty and Ludmilla or The Harbinger Report*, Glasgow: Dog & Bone

Gray, Alasdair (1990b) *Something Leather*, London: Jonathan Cape

Gray, Alasdair (1990c) 'Questionnaire', *Contemporary Authors* 126: 140–4.

Gray, Alasdair (1992) *Poor Things, Episodes from the Early Life of Archibald McCandless MD, Scottish Public Health Officer*, London: Bloomsbury

Gray, Alasdair (1993) *Ten Tales Tall and True*, London: Bloomsbury

Gray, Alasdair (1994) *A History Maker*, Edinburgh: Canongate

Gray, Alasdair (1996) *Mavis Belfrage: A Romantic Novel*, London: Bloomsbury

Gray, Alasdair (2000) *The Book of Prefaces*, London: Bloomsbury

Gray, Alasdair (2003) *The Ends of Our Tethers*, Edinburgh: Canongate

Jameson, Fredric (1983) 'Postmodernism and Consumer Society' in Hal Foster (ed.), *The Anti-Aesthetic: Essays on Postmodern Culture*, Seattle, Washington: Bay Press

King, Elspeth (2002) 'Art for the Early Days of a Better Nation' in Phil Moores (ed.), *Alasdair Gray: Critical Appreciations and a Bibliography*, Boston Spa: British Library: 93–121

Laing, R. D. (1967) *The Politics of Experience and The Bird of Paradise*, Harmondsworth: Penguin

Lee, Alison (1990) *Realism and Power: Postmodern British Fiction*, London: Routledge

McHale, Brian (1987) *Postmodernist Fiction*, New York: Methuen

Marcuse, Herbert (1956) *Eros and Civilisation*, London: Routledge & Kegan Paul

Milton, John (1973 [1644]) *Areopagitica and Of Education*, Oxford: Clarendon

Moores, Phil (ed.) (2002) *Alasdair Gray: Critical Appreciations and a Bibliography*, Boston Spa: British Library

Murray, Isobel and Tait, Bob (1984) *Ten Modern Scottish Novels*, Aberdeen: Aberdeen University Press

Oliver, Cordelia (1991) 'Alasdair Gray: Visual Artist' in Robert Crawford and Thomas Nairn (eds), *The Arts of Alasdair Gray*, Edinburgh: Edinburgh University Press: 22–36

Pittin, Marie Odile (1996) 'Alasdair Gray: a Strategy of Ambiguity' in *Studies in Scottish Fiction: 1945 to the Present*, Frankfurt: Peter Lang: 199–215

Reich, Wilhelm (1950) *Character Analysis*, London: Vision (translated by Theodore P. Wolfe)

Reich, Wilhelm (1969) *The Sexual Revolution: Towards a Self-Governing Character Structure*, London: Vision (translated by Theodore P. Wolfe)

Sassoon, Rosemary (1999) *Handwriting of the Twentieth Century*, London: Routledge

Smith, Penny (1995) 'Hell Innit: the Millennium and Alasdair Gray's *Lanark*, Martin Amis's *London Fields*, and Shena MacKay's *Dunedin*', *Essays and Studies*, Cambridge: Brewer: 115–28

Stevenson, Randall (1991) 'Alasdair Gray and the Postmodern' in Robert Crawford and Thomas Nairn (eds), *The Arts of Alasdair Gray*, Edinburgh: Edinburgh University Press: 48–63

Sutherland, John (1996) 'Review of *Mavis Belfrage*', *Times Literary Supplement*, 17 May: 22a

White, Glyn (2000) 'The Critic in the Text: Footnotes and Marginalia in the Epilogue to Alasdair Gray's *Lanark: A Life in Four Books*' in Joe Bray, Miriam Handley and Anne C. Henry (eds), *Ma(r)king the Text: The Presentation of Meaning on the Literary Page*, Aldershot: Ashgate: 55–70

Williamson, Kevin (2002) 'Under the Influence' in Phil Moores (ed.), *Alasdair Gray: Critical Appreciations and a Bibliography*, Boston Spa: British Library: 165–87

CONCLUSION

The previous chapters should have conveyed the usefulness of a critical awareness of the graphic surface. I have outlined the practical and theoretical concerns that have tended to obscure the graphic surface from critical scrutiny and given detailed analyses of a number of problematical texts showing how the graphic surface can contribute to interpretation. It remains only to review some of the implications of the project.

The graphic surface of the page is a free two-dimensional space on which text appears either mechanically (as a result of the translation of the manuscript into print) or consciously (when the author wishes to adapt it for specific purposes). As visual arrangements of printed text on the graphic surface, graphic devices can contribute to the process of reading, combining with the semantic content within the context which that text creates. The graphic surface thus allows authors a second mode of signification, one which may point out the constraints of normal printed language, but which may simultaneously supplement that language and contribute to the generation of meaning.

Throughout I have stressed that among these capabilities the use of the graphic surface can add to the representational qualities of the text. Postmodernist criticism has, however, established a critical convention in which the use of the graphic surface always self-consciously or self-reflexively signifies the materiality of the text. More traditional criticism rejects reminders of the presence of the book as a distraction from literary realism, but precisely because the graphic surface is such a vital part of every text the use of it cannot be dismissed as aberrant, unreadable or ornamental. The texts we have studied all use the graphic surface in vital, but very different, ways which demonstrably relate to the real world. I suggest that while the graphic surface is a constant of printed fiction its calculated use is often critically confused with the fact that it *incidentally* defamiliarises the conventional layout of text, and such confusion obscures the fact that the 'defamiliarising' devices are often directly mimetic.

I have used mimesis in the sense outlined above as a thread linking difficult texts by a series of 'awkward' authors, but we have not drawn the same conclusions from each analysis. This project has not been intended to assimilate and so shut down the generation of meaning by the texts discussed, but rather to put into perspective some of the hysterical reaction to graphic disruption which has been the usual response to innovations of this kind. Panic or sheer indifference to the defamiliarisation of the graphic surface – this known, but misunderstood, element of every text – is partially understandable (as we have shown in Chapters 1–4), but not to the credit of literary criticism in general. Our examination of the graphic surface has shown how it is possible for criticism to mask elements of narrative texts which we *need* for interpretation. The implications of this are to remind us of the danger of facile labels which obscure rather than inform such as 'experimental' or 'self-reflexive' or 'postmodern'. By contrast our term, 'the graphic surface', indicates a fundamental aspect of the presence of the book and describes the arena on which all printed texts meet their readers.

In addition to their use of the graphic surface, the texts I have studied share a compulsion to make the reader re-evaluate what they have already read. We see this in *Watt*'s 'Addenda', in *Albert Angelo*'s Disintegration, in *Thru* with the repeated question 'who speaks?' and the 'hidden' vertical text, and in *Lanark*'s conspicuous non-numerical ordering of its four books. These challenges to the reader's interpretative powers are, however, balanced by the texts' desire for closer communion. This is clear where we see the reader's experience paralleled by the central character in *Watt*, by the effort to remove the impediment of the objective correlative character in *Albert Angelo*, by the dramatised textual-sexual parallels which structure *Thru*, and the various devices which generate rereading and intimate knowledge of *Lanark*. To become live to the graphic surface of a text we are reading adds immediacy and intimacy to that reading. The book form transports the text to the reader, and their interaction (reading) is an event: 'a coming-together, a compenetration' (Rosenblatt 1978: 12). Though the quotation relates to poetry the same is true, over a longer period, of prose fiction and its readers. A critical awareness of the graphic surface has the potential to help us recover a significant aspect of this relationship.

Beyond implications with regard to the fundamental contact of literature, the meeting of text and reader, there is much close reading still to be done of texts which present a distinctive graphic surface. This applies to the work of the authors discussed in this book, that of many others within and outside the British Isles and many non-English writers, past and present. The Further Reading section which follows points to some of these authors and specific novels of interest.

Overall, there are many critical gaps and new opportunities and much more work to do. An awareness of the graphic surface may offer methods by which to tackle and include elements of texts that might otherwise seem to fall outside the remit of the literary critic (graphic forms from hieroglyphs to comics), and the presence (and absence) of the book deserves to be pursued in forms of textual narrative even less familiar, such as hypertext. But there is no necessity for literary critics to flee into these territories. If the book form is under threat it will be only because other media can do what it does better and I have yet to be convinced that any new media are even coming close. Prose fictions which utilise the graphic surface do not announce the end of the novel, as some of the detractors seem to worry; they take advantage of the potency of the book and the flexibility of fiction to communicate with readers in a variety of stimulating ways. The point is that criticism must keep up and be as flexible and adaptable as novelists and readers. To dismiss graphic devices as meaningless gimmicks or to immediately reduce innovations to postmodern concepts of self-reflexive play is to divisively defend a particular critical position at the expense of literature itself.

Reference

Rosenblatt, Louise M. (1978) *The Reader, the text, the Poem: The Transactional Theory of the Literary Work,* Carbondale: Southern Illinois University Press

FURTHER READING

This section lists some relevant literary works which utilise their graphic surfaces. It is not intended to be exhaustive and focuses mainly on the twentieth century. I have noted the original date(s) of publication where I feel this information is useful. Details of works by authors studied in detail in this book appear in the references for the relevant chapters.

Alexis, Andre (1998) *Childhood: A Novel*, New York: Holt
Amis, Martin (1990) *London Fields*, London: Penguin
Apollinaire, Guillaume (1986) *Selected Poems*, London: Anvil [first published 1906–18]
Auster, Paul (1988) *The New York Trilogy*, London: Faber
Bailey, Paul (1973) *A Distant Likeness*, London: Cape
Bester, Alfred (1966) *The Demolished Man*, London: Penguin [first published 1953]
Bester, Alfred (1956) *Tiger, Tiger*, London: Sidgwick and Jackson
Bester, Alfred (1981) *Golem 100*, London: Pan
Bester, Alfred (1983) *The Deceivers*, London: Pan
Blake, William (1970) *Songs of Innocence and of Experience*, Oxford: Oxford University Press [first published 1794]
Blake, William (1994) *The Marriage of Heaven and Hell*, New York: Dover [first published 1794]
Brophy, Brigid (1969) *In Transit*, London: Macdonald
Burns, Alan (1969) *Babel*, London: Calder and Boyars
Burns, Alan (1972) *Dreamerika!*, London: Calder and Boyars
Burns, Alan (1981) *The Day Daddy Died*, London: Allison and Busby
Cixous, Hélène and Calle-Gruber, Mireille (1997) *Hélène Cixous, Rootprints: Memory and Life Writing*, London: Routledge (translated by Eric Prenowitz)
Cortazar, Julio (1966) *Hopscotch*, New York: Avon (translated by Gregory Rabassa)
Cortazar, Julio (1976) *62: A Model Kit*, London: Boyars (translated by Gregory Rabassa)
Cummings, Edward Estlin (1973) *Collections: Poems 1905–62; An Authorised Typewriter Edition*, London: Marchim Press
Danielewski, Mark Z. (2000) *House of Leaves*, London: Anchor
Eggers, Dave (2003) *You Shall Know Our Velocity*, London: Hamish Hamilton
Ellmann, Lucy (1988) *Sweet Desserts*, London: Virago
Ellmann, Lucy (1991) *Varying Degrees of Hopelessness*, London: Hamish Hamilton
Ellmann, Lucy (1998) *Man or Mango? A Lament*, London: London Review
Faulkner, William (1987) *The Sound and the Fury*, New York: Norton [first published 1929]
Faulkner, William (1990) *As I Lay Dying*, London: Vintage [first published 1930].
Flanagan, Richard (2002) *Gould's Book of Fish: A Novel in Twelve Fish*, London: Atlantic
Gass, William H. (1989) *Willie Masters' Lonesome Wife*: Illinois: Dalkey Archive
Hamilton, Patrick (1953) *The West Pier*, London: Constable
Harris, Wilson (1965) *The Eye of the Scarecrow*, London: Faber

Heppenstall, Rayner (1939) *Blaze of Noon*, London: Secker and Warburg
Heppenstall, Rayner (1977) *Two Moons*, London: Allison and Busby
Joyce, James (1992) *Ulysses*, London: Penguin [first published 1922]
Joyce, James (1992) *Finnegans Wake*, London: Penguin [first published 1939]
Jones, David (1955) *The Anathemata: Fragments of an Attempted Writing*, London: Faber
Josipovici, Gabriel (1968) *The Inventory*, London: Michael Joseph
Josipovici, Gabriel (1974) *Mobius the Stripper*, London: Gollancz
Knight, Stephen (2000) *Mr. Schnitzel*, London: Viking
Leland, Jeremy (1994) *Voices*, Norwich: Rampant Horse
Llosa, Mario Vargas (1992) *In Praise of the Stepmother*, London: Faber (translated by Helen Lane)
Machado de Assis, Joaquim Maria (1997) *The Posthumous Memoirs of Brás Cubas*, Oxford: Oxford University Press (translated by Gregory Rabassa) [first published 1880]
Machado de Assis, Joaquim Maria (1998) *Quincas Borba* [a.k.a. *Philosopher or Dog?*], Oxford: Oxford University Press (translated by Gregory Rabassa) [first published 1892]
Mallarmé, Stéphane (1985) *Oeuvres de Mallarmé*, Paris: Garnier
Nabokov, Vladimir (1991) *Pale Fire*, London: Penguin [first published 1962]
O'Brien, Flann (1967) *At Swim-Two-Birds*, London: Penguin [first published 1937]
O'Brien, Flann (1987) *The Third Policeman*, London: Granada
Ondaatje, Michael (1989) *The Life and Times of Billy the Kid: Left Handed Poems*, London: Picador [1970]
Ondaatje, Michael, (1984) *Running in the Family*, London: Picador
Pérez de Ayala, Ramón (1926) *Tigre Juan* [part 1], Madrid: Pueyo
Pérez de Ayala, Ramón (1926) *El Curandero de su Honra* [*Tigre Juan* part 2], Madrid: Pueyo
Phillips, Tom (1980) *A Humument: A Treated Victorian Novel*, London: Thames and Hudson: (1987) 1st revised edition, London: Thames and Hudson; (1997) 2nd revised edition, London: Thames and Hudson
Poe, Edgar Allan (1986) *The Narrative of Arthur Gordon Pym of Nantucket*, London: Penguin Classics [first published 1838]
Pound, Ezra (1954) *Cantos*, London: Faber
Quin, Ann (1964) *Berg*, London: John Calder
Quin, Ann (1966) *Three*, London: Calder and Boyars
Quin, Ann (1969) *Passages*, London: Calder and Boyars
Quin, Ann (1972) *Tripticks*, London: Calder and Boyars
Reading, Peter (1989) *Perduta Gente*, London: Secker and Warburg
Reading, Peter (1994) *Ukelele Music / Perduta Gente*, Evanston, Illinois: Northwestern University Press
Richardson, Samuel (1985) *Clarissa*, London: Viking [first published 1747–8].
Rowson, Martin (1996) *The Life and Opinions of Tristram Shandy, Gentleman*, London: Picador [graphic novelisation]
Rubin, Jerry (1970) *Do It: Scenarios of the Revolution*, London: Cape
Saporta, Marc (1962) *Composition No. 1*, Paris: Éditions du Seuil
Sebald, W. G. (1996) *The Emigrants*, New York: New Directions (translated by Michael Hulse)
Sebald, W. G. (1998) *The Rings of Saturn*, London: Harvill (translated by Michael Hulse)
Shell, Ray (1993) *Iced*, London: Flamingo
Sukenick, Ronald (1973) *Out*, Chicago: Swallow Press,
Sukenick, Ronald (1975) *98.6*, New York: Fiction Collective
Swift, Jonathan (undated) *A Tale of a Tub, The Battle of the Books, and Other Satires*, London: Dent
Swift, Jonathan (1985 [1726]) *Gulliver's Travels*, London: Penguin Classics
Thorpe, Adam (1992) *Ulverton*, London: Minerva
Vonnegut, Kurt (1973) *Breakfast of Champions*, London: Cape
Welsh, Irvine (1995) *Marabou Stork Nightmares*, London: Cape
Welsh, Irvine (1998) *Filth*, London: Cape

INDEX

This index has been prepared by the author. With limited space available there are no headings with a single page reference only. Titles are indexed under their authors *apart from* novels studied in depth in this book which get their own headings. The terms 'graphic surface' and 'prose fiction' are not indexed but 'reading', 'book' and 'graphic devices' are given space. Where references to footnotes appear, the number following 'n' refers to the number of the note. Both of us may wonder whether a professional indexer may have done a better job but I have tried my best to make this index work and, as with the rest of the book, I hope the reader finds it helpful.

CPSIA information can be obtained at www.ICGtesting.com
Printed in the USA
LVOW11s1808130614

389977LV00002B/289/P